Small Group Instruction

Small Group Instruction

A Forum for Teaching Students with Learning Challenges

Timothy E. Morse

ROWMAN & LITTLEFIELD
Lanham • Boulder • New York • London

Published by Rowman & Littlefield
A wholly owned subsidiary of The Rowman & Littlefield Publishing Group, Inc.
4501 Forbes Boulevard, Suite 200, Lanham, Maryland 20706
www.rowman.com

6 Tinworth Street, London SE11 5AL, United Kingdom

Copyright © 2020 by Timothy E. Morse

All rights reserved. No part of this book may be reproduced in any form or by any electronic or mechanical means, including information storage and retrieval systems, without written permission from the publisher, except by a reviewer who may quote passages in a review.

British Library Cataloguing in Publication Information Available

Library of Congress Cataloging-in-Publication Data Available

ISBN 978-1-4758-4410-8 (cloth)
ISBN 978-1-4758-4411-5 (pbk.)
ISBN 978-1-4758-4412-2 (electronic)

To the members of the Morse, Smith, Bowers, and Jackson families who "have gone before," and whose legacies made this work possible.

Contents

Preface　xi

Acknowledgments　xix

Introduction　1

1　Small Group Instruction: Establishing the Conditions for Presenting Effective Instruction　7
　Overview　7
　The Case for Needing to Present Intensive Small Group Instruction　8
　Scenarios Supporting the Relevance of Group Configuration to the Presentation of Effective Instruction　13
　Small Group Instruction: The What, Who, Where, When, Why, and How　14
　Key Terms and Concepts　17
　Intensive Small Group Instruction and Its Relationship to a Fundamental Philosophy About Teaching and Learning　20
　Chapter 1 Comprehension Check　24

2　General Education Classroom Instruction: The Reference Point for Intensive Small Group Instruction　27
　Overview　27
　Introduction　28
　High-Quality General Education Instruction as the Reference Point for Intensive Small Group Instruction　30
　High-Quality Instruction: Effective and Multi-Dimensional　32

	Dimensions of High-Quality Instruction	33
	Chapter 2 Comprehension Check	49
3	Features of Intensive Small Group Instruction	53
	Overview	53
	Ways Intensive Small Group Instruction Is Related to High-Quality Instruction in General Education Classrooms	55
	Intensive Small Group Instruction: The Details	59
	Explicit, Teacher-Directed, Intensive, and Remedial Small Group Instruction	65
	Providing Ultra-Intensive Tier 2 Services	75
	Chapter 3 Comprehension Check	77
4	Preparing for Small Group Instruction	81
	Overview	81
	Preparation Considerations for Intensive Small Group Instruction	82
	Chapter 4 Comprehension Check	99
5	Small Group Instructional Strategies	101
	Overview	101
	Introduction	103
	Review of Key Concepts	104
	Basic Instructional Strategies	107
	Instructional Strategies Unique to Small Group Arrangements	108
	Small Group Behavior Management Strategies	122
	Putting It All Together: Direct Instruction Lesson Plan	130
	Chapter 5 Comprehension Check	133
6	Assessment and Small Group Instruction	135
	Overview	135
	Introduction	136
	Key Terms: Assessment, Testing, and Evaluation	138
	A Few More Key Assessment Terms and Concepts	139
	Rationale for Assessment: Informing Instruction or Acting as a Barrier	142
	Assessments Specific to Intensive Small Group Instruction	142
	Tangential Measures of Student Progress	148
	Ensuring Valid Information is Obtained from Assessments	150
	A School's Assessment Milieu and Accommodations	152
	Chapter 6 Comprehension Check	154

7 Teaching Functional Content by Way of Small Group Instruction	157
Overview	157
Introduction	159
Teaching Functional Content as One Part of Special Education	161
Functional Content	164
Chapter 7 Comprehension Check	175
Epilogue	177
Glossary	179
Bibliography	197
About the Author	205

Preface

My work as a special educator began forty years ago, which was two years after the first set of regulations for our nation's initial special education law was passed. This law, the Education for All Handicapped Children Act (EAHCA), has since been renamed and is presently known as the Individuals with Disabilities Education Act (IDEA).

During the past forty years, I have completed several degree granting programs and accumulated a wealth of professional experiences that have enabled me to see, from numerous vantage points, how the field of special education operates and the need for this book. These programs and experiences include the following:

a. Bachelor's, master's, and doctorate degrees in special education. These degrees pertain to students with mild disabilities, moderate-significant disabilities, special education administration, assistive technology applications in special education, and instructional design.
b. Various positions as a special education teacher, prekindergarten through twelfth grade, in resource and self-contained classrooms. I also have provided support to students with disabilities in general education classrooms.
c. Employment as an Assistant Director of Special Education in a school district with twenty thousand students.
d. Experiences as both an Assistant and Associate Professor of Special Education.
e. A seven-year-long stint as the Director of Training/Positive Behavior Support Specialist for an Autism Demonstration School that I founded.

I also have several family members who have disabilities and who were provided special education services while they were in school. With respect to a couple of these individuals, I have witnessed how a disability impacts a person throughout the life-span, meaning both when they were in school and during their post-secondary years.

As a result of the experiences noted previously, I have varied reasons for writing this book. The primary reason is to document the detailed, painstaking work that must be performed by educators to establish the conditions that afford students who demonstrate the most significant, persistent learning challenges the highest probability for demonstrating mastery of targeted learning outcomes. These students include some who have disabilities and are receiving special education services and some who do not. This latter group of students consists mostly of those with demonstrated low average ability and concomitant significant, ongoing learning challenges.

I have witnessed students who, although they were called "our throwaways" by the school administrators with whom I was working, made unexpected growth when placed in the right conditions. I have noted that these conditions quite often resulted from the use of a small group arrangement and the manipulation of other relevant instructional variables. The most relevant variables were those that pertained to teacher and student engagement.

Yet through my work I have noted that the creation and employment of these conditions have been the exception rather than the rule with respect to students who present significant, ongoing learning challenges. Instead what I have been able to witness with relative ease and consistency is an incredible amount of these students' time being wasted during the school day.

Their time was wasted in one of two ways. One way was when absolutely no instruction was being presented to them. The other way was when instruction was being presented but the mismatch between the type of instruction that was being presented and the type of instruction that the students actually needed to receive was so great that, for all intents and purposes, no instruction was being presented.

These experiences have caused me to ask and answer some pertinent questions. The questions that I have posed, and my answers to those questions, provide additional insight as to why I wrote this book.

Question #1: "Why are these conditions not being created when they are central to the provision of effective instruction to this relatively small number of students?"

I believe that a satisfactory answer to this question is related to the struggles of educators who have grappled with the philosophical perspective of full inclusion. I believe that an over-emphasis, by some, on the philosophy of full inclusion has diminished the use of the type of small group instruction that is the focus of this book. Specifically, I am referring to those (whose numbers are not known) who advocate for the full-time placement of every student in a general education classroom. In some instances I have noted that maintaining this placement has come at the expense of a student being afforded opportunities for more appropriate academic engagement elsewhere—meaning in a location outside of a general education classroom.

As I have noted already, I have witnessed, first-hand, students make unexpected progress once conditions were created such that the students experienced high rates of engagement and focused on instructional-level content. Conversely, I have witnessed students experience noteworthy emotional distress when they have been put in situations in which, day after day, they are overwhelmed with having to try to learn academic content that is well beyond their present level of performance and their instruction is presented under conditions that do not provide them with any chance to learn the content—nor anything else of substance.

Not surprisingly, this latter circumstance sets the occasion for these students to be ridiculed by their peers. Worse still, I have watched teachers berate students for their lack of progress and erroneously imply that it mostly is due to their lack of effort.

So one basis for having written this book is my strongly held belief that the special education services that are available through the IDEA need to be valued rather than ridiculed. Specifically, I believe that stakeholders need to ask and satisfactorily answer the following question, "Are we celebrating the continuum of alternative placements that are available to teachers and students as a result of the IDEA, or are we defaming their legitimacy in the name of a theoretical perspective—full inclusion—that is divorced from the conditions certain students need to experience to be able to attain targeted learning outcomes?"

Simply stated, in many general education classrooms the pace of instruction and the manner in which it is presented amounts to a state of affairs where events are "moving at the speed of light" from the perspective of students who present significant, ongoing learning challenges.

Question #2: "How are these conditions special education, and how is this special education interconnected to general education?"

I, like other special educators, continually ask myself, "What's special about special education?" In other words, what work can special educators perform that is truly different from the work other educators—general education teachers, in particular—perform and subsequently results in the presentation of effective instruction to the students who special educators teach?

The IDEA defines special education, in part, as specially designed instruction that involves the use of methodologies that address the unique needs of a student with a disability. I believe that the explicit, intensive, remedial, small group instruction that is the focus of this book meets this aspect of the definition for special education.

Furthermore, I have come to view special education as the avenue through which the micro-analysis of teaching is performed. By this I mean to say that special educators need to examine every variable that is relevant to the design and implementation of instruction in their attempt to present effective instruction to their students who, due to the manifestations of their disabilities, present numerous learning challenges. Every detail, no matter how small or apparently insignificant, is worthy of examination. A small group arrangement presents a venue that is particularly well-suited for this type of analysis.

However, I have always considered special education within the larger context of a public education that is afforded to every student in the United States. Consequently, as you read this book you need to remain mindful of how its content has broad applicability. General and special education teachers, as well as the students they instruct, can benefit from the content that is presented in this book. In fact, a concerted effort is made to tie the primary focus of the book's subject matter to the type of fundamentally sound, effective instruction that is presented in general education classrooms.

Question #3: "What are the features of these conditions that allow for optimal learning?"

As was just mentioned and is highlighted in this book, small group instruction is tightly coupled with the instruction that is presented to students in large group arrangements that predominate in general education classrooms.

The features of fundamentally sound, effective instruction that is presented in general education classrooms should serve as the reference point for the explicit, teacher-directed, intensive, remedial, small group instruction that is the focus of this book. However, this small group instruction needs to be uniquely configured to meet students' needs and not essentially be "more of the same" instruction that was presented in the general education classroom and was ineffective.

Accordingly, those who argue vehemently in favor of full inclusion need to be able to explain how the features of a student's special education services that allegedly support their placement in a general education classroom are more than just a simple variation of the instruction that is being presented. Some of my professional experiences have involved observing students with disabilities receive accommodations or modifications as their special education services for the purpose of enabling them to be a member of a general education classroom. This phenomenon has been described as special education as accommodations rather than the individualized, intensive instruction a student needs.

Not surprisingly, these students' assessment data indicated that they had not made appropriate progress in light of their circumstances. A recent United States Supreme Court decision calls into question whether these students were provided an appropriate education in accordance with the IDEA. I contend that this situation is directly attributable to the fact that the students were not provided the explicit, teacher-directed, intensive, remedial instruction that they needed to receive—and under the conditions that they needed to receive it—in order to be able to attain meaningful and challenging targeted learning outcomes.

Question #4: "Who needs to learn about this topic?"

Based on my professional and personal experiences I believe, quite strongly, that every educator—general and special education teachers, teaching assistants, related services personnel, and administrators—needs to learn about this topic. This belief stems from my perspective regarding how the work of all educators in a school is interconnected.

One thing that I have learned about myself is that what I enjoy doing the most is working with educators in ways that enable them to develop solid foundational teaching skills while also understanding how what they do "in the trenches" fits into a school's grand vision. For a school to be able to meet the needs of each student, every teacher must be successful in their work, and the work of every teacher must interconnect properly with every other educator's work. Hence, every educator needs to learn about this topic.

Question #5: "Why is this topic important to both students and teachers?"

As I note at the outset of this book, the primary reason that I decided to write a book that addresses this topic is because my professional experiences have led me to conclude that small group arrangements allow for the conditions that need to be established to afford certain students the circumstances under which they can master targeted learning outcomes. My recollections of these experiences account for the perspectives of both students and educators.

Regarding students' perspectives, it is critically important to note that nearly every student I have taught directly or provided support services on behalf of has demonstrated an intense desire to be successful. Furthermore, a number of these students have taken the lead in terms of self-advocating for what they need to be taught and how they need to be taught. In this book I document some of this self-advocacy as a reason in support of the use of explicit, teacher-directed, intensive, remedial, small group instruction.

Regarding educators' perspectives, this topic is important because it validates their profession. Recognizing that the examination of numerous instructional variables can lead to the development of teaching strategies that are reasonably calculated to result in the presentation of effective instruction to students who have not attained targeted learning outcomes in general education classrooms validates the role a teacher fulfills. Teachers can, and do, make a significant difference with respect to the design and implementation of effective, efficient instruction.

Accordingly, I believe that every teacher needs to remain mindful about the essence of teaching, which is to impart knowledge and skills to students. Contrast this definition of teaching with one for babysitting. Babysitting can be defined as adult supervision that ensures the welfare of the children whose safety and security has been entrusted to the adult.

Note that a key distinction between basic definitions for teaching and babysitting is that the definition for the former requires some type of direct, active engagement between an adult and a child. Babysitting, on the other hand, can be accomplished by passive activities, such as observation. Even when adult action is required—such as when an adult picks up a child who is crawling toward a hazard—there does not have to be any engagement that results in imparting knowledge or skills. Thus, when I have observed in classrooms during times when no instruction was be presented, what I was witnessing was the provision of babysitting.

One reason for putting as many details as I have in this book is to provide educators with a wealth of information that they can consider in an attempt to further the development of their profession and provide every student with some type of effective instruction. The information will enable educators to engage in thoughtful discussions about teaching and learning that go beyond general pronouncements, such as "He's doing amazing," to more substantive remarks that, hopefully, continue to result in the presentation of effective instruction (e.g., "He has doubled the number of high frequency words he can read—from three to six. Now that he is in a small group of three students and all of them are working to learn how to read the same words, he is getting five times as many trials as he used to. This has been made possible through direct instruction that includes specific and immediate feedback, and opportunities for observational learning.").

In closing, I believe that I need to address one other modern-day phenomenon that has served as an impetus for writing this book. It is the mantra, "College and Career Ready."

The use of small group instruction as described in this book is not intended to make most of the students who receive it "college ready." Yet it is intended to make them career ready. Likewise, this type of instruction can go a long way toward making other students who will not attend college career ready.

I say this because, personally, I believe that the "College and Career Ready" statement needs to be stated in the reverse for the betterment of everyone. That is to say, every student needs to be prepared to assume a career but not every student needs to be prepared to successfully complete college.

Consequently, we need to begin talking about the concept of "Career and College Ready." This stance also highlights how the content that is presented in this book has appeal for a wider audience than, upon first glance, one may assume it does.

Acknowledgments

Like many worthwhile undertakings, the completion of this endeavor resulted from the contributions of a group of competent colleagues. Thanks go to Dr. Beverly Morse, Dr. Kathryn Gift, Marie Wicks, Sarah Wicks, and Michelle Andrews for reviewing the book for clarity and content. Additionally, I am thankful to Dr. Beverly Morse and Sarah Wicks for the work they performed to ensure that the book was properly formatted.

Finally, I am grateful for the request to write this book from the extremely patient staff at Rowman & Littlefield. They kept this project going while, at various times, I addressed other issues that resulted in a delay of the finished product.

Introduction

This book is intended to be a handbook for presenting effective instruction in a small group arrangement. In particular, this instruction is intended to meet the needs of two categories of students: (a) those who have not attained targeted learning outcomes after primarily receiving large group instruction in a general education classroom and (b) those who receive instruction in a self-contained classroom on the basis of the manifestation of their disability. Consequently, this handbook presents information that pertains to remedial instruction that also may or may not be special education. Furthermore, its content focuses on the presentation of remedial instruction that is explicit, teacher-directed, and intensive.

There are two primary reasons for this focus. One reason is that research supports the topic that is the focus of this book.[1] A second reason is the concern others have expressed about the instructional needs of students who are not meeting targeted learning outcomes after receiving what has been characterized as high-quality instruction in a general education classroom where large group arrangements predominate.[2]

While the content that is presented in this book focuses on what can be referred to as intensive basic skills instruction in a small group arrangement, this content can readily be extended to teaching students higher-order thinking and problem-solving skills. For instance, reading comprehension strategies, such as predicting and visualizing, can be taught using the content that is presented. Addressing this matter in detail, however, is beyond the scope of this book.

From the outset it is important for you to know that the approach to small group instruction that is presented in this book is a labor-intensive endeavor. This book addresses the assiduous tasks of designing and presenting effective instruction in a small group arrangement to students who demonstrate significant, persistent learning challenges. This effective instruction results from the provision of intensive intervention rather than other protocols such as (a) special education as accommodations or (b) providing students exposure to the core curriculum.

Special education as accommodations refers to altering the conditions under which instruction is presented or how a student responds without changing the targeted learning outcome. Exposing students to the general education curriculum means that it is shown to them but it does not necessarily mean that they will be required to demonstrate that they have independently attained all of the curriculum's targeted learning outcomes.

Presently a student could be provided accommodations that enable them to be exposed to their school's grade-level, core curriculum but not result in their mastery of the majority of the curriculum's learning standards. An example of this outcome would be when a student with a disability barely earns the lowest passing grade (i.e., a D) for their Algebra 1 class and passes the required concomitant state exam by earning the required percentage of points (e.g., 31 percent) necessary to get a passing score. It is possible that accommodations and exposure to the core curriculum are provided as part of a good-faith effort to enable a student to demonstrate mastery of the grade-level curriculum while remaining in the general education classroom. This approach would be in keeping with the philosophy of full inclusion.

However, global constructs, such as the philosophy of full inclusion and the perspective that a student's low achievement is simply an outcome of a teacher's low expectations regarding what the student is capable of achieving, divert attention and efforts away from addressing numerous issues that must be addressed to set the occasion for the presentation of effective, intensive instruction. These issues include:

1. Establishing an appropriate environmental arrangement
2. Addressing students' dispositions toward receiving this instruction[3]
3. Providing students with the relatively high number of repetitions they need to engage in to learn a task
4. Planning for the presentation of multiple levels of content that match the instructional level of each student who is a member of a small group (e.g., a resource room with nine students and five distinct instructional reading levels)

The comments that have been attributed to a professor at a major research university are particularly germane. He reportedly often told his graduate students that "90% of the work involved in any worthwhile endeavor is grunt work." Grunt work, according to this individual, is work that involves attention to numerous, tedious details. When conducted properly, this work leads to the completion of a larger finished product that is both well done and highly valued. In his line of work this might have been the publication of a meta-analysis of all of the research that had been published about effective instruction for teaching first-grade students basic addition facts.

His remarks are relevant to this book, which focuses on what can be considered as the grunt work (i.e., tedious, necessary details) that must be attended to so that students who display significant, ongoing challenges mastering targeted learning outcomes are presented with effective instruction. In particular the targeted learning outcomes that result from this tedious work are outcomes that are appropriate and challenging for the students, and are connected to the general education curriculum.

This last point is a very important one to understand during a time when educators grapple with what rightfully can be considered as conflicting messages. One message is that educators should focus on developing each student's college and career readiness by getting them to achieve every grade-level curriculum standard.

The other message is that certain students, such as those with disabilities who are being provided special education services, are to be provided an individualized education that, among other things, focuses on providing them instruction that has been configured to account for their characteristics of thinking and learning plus the curriculum content that is at their instructional level. This instructional level may be far removed from the aforementioned grade-level standards.

Part of presenting effective small group instruction is measuring students' progress toward, and their ultimate attainment of, targeted learning outcomes. Consequently, the content that is presented in this book does present guidance for measuring a student's progress relative to a targeted learning outcome.

In particular, the book emphasizes measuring a student's progress relative to measures of performance prior to the presentation of instruction in a small group arrangement. These are called intra-individual measures that pertain to the student's performance of targeted academic and school social behaviors. In some instances the measures will focus on minute aspects of a student's behavior, such as a reduction in response latency, in addition to typical measures of academic achievement.

Thus, whereas general outcome measures that monitor a student's progress toward mastery of the entire curriculum that will be taught during the school year are as important to these students as they are to their peers, these measures are not the focus of this book. Effective small group instruction for these students will be realized when meticulous attention is paid to every detail that could be relevant to the presentation of instruction or the conduct of assessment. This book is meant to serve as a starting point for your understanding of this type of instruction although, in some instances, it may be a resource for refresher training. Hopefully it will serve as a starting point for more investigation about the topic.

Chapter 1 establishes the rationale for addressing both the topic of small group instruction as well as its particular use as a platform for providing explicit, teacher-directed, intensive, remedial instruction to students who demonstrate significant and ongoing challenges mastering targeted learning outcomes. The outcomes include mastery of academic and functional content, plus school social behaviors. For the sake of simplicity, throughout the book the term intensive instruction is used to refer to instruction that is explicit, teacher-directed, intensive, and remedial.

Chapter 2 lays the groundwork for connecting the instruction that is presented in general education classrooms with what is most often supplemental instruction in the type of small group arrangements that are the focus of this book. Specifically, chapter 2 explains basic, fundamental, effective teaching practices in terms of the high-quality instruction that is called for in discussions of multi-tier systems of support.

This instruction is intended to be presented in general education classrooms in which large group arrangements predominate. Students who do not attain targeted learning outcomes after receiving this instruction comprise the pool of candidates for whom intensive, small group instruction may be appropriate.

Chapter 3 addresses the features of this type of small group instruction that ensure that it is distinguishable from the large group instruction that proved to be ineffective. These features ensure that this type of instruction is something other than "more of the same" and is, therefore, calculated to offer teachers and students the highest probability that this type of instruction will prove to be effective.

Chapter 4 identifies and discusses considerations that a teacher must address as they prepare to present intensive, small group instruction. For example, the teacher will need to account for the characteristics of thinking and learning that are exhibited by the students. These characteristics might include features such as sensory differences, being prone to distractions, impulsivity, and preferences for routines. Accordingly, the teacher may arrange the environment with dividers and solid color curtains to eliminate potential visual distractions, and follow a direct instruction lesson plan as a way to establish a functional routine.

Next, chapter 5 explains one protocol for presenting this type of instruction. This protocol allows for the incorporation of various instructional strategies that enable intensive, small group instruction to be "uniquely different" from the large group instruction that is presented in a general education classroom and was discussed in chapter 2.

Chapter 6 addresses the topic of assessment. First, general terms, concepts, and issues pertaining to assessment are discussed. This discussion focuses on assessment from a school-wide perspective in the sense that measures of large groups of students are being obtained and evaluated (i.e., determining how the first-, second-, third-, and fourth-grade students are doing).

Second, terms, concepts, and issues that are specific to assessment as it applies to intensive, small group instruction are discussed. Emphasis is placed on the assessment of individual students as opposed to groups of students.

Chapter 7 focuses on teaching what is referred to as functional content to students with disabilities who have been determined to be eligible to receive special education services. The federal law that directs how educators are to design and implement appropriate educational programs for these students states that if they need to be taught this content, then public schools must do so.

Small group arrangements can prove to be an effective and efficient forum for teaching this content. Additionally, the characteristics of thinking and learning that are exhibited by some of the students who need to learn this content necessitates the use of intensive small group instruction or, in some cases, a 1:1 arrangement (i.e., one student with one teacher). Most of the content that is presented in this book can be applied to the latter situation, although it is not addressed directly in this manuscript.

NOTES

1. Belva C. Collins, David L. Gast, Melinda J. Ault, and Mark Wolery, "Small Group Instruction: Guidelines for Teachers and Students with Moderate to Severe Handicaps," *Education & Training in Mental Retardation* 26, no. 1 (1991): 1–18.

2. Douglas Fuchs and Lynn S. Fuchs, "Introduction to Response to Intervention: What, Why, and How Valid is It?" *Reading Research Quarterly* 41, no. 1 (2006): 93–99.

3. National Center on Intensive Intervention (NCII) at American Institutes for Research, *Data-Based Individualization: A Framework for Intensive Intervention*, ERIC Clearinghouse, 2013.

Chapter One

Small Group Instruction

Establishing the Conditions for Presenting Effective Instruction

OVERVIEW

In this chapter you will learn about the rationale for providing small group instruction and its primary features. You also will be introduced to the type of instruction—explicit, teacher-directed, intensive, and remedial—that is the focus of small group instruction as it is explained in this book.

Key points from this chapter include the following:

1. Among the variables that a teacher might consider, and subsequently plan for, when they set out to present effective instruction include (a) the time allocated for instruction, (b) the curriculum that is to be taught, (c) the instructional materials that will be used, (d) the way that the instructional setting will be configured, and (e) exactly which students and staff will be present during a lesson.
2. For various reasons not every student is able to demonstrate adequate progress in the general education classroom where large group instruction is presented. Hence, small group arrangements are called for—either explicitly or implicitly—in the professional literature and relevant laws.
3. In most cases the intervention of changing the size of the instructional group, in and of itself, will not be sufficient to produce changes in a student's behavior. Rather, the thoughtful, meticulous manipulation of numerous variables that pertain to a small group instructional arrangement—and that are possible because of it—will have the highest probability of subsequently resulting in a student's attainment of targeted learning outcomes.

4. One approach to presenting effective instruction while using a small group arrangement involves the use of explicit, teacher-directed, intense, remedial instruction. This type of instruction is the focus of the content that is presented throughout this book.
5. Small group instruction refers to an arrangement in which there is a pupil:teacher ratio of at least two, but not more than eight, students with one teacher.
6. Just about any student can benefit from small group instruction. This type of instruction can be presented in various locations within a school or on the school's grounds, and can be presented before, during, or after school.
7. Reasons for presenting small group instruction include the facts that (a) a student's particular characteristics of thinking and learning necessitates this type of arrangement, (b) public schools cannot afford a 1:1 instructional arrangement for every student who is demonstrating a learning challenge, and (c) small group instruction prepares students for instruction in other school (e.g., general education classrooms) and non-school locations (e.g., Sunday school) where large group arrangements are employed.
8. The meanings for key vocabulary as they are used in this book are presented in this and subsequent chapters to provide you with an opportunity to fully understand the content that is presented. In this chapter some of the key vocabulary that are defined include explicit, effective, efficient, and intense instruction, as well as learning, mastery, and accommodations.
9. One's philosophy refers to their thoughts regarding the fundamental features and principles about some phenomenon. Aspects of a philosophy pertaining to the relationship that exists between teaching and learning are presented at the end of this chapter. These include beliefs that (a) a teacher who is knowledgeable about their subject matter and is skillful in the presentation of effective instruction is a student's most valuable asset, (b) the time that has been made available for the presentation of instruction is the student's second most valuable asset, (c) students learn by doing, and (d) some students will be able to make meaningful progress in mastering targeted learning outcomes only by participating in small group instructional arrangements most of the time.

THE CASE FOR NEEDING TO PRESENT INTENSIVE SMALL GROUP INSTRUCTION

Professional sports coaches and business owners often remark that their primary job is to determine how to put each of their employees in a position that affords them the highest probability to be successful. Likewise, public school teachers—whose students' job is to attend school and master the content that is taught—continually seek ways to create instructional settings that afford their students the highest probability to be successful in their work. Currently this success is primarily measured by each student's performance on standardized assessments that have been designed to determine whether the student has learned the academic content they have been taught.

Consequently, when teachers plan for, and subsequently present, what they trust will be effective instruction, they consider a plethora of variables that they surmise can have a noteworthy impact on a student's ability to demonstrate mastery of the curriculum. The bases for their belief include supporting research as well as professional and personal experiences. The variables teachers might consider include, but certainly are not limited to, the following:

1. the time allocated for instruction;
2. the curriculum that is to be taught—particularly its scope and sequence;
3. the instructional materials that are available for use and, more specifically, the ones that will be used;
4. the pace at which instruction will be presented;
5. the type and amount of active student responding that will be solicited;
6. the mode of responding that will be required from the student;
7. the type and amount of feedback that will be presented following correct and incorrect responding;
8. how the instructional setting will be configured; and,
9. exactly which students and staff will be present during a lesson, and the roles they will fulfill.

The last variable (i.e., the number of people who will be in an instructional setting) is an issue that is relevant to all types of educators—both general and special education teachers as well as related service providers, such as speech-language pathologists, occupational therapists, and physical therapists. Given how most schools are structured, the general education classroom is the default placement for all students and, as such, represents a location where instruction typically is presented to relatively large groups of students (i.e., twenty to more than thirty students at a time).

The term "class size" is often used to refer to the number of students in a general education classroom, and the term's use is predicated on the assumption that these students will be taught by one teacher. Quite often fiscal constraints largely influence the typical class size in a school irrespective of sound, pedagogical arguments in favor of other—most often smaller—class sizes.

However, for various reasons, not every student is able to demonstrate adequate progress in the general education classroom when large group instruction is presented, and this circumstance results in educators being tasked to determine how instruction can be presented differently to these students so that they can master the content they are taught. The use of small group instructional arrangements with these students is one intervention educators employ to address this circumstance.

These groups may consist of multiple students and only one instructor who either remain in the general education classroom or else go to another location within the school (e.g., a setting where special education services are presented exclusively, such as a resource room). Conversely, these groups may consist of both multiple students and multiple instructors, as may be the case in one type of setting where special education services are provided exclusively: a self-contained classroom.

Consequently, the term "pupil:teacher ratio" is used to describe situations where small groups of students may be receiving instruction from one teacher (e.g., a 5:1 pupil:teacher ratio describes a situation in which five students receive instruction from one teacher), or one teacher as well as one or more teaching assistants (e.g., an 8:3 pupil:teacher ratio describes a situation in which eight students receive instruction in a setting where three instructors are present, such as a teacher who presents the lesson while two teaching assistants support the teacher by monitoring the students for displays of appropriate behavior and provide appropriate prompts to insure correct responding).

Small group arrangements are called for—either explicitly or implicitly—in the professional literature and relevant laws. For instance, recent advocacy for the use of response-to-intervention models that are intended to remediate students' academic deficits and provide data that can be used to determine a student's eligibility for special education services specifically call for the use of small group instructional arrangements. Likewise, the continuum of alternative placement options that are put forth in the nation's federal special education law, the Individuals with Disabilities Education Act (IDEA),[1] implicitly call for the provision of instruction in small group arrangements.

Hence, educators need to know about interventions that are provided beyond those that involve large group arrangements and will result in a student demonstrating appropriate progress in the core curriculum. A basic definition for an educational intervention is a change of the environment. Therefore, placing a student in a small versus a large group arrangement to receive instruction would be an intervention. However, in most cases, the intervention of changing the size of the group, in and of itself, will not be enough to produce changes in a student's behavior.

Rather, the thoughtful, meticulous manipulation of numerous variables that pertain to a small group instructional arrangement—and that are possible because of it—will have the highest probability of subsequently resulting in a student's attainment of targeted learning outcomes. Thus, the employment of a small group instructional arrangement would be one element in a multicomponent intervention that must allow for the manipulation of numerous variables, simultaneously, that have been shown to produce favorable learning outcomes.

How, then, can small group instruction allow for the provision of instruction that is notably different from the large group instruction that is presented in a general education classroom but is ineffective with students without disabilities who demonstrate learning challenges, as well as children with disabilities who receive special education services that are, by law, required to consist of specially designed instruction? Answers to this question are the focus of this book.

More specifically, this book focuses on the design and implementation of effective small group instruction that is explicit, teacher-directed, intense, and remedial. Each of these four terms is defined below.

1. *Explicit.* A type of teacher-directed instruction during which all aspects are made known to the learner. Central features of explicit instruction include the teacher selecting the learning objective and then designing a structured lesson that is comprised of (a) direct explanation and modeling by the teacher, (b) guided practice, (c) independent practice, (d) assessment, and (e) lesson review. Each feature incorporates evidence-based strategies that enhance student learning, such as the use of clear and concise language by the teacher when they present a direct explanation and modeling, and opportunities for frequent and varied active student responding during guided practice.

    This definition indicates that the instruction that is presented in small group arrangements will be teacher-directed. Also, the definition identifies variables that can be skillfully controlled for the purpose of refining instruction to be as effective as possible. This sets the occasion for teachers to think about the large number of relevant external variables that they can change in order to make their instruction effective rather than simply explaining a student's learning challenges as a child-centered phenomenon.

2. *Teacher-directed.* The work that a teacher performs is central to the type of small group instruction that is explained in this book. As was noted previously, the teacher's role involves the teacher taking the lead in a number of ways, which include selecting a curriculum standard, writing a relevant learning objective, modeling how to successfully perform the

activity that is the focus of the learning objective, and supporting students in their initial attempts to do the same.

While interventions that are not teacher-directed, such as the use of computer-based instruction, can be effective within a small group instructional arrangement, these interventions are not the focus of this book. Similarly, the use of cooperative learning groups in which peers are intimately involved in directing each other's learning are not addressed.

3. *Intense.* Intensive instruction refers to strategically designed interventions that address elements that allow for more individualized and prolonged student engagement.[2] Engagement refers to a student's cognitive processing of the content that is the focus of a lesson. Intensive interventions evolve from an examination of the large group instruction that is presented in a general education classroom. This instruction is made more intense by changing certain aspects such as the size of the group, affording students more opportunities to practice performing targeted skills, and providing immediate and specific feedback to each student response.

4. *Remedial.* Remedial instruction is provided to rectify, or resolve, a student's significant and ongoing challenge learning targeted academic, functional, or school social behavior content. In most cases the student needs to learn content that is at their current age-appropriate grade level because they have not done so as a result of receiving instruction in the general education classroom through the presentation of instruction in a large group arrangement.

In many instances, irrespective of the student's age, remedial instruction can be equated to instruction the focuses on what are referred to as basic skills (e.g., learning multiplication and division facts, decoding one- and two-syllable words). Yet care should be taken to avoid equating the meanings of words such as basic and fundamental to the meaning of the word easy. The considerable effort that is required by a student to learn this content, as well as the labor-intensive work that a teacher must engage in to prepare for—and present—effective remedial instruction, explains why a word such as challenging is more accurate and appropriate.

For the sake of clarity, the phrase "intensive small group instruction" is used throughout this book to refer to the explicit, teacher-directed, intense, remedial instruction that was just described. One reason for using this convention is that the intensive instruction that students who present long-standing, significant learning challenges will need to receive will nearly always have to be explicit, teacher-directed, and remedial in addition to being intensive in ways that are student-specific.

SCENARIOS SUPPORTING THE RELEVANCE OF GROUP CONFIGURATION TO THE PRESENTATION OF EFFECTIVE INSTRUCTION

The following three stories about the impact of group arrangements on students' learning outcomes lend credence to the argument that educators need to consider the potential significance of small group instruction. In fact, it could be argued that these types of reports from the field are examples of expert validity in terms of how group configurations are a key element of a multi-component intervention that results in effective instruction.

1. A professor remarked about a practicum in which he supervised aspiring special education teachers. In this practicum each aspiring teacher was required to present instruction to two to three third-grade students in a small group arrangement. Otherwise, these students primarily received instruction in a large group arrangement in a general education classroom.

    One of these students entered his group demonstrating that he could read three of the 220 words from a high frequency word list (i.e., the Dolch Word List). After participating in his small group practicum for two days per week, thirty minutes per day, for a total of eight weeks, the student was able to read fifty-three of the words from this list.

    His progress certainly raised the question of what, exactly, happened in this small group that apparently did not happen in his four years of prior schooling that enabled him to make such remarkable progress with respect to this one skill. Similarly, another question that was raised was what other kinds of remarkable progress could this boy have made with respect to mastering other academic content if he were provided similar instructional experiences.

2. A special education teacher reported his experience involving a high school student who the teacher worked with, daily, in a small group setting after the student had participated in his Algebra 1 class the very same day. Unsolicited, the student told the teacher that he (the student) needed the teacher to show him eighteen times how to solve a new problem as opposed to the four times he was shown how to do a new problem on a typical day in his Algebra 1 class.

    In other words, the student was able to clearly discern at least one way that instruction within a small group arrangement should differ from the way that instruction was being presented in a traditional general education class with twenty to thirty students in order to enable him to master the content. Put another way, he was aware that he was going to struggle in his Algebra 1 class given how it was structured and operated compared to the way he needed the instructional environment to be configured.

3. Some students with disabilities are provided services beyond the traditional school calendar in what commonly is referred to as an extended school year program. Essentially these services are provided during the traditional summer break to enable the students to maintain the progress they demonstrated during the school year. Yet in one instance school staff reported that their students with autism made noteworthy progress, rather than just maintained skills, when the students and staff had to occupy smaller classrooms because the larger classrooms that they typically occupied were under repair.

This circumstance resulted in smaller group arrangements than were in place during the school year. Within these arrangements, staff and students not only interacted more frequently but staff also were able to provide more individualized instruction—particularly with respect to the feedback they presented to the students.

SMALL GROUP INSTRUCTION: THE WHAT, WHO, WHERE, WHEN, WHY, AND HOW

In the following, an overview of small group instruction is presented in the form of limited answers to the following what, who, where, when, why, and how questions. Throughout the book the answers to these questions are developed in greater detail.

What Is Small Group Instruction?

In this book small group instruction refers to an arrangement in which there is a pupil:teacher ratio that consists of at least two, but not more than eight, students with one teacher. Because there is not a universally agreed upon definition for small group instruction you may come across other definitions that extend the upper limit of the number of students in the group. For instance, other authors have defined small group instruction such that as many as ten students can be in the group.[3]

Arguably one component of any definition of small group instruction must be that there is a minimum of two students so as to ensure that a group does, in fact, exist. Furthermore, since the rationale for providing instruction to students in a small group arrangement is often that the students are not able to demonstrate mastery of targeted learning outcomes when provided instruction in a typical large group arrangement in a general education classroom (i.e., an arrangement in which the pupil:teacher ratio is 20-30+:1), definitions for small group instruction should establish a limit for the total number of students that is significantly lower than that for a typical general education classroom.

Who Can Benefit From Small Group Instruction?

Just about any student can benefit from small group instruction. Many students with significant disabilities who had been thought to be able to learn only by being provided effective instruction in a 1:1 arrangement subsequently demonstrated that they can participate appropriately and master targeted learning outcomes when they were in a small group.[4]

Likewise, students who have made limited or less-than-expected progress after participating in large group arrangements in general education classrooms have demonstrated that both their rate and level of learning can increase after they have received what is referred to as more intense instruction in a small group arrangement.[5] These are students who have been described as presenting significant, persistent challenges to learning academic content or school social behaviors.

Even though they are not the subject of this book, students who perform above average also can benefit from small group instruction. Small group arrangements are often used when these students participate in tutorials.

Where Can Small Group Instruction Be Presented?

Small group instruction can be presented in any location on a school's campus that can be configured (a) to accommodate the number of students and staff who comprise the group and (b) in a way that physically supports the provision of effective instruction. This means that this type of instruction can be presented within a properly constructed sub-environment in a general education classroom as well as a classroom that has much less floor space because it has been specifically designed for small group arrangements. Small group instruction also can be presented in common areas, such as a cafeteria or on the stage in an auditorium—provided the physical space has been properly configured.

When Can Small Group Instruction Be Presented?

In terms of the exact time during the school day, small group instruction can be presented at any point within the total time that has been allotted for the school day, as well as immediately before or after this time. Oftentimes small group arrangements are used to present remedial instruction or instruction to students who have been absent from school during tutorial sessions that are conducted either right before the start of the school day or immediately after it ends.

With respect to curriculum content and when it would be taught, small group arrangements can be used to teach students both academic knowledge and skills, school social behaviors, and what are referred to as functional tasks (which are also referred to as life skills or activities of daily living). One example of when a small group arrangement would be used to teach academic content would be when a group of students needs to receive intensive, remedial instruction because they have demonstrated persistent challenges acquiring grade-level content. An example of when this arrangement would be used to teach a functional skill is when students need to learn a cooking skill, but it is not feasible financially for each student to be able to prepare an item or meal that is the focus of the cooking activity.

Why Would You Use Small Group Arrangements?

In general, there are four reasons why small group arrangements are used. One is because students have not been successful—meaning they have not attained targeted learning outcomes—after receiving large group instruction in a general education classroom. A second reason is because a student needs to learn how to participate in some type of group instructional arrangement other than a 1:1 arrangement. There are a couple of reasons this is so.

First, for financial reasons public schools cannot afford a 1:1 instructional arrangement for every student, or even a significant number of students. Thus, school personnel need to know how to provide effective, efficient small group instruction.[6] Second, small group instruction prepares students for instruction in other school (i.e., the general education classroom) and non-school settings (e.g., Sunday school, summer camps) where various forms of large group instruction are presented and considered to be the norm.

A third reason why you would use small group arrangements is because a student's characteristics of thinking and learning necessitates this type of arrangement. A student who exhibits sensory differences and is hypersensitive to sound and the movements of others may not be able to focus properly in a large group arrangement. Finally, in accordance with aspects of the provision of special education services to students with disabilities, there is an expectation that small group arrangements will be used in certain locations. These include resource and self-contained classrooms that are a part of what is called the continuum of alternative placements.

Who Can Present Instruction in a Small Group Arrangement?

A wide variety of individuals can present instruction to students in a small group arrangement. This circumstance is partly the result of one type of approach that is available for presenting small group instruction: a standard treatment protocol. This approach involves the use of a pre-packaged, commercial program that has been designed to be presented in a small group arrangement and comes with detailed presentation instructions.

Thus, in addition to licensed personnel—including general and special education teachers and speech-language pathologists—teacher assistants, adult volunteers, school support personnel (e.g., clerical staff), and certain students (e.g., preservice teachers or high school students seeking to fulfill community service hours) can present small group instruction.

How Do You Present Small Group Instruction?

The focus of this book is how to present explicit, teacher-directed, intensive, remedial instruction in small group arrangements. In particular, the focus is on the use of instructional strategies that enhance students active responding during academic learning time as well as the amount of engagement between the teacher and the students.

A related matter pertains to the general protocol that will be followed when instruction is presented to students in a small group arrangement. It is important to note the two basic approaches to small group instruction: standard treatment protocol and problem-solving protocol. The standard treatment protocol was described previously. The problem-solving protocol involves the development and implementation of intervention services that are predicated on a case study approach.

The information presented in this book is applicable to both protocols. However, it is more clearly related to a problem-solving protocol, which entails building individualized small group instruction from "the ground up." Also, when functional content is the focus of small group instruction there are very few commercial programs available, so standard treatment protocols are rarely an option.

KEY TERMS AND CONCEPTS

Sometimes in the field of education multiple definitions are offered for a single term or phrase. One example of this phenomenon is the term explicit instruction. In addition to how it was defined previously, explicit instruction also has been defined as follows:

1. Demonstration of a step-by-step plan that is specific for a set of problems; students use the same steps to solve the problem[7]
2. Segmenting of complex skills, using modeling or think aloud, systematically fading supports or prompts, providing opportunities for students to respond and receive feedback, and creating purposeful practice[8]
3. Unambiguous and direct approach to teaching; includes both instructional design and delivery procedures[9]

Furthermore, different terms can, in some people's minds, refer to the same concept.[10] For instance, some educators think that the terms explicit instruction, systematic instruction, and direct instruction are synonymous. Altogether, these circumstances can lead to confusion.

A quotation that has been attributed to the philosopher Voltaire is relevant to the current discussion. He reportedly said, "If you wish to converse with me, define your terms." One plausible interpretation of this statement is that two people will be more likely to agree on the meaning of the topic they are discussing if they first settle upon the meanings for the words they are using.

While this book's glossary provides definitions for a wide variety of noteworthy terms and phrases that are used in this book, some key terms and concepts are listed and defined in the following. As you read the content, remain mindful of the fact that the purpose of this section is not to get you to agree with how the key vocabulary in this book has been defined. Rather, the purpose is to make transparent to you the meanings of these key vocabulary. To be able to comprehend the overall meaning of the connected text you must first understand the meanings of individual words.

1. *Effective instruction.* Instruction that results in a student demonstrating mastery of the targeted learning objective.
2. *Efficient instruction.* Efficient instruction is effective instruction that, relative to one or more other means of presenting effective instruction, requires less time, teacher effort, or financial or tangible resources.
3. *Learning objective.* A statement that describes the knowledge or skill from the curriculum that the student will acquire after being presented effective instruction. This statement includes (a) the student's name; (b) an observable, measurable explanation of the knowledge or skill they will acquire; (c) the conditions under which the student will acquire the knowledge or skill; and (d) the criteria for mastery.

An example of a learning objective is as follows: "When presented with ten index cards on which one numeral, zero to nine, is written, Jaquan will state the name of each numeral correctly within two seconds across three consecutive daily probes."

4. *Curriculum.* A comprehensive listing of the knowledge and skills that students are expected to learn through the instruction they are presented at school. In this book a curriculum may refer to academic content, functional content, or school social behaviors.

   Academic knowledge and skills pertain to traditional disciplines such as math, English, science, and social studies. Functional content addresses what are referred to as the activities of daily living, such as dressing and cooking skills. School social behaviors pertain to the observable actions a student engages in to share space appropriately with others—both on school grounds and in locations considered to be school grounds, such as the school bus that transports students to and from school.
5. *Learning.* A relatively permanent change in behavior resulting from experience (i.e., a change in behavior that results from receiving instruction). This definition differentiates learning from other changes in behavior that are the result of some factor other than teaching. An example is a change in one's behavior that is the result of physical maturation. Whereas a student can be taught how to add two single-digit numbers, after learning how to pick up a bag of sand they cannot be taught how to pick up a ten-pound bag instead of a five-pound bag if they have not physically matured to the point of being able to do so.
6. *Mastery.* A student is said to have demonstrated mastery when they have acquired the knowledge or skill that is defined in a learning objective in accordance with the established criterion for correct responding (e.g., reading ten high frequency words within thirty seconds across three consecutive assessment sessions or complying with all of the rules for appropriate behavior while eating lunch in the cafeteria on 95 percent of the days during a nine-week grading period).
7. *Instructional strategy.* The planned actions a teacher executes when they present a lesson. Synonymous terms include teaching procedure, teaching strategy, and teaching method. (See the discussion regarding the four basic instructional strategies.)
8. *Teaching.* Teaching involves imparting knowledge and skills to others. It results from the actions, or behaviors, a teacher exhibits to enable their students to master their learning objectives and, hence, their curriculum.
9. *Accommodations.* Changes to the conditions under which a student is expected to acquire knowledge or perform an academic skill, rather than an

alteration of the standard that has been set for performance. A change to the standard is a modification. Accommodations may include, but are not necessarily limited to, the time that a student is given to complete a task, the manner in which the task is presented to the student (e.g., in writing rather than an oral presentation), the mode of responding that is required from the student (e.g., typewritten rather than handwritten answers), and the arrangement of the setting in which the task is to be performed (e.g., in a small rather than large group).

The purpose for providing an accommodation is to ensure that a student's performance is a valid reflection of their ability. Accommodations are provided to allow for an equitable, as opposed to advantageous, situation for a student.

INTENSIVE SMALL GROUP INSTRUCTION AND ITS RELATIONSHIP TO A FUNDAMENTAL PHILOSOPHY ABOUT TEACHING AND LEARNING

At the heart of this book is a discussion of the numerous details that need to be considered when a teacher prepares for, and then presents, effective small group instruction to students who demonstrate significant, persistent challenges mastering targeted learning outcomes. This content, however, is related to a broader philosophy about teaching and learning with respect to this book's focus.

This philosophy is presented here to enable you to fully appreciate the overarching perspective that is put forth in this book. As you read this philosophy, consider how it compares to yours. Then when you finish the book revisit this philosophy and reconsider its relationship to yours.

1. A teacher who is knowledgeable about their subject matter and is skillful in their presentation of effective instruction is the most valuable asset to a student who is working to master targeted learning outcomes. This type of teacher needs to be put in a position that provides them with the highest probability that they will be able to use their knowledge and skills to be effective. In some instances, allowing the teacher to design and implement small group instruction will be what is necessary to enable them to be effective.
2. The time that has been made available for the presentation of instruction is the second most valuable asset to a student who is working to master targeted learning outcomes. Consequently, educators must be able to

justify their use of allotted time for any purpose other than presenting instruction.
3. Students learn by doing.[11] Therefore, throughout a lesson every student must be permitted a maximum number of opportunities to engage in active responding. More specifically, students who demonstrate significant, persistent learning challenges and need to be provided intensive small group instruction often will require an exceedingly high number of opportunities to actively respond.

    Reportedly there is a Russian saying regarding effective teaching, which is, "Repetition is the mother of all learning." Likewise, John Wooden, the college basketball coach of renown, reportedly said that the teaching process consists of four steps: demonstration, imitation, repetition, and correction. Educators need to be prepared for the tremendous number of practice opportunities that some students will require before they are able to meet the criteria for mastery of a targeted learning objective.
4. Educators must make certain that the use of accommodations or modifications do not mask a student's need for intensive instruction to remediate their challenges to learning academic or functional content, or school social behaviors. Among other things, this issue highlights the fact that, first and foremost, educators must be able to make a distinction between an accommodation and a modification. Additionally, particularly with respect to the use of accommodations, educators must be able to show that the reasoned, systematic, data-based use of an accommodation results in a more valid demonstration of a student's mastery of the curriculum than would otherwise be the case absent the accommodation.
5. Peer-reviewed research (i.e., "the literature"), as well as evidence-based practices, are among a number of sources of information that can provide educators with guidance concerning the provision of effective instruction.[12] Additional sources include the data educators collect on the students they teach and these educators' professional and personal experiences—which include the interventions that arise from them.

    The recent, concerted emphasis by some regarding the use of evidence-based practices neglects a noteworthy limitation of published peer-reviewed research, which is that it is overwhelmingly populated by studies that present positive outcomes. Consequently, what will never be known is how many studies have been conducted using the same—or very similar—interventions and in which positive outcomes were not achieved because these studies are not readily available for examination.
6. Resources matter, so the feasibility of any proposed intervention must be considered with respect to whether it can be implemented "to scale" in a

public school system in which there is fierce competition for the available, albeit limited, resources. That is to say, an effective intervention that is based upon a 1:1 pupil:teacher ratio most likely is not scalable in most public school settings. Conversely, the higher the pupil:teacher ratio in a small group arrangement in which effective instruction can be presented, the higher the probability that it can be implemented to scale in a public school system.

7. Some students will be able to make meaningful progress in mastering targeted learning outcomes only by participating in small group instructional arrangements most of the time. For these students, small group instruction will be a mainstay of their public school programming. This might be the case for certain students with disabilities who have been placed in a self-contained classroom.

    Conversely, plans need to be developed and implemented for the purpose of enabling students who are successful in small group arrangements to also be successful in general education settings in which large group instruction is presented. This will mean that some students will always need to receive instruction in a combination of large and small group instructional arrangements.

    This latter circumstance highlights the need to be cautious about adopting an "automobile engine repair" philosophy when using some type of response-to-intervention framework. As was just noted, while the use of small group instruction to address a student's academic or social behavior deficits will result in some students returning to a general education classroom where they will forevermore make appropriate progress without having to receive supplemental instruction, this instruction may never result in other students being able to function just like their grade-level peers in a general education classroom. This situation stands in sharp contrast to what happens when an automobile engine needs to be repaired.

    A short stay in a repair shop during which a targeted fix is performed to the engine most likely is all that is needed to enable a car to get back on the highway and perform similarly to other vehicles for the rest of the car's existence. A student, however, may never be "fixed" in a manner that can be implied through the use of small group arrangements in a response-to-intervention framework. Instead the student will always need to receive instruction in a combination of large and small group instructional arrangements.

8. Both antecedent- and consequence-based interventions must be employed simultaneously to teach students how to master targeted learning objectives. Historically, school personnel who have worked with stu-

dents who have demonstrated significant, persistent learning challenges have relied heavily upon consequence-based interventions to teach students targeted learning objectives, particularly those that address school social behaviors.[13]

However, more attention needs to be paid to the use of effective antecedent-based interventions because these interventions highlight the essence of a proactive, teacher-directed approach that sets the occasion for correct student responding and, ultimately, the presentation of effective instruction.[14]

9. What gets taught is what gets learned. On the one hand this statement highlights the importance of clearly defining the content that is to be taught,[15] as well as the need to make clear to students what they are to learn. On the other hand, this statement reminds educators to be cognizant of the hidden curriculum that is being presented to students and is being learned by them.

For example, the content that comprises a traditional academic curriculum is readily available to those who desire to know it for no other reason than it is published in various locations that allow ease of access, such as a school district's website. Conversely, some behaviors are not explicitly stipulated as being a part of this formal curriculum but are, nonetheless, learned by students as a result of the way instruction is presented when the traditional curriculum is taught. For instance, a student may learn that they do not have to develop sound study habits for the purpose of passing an exam because, if the class performs extremely poorly on the exam, the teacher will grade it on a curve or allow the students some other means to raise their grade.

10. Recognize the fact that academic and school social behaviors must be addressed simultaneously. Some professionals who have been employed to work with students who have been identified as having a disability that manifests as displays of noteworthy inappropriate school social behaviors have asserted that they (the professionals) could not be held responsible for teaching the students' academic behaviors until the students' inappropriate school social behaviors were "under control." For a number of reasons this stance is indefensible.

One reason this stance is indefensible is because the academic knowledge and skills these students are being taught may, in fact, serve as the basis for their displays of inappropriate school social behaviors. That is to say, these students may either act out or withdraw from engaging with their environment as a direct result of their frustration or angst that results from instruction that they perceive to be inappropriate. It could be that the instruction addresses content that is well beyond the student's instructional level or the various features of the instruction do not appeal to the students (i.e., it is boring).

A second reason this stance is indefensible is because behavior, by definition, refers to one's observable actions: anything a person says or does. Therefore, if someone is hired to address a student's behavior, then behavior, by definition, includes actions pertaining to academics and school social behaviors. Some of the relatively recently published literature that pertains to response-to-intervention protocols raises this very point.[16]

11. The conditions that result in the provision of effective instruction are a much more important consideration than is the designation of the location where these conditions exist. Some school personnel are more committed to ensuring that all students are in a general education classroom for nothing more than "the sake of full inclusion" than they are to providing students with the conditions that result in the provision of effective instruction, particularly when these conditions involve placements that are associated with a student having a disability, such as resource or self-contained classrooms.

A commitment to theoretical constructs such as full inclusion and universal design can divert attention from the matters that can be, and need to be, readily addressed by teachers for the purpose of providing effective instruction to students who present significant, persistent challenges learning academic and functional content, plus school social behaviors.

CHAPTER 1 COMPREHENSION CHECK

Now that you have finished reading the chapter, you should be able to:

List the variables that a teacher might consider, and subsequently plan for, when they set out to present effective instruction.
Explain how small group arrangements are called for—either explicitly or implicitly—in the professional literature and relevant legislation.
Define the terms explicit, teacher-directed, intense, and remedial in terms of the type of small group instruction that is described in this book.
State the definition for small group instruction that is presented in this book.
List three reasons for presenting small group instruction.
Define what have been designated in this book to be key terms: effective instruction, efficient instruction, teaching, learning, mastery, and accommodations.

NOTES

1. Mitchell L. Yell, *The Law and Special Education*, fourth edition, edited by Jeffrey Johnston, (New York: Pearson, 2016); Frederick J. Brigham, Thomas E. Scruggs, and Margo A. Mastropieri, "Teacher Enthusiasm in Learning Disabilities Classrooms: Effects on Learning and Behavior," *Learning Disabilities Research & Practice*, (1992).

2. Lynn S. Fuchs, Douglas Fuchs, and Amelia S. Malone, "The Taxonomy of Intervention Intensity," *TEACHING Exceptional Children* 50, no. 1 (2017): 35–43; The IRIS Center. Intensive Intervention (Part 1): Using Data-Based Individualization to Intensify Instruction. Retrieved from https://iris.peabody.vanderbilt.edu/module/dbi1/. (2015).

3. Belva C. Collins, David L. Gast, Melinda J. Ault, and Mark Wolery, "Small Group Instruction: Guidelines for Teachers and Students with Moderate to Severe Handicaps," *Education & Training in Mental Retardation* 26, no. 1 (1991): 1–18.

4. Belva C. Collins, David L. Gast, Melinda J. Ault, and Mark Wolery, "Small Group Instruction: Guidelines for Teachers and Students with Moderate to Severe Handicaps," *Education & Training in Mental Retardation* 26, no. 1 (1991): 1–18; Debra M. Kamps, Dale Walker, Erin P. Dugan, Betsy R. Leonard, Susan F. Thibadeau, Kathleen Marshall, Laurie Grossnickle, and Brenda Boland, "Small Group Instruction for School-Aged Students with Autism and Developmental Disabilities," *Focus on Autistic Behavior* 6, no. 4 (1991): 1–18; Edward A. Polloway, Mary E. Cronin, and James R. Patton, "The Efficacy of Group Versus One-to-One Instruction: A Review," *Remedial and Special Education* 7, no. 1 (1986): 22–30; Dennis H. Reid and Judith E. Favell, "Group Instruction with Persons Who Have Severe Disabilities: A Critical Review," *Journal of the Association for Persons with Severe Handicaps* 9, no. 3 (1984): 167–77. David A. Rotholz, "Current Considerations on the Use of One-to-One Instruction with Autistic Students: Review and Recommendations," *Education and Treatment of Children* (1987): 271–78; Debra M. Whorton, Joseph Delquardri, and R. Vance Hall, "Classroom Instructional Programs with Autistic Children: Group Structures and Tutoring Models, Final Report, Federal Grant #G008300068, (University of Kansas, Bureau of Child Reseach), ERIC Document ED 295 401, EC 202 840, (1986); Janis L. Johnson, Kelly Flanagan, Mary E. Burge, Sharon Kauffman-Debriere, and Charles R. Spellman, "Interactive Individualized Instruction with Small Groups of Severely Handicapped Students," *Education and Training of the Mentally Retarded* (1980): 230–37.

5. Douglas Fuchs and Lynn S. Fuchs, "Critique of the National Evaluation of Response to Intervention: A Case for Simpler Frameworks," *Exceptional Children* 83, no. 3 (2017): 255–68.

6. T. E. Morse, "Response to Intervention and the Cost of Student Achievement," *School Business Affairs* 82, no. 8 (2016): 18–20.

7. Russell Gersten, David J. Chard, Madhavi Jayanthi, Scott K. Baker, Paul Morphy, and Jonathan Flojo, "Mathematics Instruction for Students with Learning Disabilities: A Meta-Analysis of Instructional Components," *Review of Educational Research* 79, no. 3 (2009): 1202–42.

8. Charles A. Hughes, Jared R. Morris, William J. Therrien, and Sarah K. Benson, "Explicit Instruction: Historical and Contemporary Contexts," *Learning Disabilities Research & Practice* 32, no. 3 (2017): 140–48.

9. Anita L. Archer and Charles A. Hughes, *Explicit Instruction: Effective and Efficient Teaching* (New York: Guilford Press, 2010); Devin Kearns, "Explicit Instruction: Modeling and Practicing to Help Students Reach Academic Goals," National Center on Intensive Intervention, Module 5, 2018.

10. Paul J. Riccomini, Stephanie Morano, and Charles A. Hughes, "Big Ideas in Special Education: Specially Designed Instruction, High-Leverage Practices, Explicit Instruction, and Intensive Instruction," *TEACHING Exceptional Children* 50, no. 1 (2017): 20–27.

11. John Hattie and Helen Timperley, "The Power of Feedback," *Review of Educational Research* 77, no. 1 (2007): 81–112.

12. P. S. Strain and G. Dunlap, "Recommended Practices: Being an Evidence-Based Practitioner," (2006): 2006, http://challengingbehavior.fmhi.usf.edu/handouts/Practitioner.pdf; James McLeskey, Council for Exceptional Children, and Collaboration for Effective Educator Development, Accountability and Reform, *High-Leverage Practices in Special Education* (Arlington, VA: Council for Exceptional Children, 2017); National Autism Center, "Evidence-Based Practice and Autism in the Schools: A Guide to Providing Appropriate Interventions to Students with Autism Spectrum Disorders," (2009); Melody Tankersley, Sanna Harjusola-Webb, and Timothy J. Landrum, "Using Single-Subject Research to Establish the Evidence Base of Special Education," *Intervention in School and Clinic* 44, no. 2 (2008): 83–90; Brandi Simonsen, Sarah Fairbanks, Amy Briesch, Diane Myers, and George Sugai, "Evidence-Based Practices in Classroom Management: Considerations for Research to Practice," *Education and Treatment of Children* (2008): 351–80; H. M. Walker, E. Ramsey, and F. M. Gresham, *Antisocial Behavior in School: Evidence-Based Practices* (Belmont, CA: Wadsworth/Thomson Learning, 2004).

13. Lee Kern and Nathan H. Clemens, "Antecedent Strategies to Promote Appropriate Classroom Behavior," *Psychology in the Schools* 44, no. 1 (2007): 65–75.

14. Lee Kern and Nathan H. Clemens, "Antecedent Strategies to Promote Appropriate Classroom Behavior," *Psychology in the Schools* 44, no. 1 (2007): 65–75; Michael Epstein, Marc Atkins, Douglas Cullinan, Krista Kutash, and K. Weaver, "Reducing Behavior Problems in the Elementary School Classroom," *IES Practice Guide* 20, no. 8 (2008): 12–22.

15. Donald M. Baer, Montrose M. Wolf, and Todd R. Risley, "Some Still-Current Dimensions of Applied Behavior Analysis," *Journal of Applied Behavior Analysis* 20, no. 4 (1987): 313–27.

16. Paul Alberto and Anne C. Troutman, *Applied Behavior Analysis for Teachers*, ninth edition (New York: Pearson, 2007); Bob Algozzine, R. Putman, and R. H. Horner, "Support for Teaching Students with Learning Disabilities Academic Skills and Social Behaviors within a Response-to-Intervention Model: Why It Doesn't Matter What Comes First," *Insights on Learning Disabilities* 9, no. 1 (2012): 7–36; George Sugai, Robert R. Horner, and F. M. Gresham, *Interventions for Academic and Behavior Problems II: Preventative and Remedial Approaches* (Bethesda, MD: National Association of School Psychologists, 2002).

Chapter Two

General Education Classroom Instruction

The Reference Point for Intensive Small Group Instruction

OVERVIEW

In this chapter you will learn details pertaining to the concept of high-quality instruction that is to be presented in a general education classroom, and its relevance to the type of small group instruction that is the focus of this book.
Key points from the chapter include the following:

1. The general education classroom and the features of the instruction that is presented in it serve as the reference point for the intensive small group instruction that is the focus of this book. Some of the reasons for this state of affairs are that (a) the general education classroom is the default placement for students with disabilities who are likely candidates for intensive small group instruction, and (b) this classroom is the only placement for students who exhibit significant, persistent learning challenges but have not been determined to be eligible to receive special education services. Accordingly, any discussion about intensive small group instruction must acknowledge how it is connected to general education instruction.
2. One way of conceptualizing the type of instruction that one expects to be presented in a general education classroom is as high-quality instruction. Hence, there is a need to operationally define this term. An operational definition is one that defines a concept in observable, measurable terms such that two or more individuals can agree upon its existence when they see it.
3. High-quality instruction can be operationally defined in a number of ways. In this chapter it is operationally defined as a multi-dimensional construct

that involves (a) the appropriate design and operation of a classroom; (b) successful time management; (c) a focus on core curriculum content; (d) the presentation of effective, evidence-based instructional strategies; and (e) the use of valid and reliable assessments.
4. A school's curriculum is a comprehensive listing of the knowledge and skills that students are expected to learn through the instruction they are presented. Broadly speaking, a school's curriculum addresses academic and school social behaviors.
5. A curriculum's academic content refers to the knowledge and skills that pertain to traditional disciplines (i.e., math, science, English/language arts, social studies), whereas its content that concerns school social behaviors refers to how students behave so as to share space appropriately with others across all school-related environments.
6. For students with disabilities, the curriculum also might address functional content. This content is also referred to as activities of daily living and life skills. Learning this content will enable an individual to live and work as independently as possible. A functional curriculum includes tasks such as maintaining appropriate personal hygiene, shopping for groceries, and using public transportation.
7. Effective instruction is defined as instruction that results in a student demonstrating mastery of targeted learning objectives.

INTRODUCTION

While the focus of this book is the provision of intensive small group instruction, the design and implementation of this instruction has to be connected to the instruction that is presented in general education classrooms. Several reasons for this circumstance are presented in the following.

1. Various protocols, including special education pre-referral to placement processes and response-to-intervention frameworks,[1] call for the provision of small group instruction to students who are not mastering grade-level content after receiving instruction in large group arrangements in general education classrooms.

    In particular, some of these protocols reference the need to provide these students high-quality instruction in general education classrooms.[2] When this occurs and the high-quality instruction proves to be ineffective, then intensive small group instruction is warranted. Therefore, to be able to explore how intensive small group instruction can be designed and presented to these students so that it is effective, it is necessary to have an in-depth understanding of the type of instruction that has proven to be ineffective.

2. The general education classroom is the default placement for students with disabilities who qualify for the receipt of special education services.[3] This means that a group of individuals who are known as a student's individualized education program (IEP) team must first determine how the program can be designed and implemented so that the student can receive an appropriate education in this setting. The majority of students who are determined to be eligible to receive special education services will be characterized as having a mild disability and will spend the majority of each school day in a general education classroom.

Yet some of these students will demonstrate a need to receive supplemental, intensive small group instruction. Many times this instruction will be presented in a location other than a general education classroom. These other locations comprise, in part, what is known as the continuum of alternative placements and have come to be regarded as special education classrooms. (This topic is addressed in more detail in chapter 7).

In these instances, two issues will be paramount:

   a. The way that general education instruction has been designed yet proven to be ineffective. An operational definition for the design and implementation of this instruction permits an analysis of its features that can be changed completely, or else modified slightly, so that intensive small group instruction can be designed and implemented differently. Moreover, this reasoned approach increases, from the outset, the probability that the intensive small group instruction will be effective.

   b. How intensive small group instruction can be designed and implemented so that students' performances in these small group arrangements have a high probability of generalizing to other locations—particularly grade-level general education classrooms. Also, the intensive small group instruction should result in students maintaining, across time, the targeted learning outcomes they mastered. This maintenance needs to occur most especially in general education classrooms.

3. The general education classroom will be the only placement for a very small number of students who exhibit significant, persistent learning challenges but have not been determined to be eligible to receive special education services yet need to be provided intensive small group

instruction. This might be the case for students who demonstrate below average ability and concomitant learning challenges.

The issues that were just discussed regarding students who receive special education services are also relevant to students without disabilities who are demonstrating ongoing, significant learning challenges. Therefore, any discussion about intensive small group instruction must acknowledge how it is connected to the instruction these students are receiving in the general education classroom.

So if general education classroom instruction is to be a foundational reference point for the provision of intensive small group instruction, through what prism should the general education classroom instruction be examined?

It is important and necessary to answer this question because how instruction is presented in general education classrooms varies widely. Consequently, in this book a construct known as high-quality instruction serves as the basis for describing, in general terms, the type of instruction that one could reasonably expect to see being presented in a general education classroom. There are two reasons for using this approach.

One reason is because discussing general education classroom instruction in this manner is in keeping with widely used protocols, including response-to-intervention frameworks[4] and similar multi-tier systems of support,[5] that call for the presentation of small group instruction to students who have not attained targeted learning outcomes when high-quality instruction has been presented to them in a general education classroom. A second reason is because it allows for the presentation of a coherent discussion about general education classroom instruction and its relationship to supplementary intensive small group instruction.

HIGH-QUALITY GENERAL EDUCATION INSTRUCTION AS THE REFERENCE POINT FOR INTENSIVE SMALL GROUP INSTRUCTION

Having identified reasons why the type of small group instruction that is described in this book needs to be referenced to the large group instruction that is being presented in a general education classroom, it is necessary to examine the features of this latter type of instruction. As was just noted, the construct of high-quality instruction serves as the basis for this discussion.

In the following, high-quality instruction is operationally defined and then discussed in terms of its relevance to effective small group instruction. An operational definition is one that defines a concept in observable, measurable terms such that two or more individuals can agree upon its existence when they see it.

In most instances it must be demonstrated that a student was provided this type of instruction prior to concluding that a student's lack of expected, or hoped for, progress in the general education classroom needs to be addressed through intensive small group instruction. An exception would be the case of a student with a disability that results in a reasonable calculation that the student would not demonstrate meaningful progress if they mainly were provided instruction in a general education classroom.

Thus, from a general education teacher's and school administrator's perspective, it is imperative that the term "high-quality instruction" is operationally defined so that one can determine if, in fact, this type of instruction has been provided in a general education classroom or, if not, what can be done so that this instruction is presented. If it is determined that high-quality instruction had not been presented, then instead of providing a student with intensive small group instruction, other work would be performed to enhance the instruction that is being presented in the general education classroom (e.g., distractions could be eliminated, the amount of active student responding could be increased, etc.).

For instance, professional development would be provided to the general education teacher with the intent of improving upon the work that they are performing in the classroom such that it can be considered to be high-quality instruction. This situation highlights a practical matter with respect to high-quality instruction, which is that a teacher needs to know how their school operationally defines high-quality instruction so that they will know what is needed to demonstrate that they are presenting it so that formal evaluations of their work will reflect this fact.

The various observable, measurable elements that combine to result in the provision of high-quality instruction are subject to debate. The discussion presented next is offered as one way to define the features that would characterize high-quality instruction.

As you consider the content that is presented, it is important for you to begin thinking about how, in a sense, there is a symbiotic relationship between high-quality general education classroom instruction and intensive small group instruction. Already you have learned that students who receive intensive small group instruction must maintain and generalize the content they master—as well as their "learning how to learn skills"—when they return to the general education classroom and its large group arrangement. Furthermore, in chapters 3 to 5 you will learn that intensive small group instruction should retain relevant elements of high-quality instruction.

HIGH-QUALITY INSTRUCTION: EFFECTIVE AND MULTI-DIMENSIONAL

High-Quality Instruction Is Effective Instruction

High-quality instruction can be characterized as effective instruction. Effective instruction is defined as instruction that results in a student demonstrating mastery of the targeted learning objective. Learning objectives are statements that describe either the academic, functional, or school social behaviors students are to be able to perform after receiving effective instruction.

Given the fact that large group arrangements predominate in general education classrooms, it is necessary to stipulate that high-quality instruction in this environment must be effective for the vast majority of the students in the class. In other words, if the instruction enables only one student to master the targeted learning objective, it would be technically accurate to say that the instruction was effective (with respect to the one student), but it also is reasonable to conclude that most educators would not characterize this instruction as being of high quality.

How many students in a general education classroom need to master the targeted learning objective in order for the instruction to be characterized as high quality? Widespread agreement on this matter does not exist. However, some who have written about schoolwide intervention protocols, such as response-to-intervention, have indicated that 75 to 80 percent of the students in a general education classroom will attain expected learning outcomes as a result of receiving high-quality instruction.[6]

As you read this book, you need to remain mindful of the fact that its content is based on the assumption that general education teachers present instruction that addresses both academic content and school social behaviors. Hence, references to students' "attainment of expected learning outcomes" is often used and encompasses both academic and school social behaviors. Further, throughout this book the term "effective instruction" is used interchangeably with high-quality instruction, particularly when doing so allows for a clearer presentation of the content.

High-Quality Instruction Is Multi-Dimensional

While there is not a universally agreed upon definition for the term "high-quality instruction," most educators certainly agree that the construct involves more than just the instructional strategy a teacher uses at the point in time when they conduct a lesson. High-quality instruction results from additional components that include work a teacher performs before and after presenting a lesson. Thus, high-quality instruction is a multi-dimensional construct. The various dimensions of instruction that intertwine to result in high-quality instruction include the following:

1. a safe, orderly classroom that is conducive to the presentation of effective instruction;
2. successful time management;
3. presentation of effective instructional strategies, which include both what are referred to as (a) core universal principles of effective teaching and (b) strategies that are specific to an academic discipline, such as the teaching of reading or math, or school social behaviors. In both cases the strategies are evidence-based practices;
4. a focus on core curriculum content plus an appropriate pacing guide (i.e., a relevant scope and sequence); and
5. the use of valid, reliable assessments to measure students' mastery of the grade-level standards in the core curriculum and their demonstration of appropriate school social behaviors. Assessment data also informs instruction.

DIMENSIONS OF HIGH-QUALITY INSTRUCTION

Each of the dimensions of high-quality instruction that were identified previously are explained in detail in the following. As you read each explanation, think about how the dimension is defined in observable, measurable terms. Additionally, consider how the aspects of each dimension could be reconfigured such that the impact of this reconfiguration could be measured in terms of effective instruction (i.e., a comparison could be made of how many students demonstrated attainment of the targeted learning outcomes before and after the reconfiguration).

High-Quality Instruction: Environmental Arrangement and Management

The classrooms within a school are the locations where teachers and students spend the most time interacting. It stands to reason, therefore, that one component of high-quality instruction is the creation of a safe, orderly general education classroom that facilitates teaching and learning.

The term "environmental arrangement" is used to refer to the appropriate configuration of this and any other location where instruction is provided to students. The discussion that is presented in this section is based on a typical, traditional general education classroom in which twenty to more than thirty students receive instruction from one teacher. This is referred to as a large group arrangement.

The importance of creating safe, orderly classrooms has been highlighted by research that has established a positive correlation between students' engagement in appropriate school social behaviors and their attainment of expected academic outcomes. Furthermore, research has documented that, in many instances, the same types of instructional strategies can be used to teach both.[7]

The following discusses some of the issues a general education teacher will need to address to be able to create and operate an environment that supports the presentation of effective instruction. The issues are discussed in sufficient detail to enable you to develop an understanding of their importance as well acquire some knowledge about how to address them.

These issues highlight the fact that universal effective teaching practices, which are explained in the following, include both interventions that are defined as changes to the environment that set the occasion for the presentation of effective instruction as well as instructional strategies that primarily involve the demonstration of behaviors by the teacher that have been shown to result in students' attainment of targeted learning outcomes.

As you consider each issue, be mindful of the fact that establishing an appropriate environmental arrangement is a dynamic, as opposed to static, undertaking. Factors such as (a) a change in the class roster or (b) a teacher's incorporation of new instructional strategies (e.g., cooperative learning groups) may result in having to change the way the teacher has arranged the environment. While a teacher does not want to waste time addressing this topic, it is necessary to recognize that it may present a reoccurring demand on a teacher's time that must be addressed to be able to present high-quality instruction.

1. Establish clear lines of sight for both the teacher and the students. Clear lines of sight enable teachers to manage students' displays of appropriate school social behaviors and assess their understanding of a lesson. Research has shown that teachers who conduct a visual scan of the entire classroom every one or two minutes have students who engage in appropriate school social behaviors more often.[8] When scanning the classroom the teacher can provide either the entire class or individual students with behavior-specific praise, thereby reinforcing them for displays of these behaviors.

Providing students with clear lines of sight allows them to both see any person or item that is central to the presentation of instruction and attend in a way that does not disrupt the lesson. A disruption refers to any event that draws attention to itself and impedes the ongoing flow of activities in a classroom. Thus, if a student gets out of their seat and moves about the room to improve their line of sight or leans to one side of a desk to do so, but also inadvertently bumps into another student, these actions may function as disruptions.

Numerous techniques can be used to check for student's understanding of the lesson. A very simple one is interpreting students' facial expressions. The display of a grimace or frown may indicate that a student does not understand the targeted learning outcome. A more objective approach to assessing students' understanding is for the teacher to periodically pose comprehension questions and have students respond simultaneously but by way of a response mode that can interpreted individually (e.g., in response to a true/false question each student either shows a thumbs up to indicate their answer is true or a thumbs down to indicate their answer is false).

2. Necessary steps should be taken to ensure that the climate is conducive to effective instruction. A student may not be able to focus on the teacher's instruction when they are uncomfortable because of some feature of the classroom's climate.

These features may include inadequate lighting (too much light or darkness), an uncomfortable temperature setting (too hot or cold), or a structural defect (e.g., water dripping from the ceiling or snow/rain being blown through a window's seal). While a teacher may not be able to control these features, they need to be mindful of their potential impact on instruction as well as how the teacher might be able to intervene to mitigate them (e.g., permit students who say it is too bright to wear a baseball cap or students who say they are cold to wear a sweater).

3. Protocols for managing high traffic areas should be created. Students frequent some areas of a classroom more than others, such as the pencil sharpener, trash can, the hanging drape with pockets where calculators are stored, and the tray where they are to turn in their homework and the assignments they complete while in class. A teacher must strategically locate these areas such that they are both out of students' direct lines of sight and easily accessible. These arrangements will serve as antecedent-based interventions that increase the probability that a student will not disrupt a lesson when accessing a high-traffic area.

To assist in the management of these areas, the teacher should establish routines and set rules for accessing them. A routine for entering an Algebra I class may be for students to first get a calculator from the storage bin and then sit in their assigned seats and begin working on a test preparation question that is written on the classroom's whiteboard. An example of a rule for accessing a high-traffic area would be that only one person at a time can be out of their seat to use the pencil sharpener.

4. Potential distractions should be limited. A teacher wants students to attend to the aspects of a lesson that they deem to be most important, such as their modeling how to solve a long division problem or how to identify key locations on a map during a geography lesson. When a student is distracted, this means they are attending to some other aspect of the environment. If the teacher then has to redirect the student's attention, the distraction would serve as a disruption.

Teachers can take a number of actions to limit distractions. Examples include positioning portable dividers in locations that eliminate visual distractions or controlling for auditory distractions by only permitting students to use a printer when doing so would not serve as a potential auditory distraction.

5. Use of both the floor and wall space should be planned out. Teachers need to address different issues that are specific to the use of either floor space or wall space which, for the purpose of this discussion, includes a classroom's ceiling space. Yet they need to coordinate their design of floor and wall space in order to create an organized classroom.

Regarding floor space, teachers need to consider the amount that is available and its configuration when planning their students' seating arrangement and the placement of classroom furniture, such as bookshelves. Two primary considerations that were addressed previously will be ensuring clear lines of sight and an efficient traffic flow.

Teachers will need to contemplate several issues when planning for the use of wall space. First, they need to decide whether this space will be used to present instruction, enhance the classroom's organization, display decorations, or reinforce students through displays of their work or performance data. Examples of how a teacher can use wall space to present instruction include creating a word wall comprised of key vocabulary from a novel the students are reading or the order of operations that need to be followed to solve an algebra problem. To enhance the classroom's organization the teacher may post a weekly and daily schedule.

Decorations could consist of students' artwork or seasonal exhibitions that pertain to upcoming holidays. Displays of students' work and performance data could include an exemplary essay and a line graph that depicts the number of sight words a student has mastered during the current grading period.

Second, if portable floor dividers are placed throughout the classroom, the teacher will have to decide if they will be used like fixed wall space. Third, the teacher will have to decide whether they will allow mobiles to hang from the ceiling. Just like other fixtures that are placed on walls, these mobiles could be informative, decorative, or reinforcing. However, care must be taken to prevent them from serving as a distraction.

The overarching consideration when deciding how to design wall space is to ensure that its design contributes to, rather than detracts from, the presentation of high-quality instruction. The space that is available on the walls that surround a classroom will exceed the room's floor space. Hence, its use warrants considerable attention.

6. Ensure that instructional materials are nearby and ready for use. Teachers need to position instructional materials so that they are readily accessible and usable. Doing so allows for effective behavior management and the efficient use of allocated time.

When instructional materials are very close by the location where the teacher will present instruction, they can continue to monitor students' behavior while accessing needed materials. Additionally the teacher will not waste instructional time as might be the case when they have to walk to another place in the room to get needed materials.

Likewise, instructional time will be lost if a teacher has to prepare materials that were not made ready in advance of a lesson. This would occur when a teacher has to take time away from a lesson to make copies of a handout that pertains to a lecture or worksheets students will be required to complete.

7. Consider how existing fixtures will be incorporated. Teachers either will not be permitted to move some fixtures in the environment or cannot move them given the school's design. Examples might include storage cabinets, electrical outlets, ports for connecting computers to the internet, chalkboards, countertops, and sinks. Teachers will have to plan for these fixtures "as is" in conjunction with all of the other considerations mentioned here.

8. Recognize the potential influence of a classroom's aesthetics on students' behavior. This aspect of an environmental arrangement refers to its overall look and feel. Simply stated, an appropriately lit, colorful, well-organized, climate-controlled room that exudes a sense of calm can set the occasion for displays of appropriate student behavior because students will be more likely to want to come to the room to work. Conversely, a poorly lit, uncomfortable, disorganized room could result in students neither wanting to enter or remain in it irrespective of the fact that they otherwise enjoy engaging in the instruction that is presented.

9. Development and use of routines that support instruction. Classroom routines are repeated sequences of actions. Routines make efficient use of allocated time and establish behavioral momentum.

An example of a routine that makes use of allocated time and, therefore, supports the instruction that is presented in a math class is as follows: upon entering the classroom a student obtains a practice test question from the teacher, who is standing at the doorway; the student then gets their calculator from its storage pocket that is on a curtain hanging on a wall in the rear of the classroom; next the student goes to their assigned seat and situates their belongings; afterward they place their homework in the "Finished Tasks" box that is located on the teacher's desk; finally, the student returns to their seat and answers the practice test question.

Behavioral momentum refers to the fact that students are more likely to continue to engage in appropriate behaviors after already exhibiting several or more appropriate behaviors back-to-back. Hence, completion of the routine just described would increase the probability that students will engage appropriately in whatever subsequent activity the teacher has planned.

High-Quality Instruction: Successful Time Management

Arguably one of a teacher's most valuable resources is the time they have been allocated to teach. The presentation of high-quality instruction depends, in part, on a teacher being cognizant of this time and properly managing it.

The breadth, or scope, of the curriculum that must be taught highlights the importance of proper time management. Those involved in curriculum design know that a noteworthy challenge is settling upon a curriculum's content. One reason for this circumstance is that one can readily identify more knowledge and skills that students probably should be taught than there is time available to teach it. Ultimately factors including available funding, the length of the school year, and the length of each school day set an upper limit with respect to how much content can be taught. Thus, teachers need to properly manage their allocated time to achieve this upper limit.

Mindful of this fact, a teacher does not want to lower this limit by improperly managing the allocated time. Likewise, students must have the same commitment. A teacher can take steps to properly manage their allocated time in a way that is designed to meet each student's needs, but each student also has the responsibility to take full advantage of the teacher's efforts by remaining appropriately engaged during a lesson.

Others[9] have devised a way to conceptualize the time that is available for instruction each school day. Their model serves as the basis for the discussion presented in the following. The model consists of four components: allotted, allocated, engaged, and academic learning time.

The term "allotted time" refers to the total amount of time in one school day that is available for teaching. If a school day begins at 8 a.m. and ends at 3:30 p.m., and the students are permitted thirty minutes to eat lunch and a total of thirty minutes to change classes, then the allotted time would be six hours and thirty minutes.

"Allocated time" is the amount of time that has been designated to teach subject matter content, such as English/language arts, math, science, and social studies. Within the amount of allotted time previously identified, in an elementary school ninety minutes may be allocated for English/language arts instruction and seventy-five minutes for mathematics instruction. In a high school that uses what is referred to as a block schedule, ninety-four minutes may be allocated for each class period. This means each subject matter teacher would be allocated ninety-four minutes for each period during which they taught their subject, such as World History.

In many instances, state departments of education establish the minimum amount of time that must be allocated each day for certain subject matter instruction. Some schools then further dictate to teachers the curriculum content they are to teach on a designated day, as well as the amount of time they are to spend teaching each subtopic. In these instances teachers have been presented what is referred to as a pacing guide.

"Engaged time" is defined as the amount of time during the allocated time when instruction is being presented that a student attends to the instruction. In turn, the term "academic learning time" refers to the amount of time that a student is taught relevant content that is at their instructional level.

In a typical public school, general education classroom students receive subject matter instruction during allocated time every day school is in session, which typically is five days per week during the months that comprise the school year. The general education teacher manages allocated time in accordance with the subject matter curriculum's scope and sequence that they must follow. As was noted previously, some schools strictly manage this task through a pacing guide.

Within this allocated time, when the teacher is presenting whole class instruction, they may use various strategies to maximize students' engaged time, such as (a) presenting an attention directive, which might consist of a statement—such as "Eyes up"—that directs the students to attend to the teacher; (b) having students use a response card, which is a small card on which an answer is displayed and a student holds up to indicate their response to a teacher's comprehension check question; and (c) using a model-lead-test routine that involves having all students respond at the same time when the teacher presents the lead, or what is also called the guided practice, portion of the lesson. Having all students respond at the same time is known by various names, including choral and unison responding.

Also, the teacher may present some amount of differentiated instruction within the allocated time for a large group lesson to maximize certain students' engaged or academic learning time, or both. These strategies would supplement the large group instruction and could include the use of learning centers, cooperative peer groups, and teacher-led small group instruction.

Although it is both appropriate and necessary for a teacher to use these strategies in a general education classroom, they will not be able to do so to the extent that is needed by students who display significant, persistent challenges mastering targeted learning objectives. This matter is addressed in chapters 3 to 5, which explain, in detail, the features of intensive small group instruction for these students.

One final point about the time that is available for the presentation of instruction, and about which school personnel should remain mindful, is the percentage of time during a student's life, from kindergarten to grade twelve, that a student spends in school. If a school day is seven hours long and one school year consists of 180 days, then a student with a record of perfect attendance during the thirteen years they attended school would have spent 14 percent of his life in school.

This relatively limited percentage of time that is available for instruction is reduced by non-instructional activities such as lunch, recess, restroom breaks, pep rallies, and transitioning from one class to the next. Altogether this information highlights the need for teachers to exercise efficient instructional time management on behalf of every student so as not to deny them an opportunity to learn if they are willing to put forth the effort that is required to do so.

High-Quality Instruction: Combining Universal Principles of Effective Teaching and Evidence-Based Practices Specific to Academic Disciplines

The third component of high-quality instruction is the use of effective teaching practices. Effective teaching practices are those that have been shown, through research, to result in students attaining targeted learning outcomes. For the purposes of this discussion about high-quality instruction, these practices result from a combination of universal effective teaching practices and evidence-based practices that are specific to an academic discipline which, in schools, is often referred to as subject matter instruction (e.g., science, social studies).

Evidence-based practices are those that have been shown through multiple, scientifically based research studies to result in effective instruction. The universal principles of effective teaching are evidence-based practices, and in order to realize high-quality instruction, they are to be used in concert with the evidence-based practices that pertain to a particular academic discipline.

Relationship Between Universal Effective Teaching Practices and Evidence-Based Practices That Are Specific to an Academic Discipline

Researchers have identified teacher behaviors that are directly related to the presentation of effective, high-quality instruction irrespective of the subject matter that is the focus of instruction.[10] For instance, an elementary school general education teacher who, daily, strives to present effective reading, math, science, and social studies lessons to the same group of students would demonstrate these behaviors in each lesson. Similarly, an Algebra I teacher would demonstrate these behaviors regardless of the topic they address, whether it be linear, quadratic, or exponential functions, or adding or factoring polynomials.

As was just noted, these universal practices are evidence-based and allow for the incorporation of evidence-based practices that are specific to a subject, such as teaching beginning reading or math. The evidence-based practices that are specific to a subject often exclusively address the specific skills that need to be taught (e.g., in beginning reading instruction these skills include both phonemic awareness and phonics), the sequence to follow to teach them (e.g., when teaching students letter names teach the names for letters whose shapes are quite dissimilar, such as f and s, before teaching the names for letters whose shapes are quite similar, such as m and n), and the types of instructional strategies that should be used (e.g., when teaching students phonemic awareness or phonics skills have the students look into a hand-mirror to see the positions of their tongue, teeth, and lips as they make different speech sounds).

Often, however, in research reports, the explanations of subject matter, evidence-based practices do not address some of the more intricate, and important, aspects of effective, high-quality instruction. These include the topics addressed previously—such as the features of an appropriate environmental arrangement and effective time management—as well as the use of universal effective teaching practices. All of these aspects of instruction, plus evidence-based practices specific to an academic discipline, combine to result in the presentation of high-quality instruction in a general education classroom. The challenge for teachers is how to interconnect them in a lesson.

Universal Effective Teaching Practices

Universal effective teaching practices mostly refer to behaviors a teacher exhibits during a lesson rather than the tasks a teacher performs to set the stage for a lesson (e.g., create an appropriate environmental arrangement) or follow up after a lesson (e.g., evaluate assessment data to inform their instruction). A teacher who engages in universal effective teaching practices:[11]

1. presents a directive to students that indicates a lesson is about to begin and requires them to respond in a way that indicates they are ready to attend to the instruction;
2. clearly states the lesson's learning objective(s);
3. ties new content to what the students already know about the lesson's topic;
4. presents material in appropriate chunks, or small enough steps, that are sequenced to enhance clarity and minimize confusion, all the while using clear and precise language;
5. solicits regular, active student responding in multiple ways (e.g., response cards, choral responding);
6. monitors students' understanding, provides immediate behavior-specific feedback rather than general statements of praise, and re-teaches as necessary—using something other than "more of the same";
7. maintains a "laser-like," seamless focus on the lesson, not allowing disruptions (either through off-topic comments or questions, or other behaviors);
8. employs visual supports (e.g., outlines, graphic organizers, study guides, task organizers) that serve multiple purposes, such as highlighting key ideas, pointing out the structure and flow of the content, depicting the strategies for solving a problem or completing a task while keeping track of the steps involved, or enabling students to retain in their short-term memory what the teacher just said;
9. conducts a review at, or near, the end of a lesson in which the main points and integrative concepts are re-stated—and previews the next, related lesson they will teach; and
10. requires the completion of follow-up assignments that enable students to practice a skill or encode the material in the student's own words.[12]

A lesson plan format that readily incorporates each of these universal effective teaching practices is explained in chapter 4. This lesson plan is comprised of a series of techniques that are based on the principles of applied behavior analysis, which is a field of study that examines the relationship between human behavior and environmental events. While this lesson plan format has been identified as an example of a direct instruction lesson plan,[13] as was noted previously, in this book the term "direct instruction" is synonymous with the term "explicit instruction." Furthermore, both of these terms are captured by the term "intensive instruction."

High-Quality Instruction: Focus on Core Curriculum Content

A fourth component of high-quality instruction is a clear focus on the content, or curriculum, that is to be taught. As a practical matter it is unrealistic to assume that a student will attain expected learning outcomes if they are not taught the knowledge and skills that comprise the school's curriculum, and that are the basis for assessing a student's attainment of targeted learning outcomes. The term "curriculum-assessment alignment" refers to ensuring that the content that is taught is the content that is assessed.

A teacher must be well-versed about the entire curriculum that they are expected to teach. While those who develop a curriculum, whether it be a diverse group of stakeholders that develops a curriculum for a state department of education or an IEP team that establishes the goals for a student with a disability, can identify more content students probably need to master than there is time allotted for schools to teach this content, this matter is, to some degree, separate from a teacher's micro-analysis of what needs to be taught in a particular context.

For instance, it is highly unlikely that a school's stated curriculum addresses teaching students routines for the transitions that are involved with respect to the presentation of intensive small group instruction. Yet explicitly teaching students how to efficiently execute these transitions enables everyone involved to maximize students' engaged and academic learning time. Further, doing so allows students to master important school social behaviors. Hence, a teacher's in-depth knowledge about both the entire curriculum they can—and should—address is central to every other task they perform.

With these considerations in mind, the specific focus of the discussion presented in the following is the expectation that a teacher needs to know the content that comprises the core curriculum that is being taught in a general education classroom in order to be able to present effective small group instruction. Specifically, when the teacher presents intensive small group instruction, they will focus on expected learning outcomes that a student has not attained through the instruction that was presented in a general education classroom.

The students who are the focus of this book will have demonstrated significant and persistent challenges learning this content. Among other things this might mean that, during intensive small group instruction, these students might be taught curriculum content that is several years below their current grade-level placement.

Hence, two topics are addressed in the remainder of this section. One topic is the definition for, and development of, a curriculum. The second topic is the need to teach, in a general education classroom, a curriculum that consists of both academic and school social behaviors. This second topic was discussed previously and is addressed in more detail in the following.

Curriculum Defined

In this book the term "curriculum" refers solely to a listing of the knowledge and skills that students are to learn. Related, but separate, terms include (a) instructional strategies, which are the planned actions a teacher executes when they present a lesson; (b) instructional materials, which refer to both the tangible (e.g., base ten blocks) and intangible (e.g., apps) items that are used during a lesson; and (c) assessments, which refer to the various means of collecting data that are then used to make decisions about past and future instruction. Some definitions for curriculum incorporate each of these terms. This, however, is not the case here.

Before discussing issues pertaining to matters such as who develops a curriculum and why they do so, an explanation of the subtle differences of the content that comprises a curriculum is presented. Heretofore in this book, this content has been distinguished in terms of knowledge and skills.

A heuristic that has been used to differentiate the knowledge and skills that comprise a curriculum is that knowledge refers to declarative information, which can be thought of as discrete pieces of information, such as the name for a letter of the alphabet or a numeral. Skills refer to procedural tasks, such as applying information one has acquired about phonics to decode and read the word "cat," performing the necessary steps to solve for the value of a variable in an Algebraic equation, and completing the actions necessary to make a peanut butter and jelly sandwich.[14]

It is important to note that overlap can exist between the two types of information just described. For example, a student might be required to decode the words "cat," "dog," and "fox" (a procedural task) before identifying one as being the correct name of an animal that is depicted in a picture that a teacher has asked the child to label (declarative information).

Development: Who Creates a Curriculum and the Ethics of Teaching It

To highlight the saliency of the curriculum, it is important to note how and why it is developed. Quite often large and diverse groups of stakeholders, including educators, parents, politicians, and business leaders, work to establish a school's curriculum.

Together they attempt to identify what they believe students should learn in kindergarten through twelfth grade so that they will be prepared for further education, employment, and living independently during their post-secondary years. In other words, they identify the knowledge and skills that they believe are critically important for students to learn to be able to live interdependently as contributing members of a society. Consequently, some believe it is unethical to disregard teaching students their school's curriculum, and research has confirmed that "what gets taught is what gets learned."[15]

Relationship Between a Curriculum and Universal Effective Teaching Practices

High-quality instruction is predicated on "teaching the right things." Therefore, the statement, "What gets taught is what gets learned," applies. "What gets learned" is referred to as students' attainment of targeted learning outcomes, and it is these outcomes that should be delineated in the curriculum. Further, this curriculum becomes the laser-like focus of a teacher's instruction.

Curriculum focus is related to several universal effective teaching practices. According to these practices, effective teachers promote students' focus on the curriculum and active engagement with its content. Furthermore, these teachers avoid diversions that alter this focus. This means that a teacher must be diligent in their efforts to focus both their and their students' work on the content that comprises the curriculum.

In conformity with this logic, a student will not master math skills if, during the time that has been allocated to teach these skills, the student is engaged in activities that may divert their attention from learning the skills that are the focus of instruction. This could occur if a student engages with computer games that purport to teach math skills but instead result in the student focusing most of their attention on how to play the game rather than learn the skills (e.g., the student focuses more of his attention on how to increase the race car's speed, which is a critical feature of the game that is used to teach basic addition facts).

Critical Subject Matter Skills Must be Targeted

In some subject matter areas research has identified the knowledge and skills that students must master to be proficient in the subject matter area.[16] One component of high-quality instruction in these disciplines would be teaching a curriculum that consisted of this content.

For example, research pertaining to teaching students how to read has identified what are referred to as the five big ideas of reading instruction: phonemic awareness,[17] phonics,[18] vocabulary, fluency,[19] and reading comprehension. Students need to master the curriculum across these five areas to become proficient, independent, skilled readers. Therefore, high-quality reading instruction in general education classrooms would focus on teaching this content.[20]

Furthermore, the sequence, or order, in which certain skills are to be taught is important. One reason for this arrangement is that the mastery of more advanced, higher order skills depends upon the mastery of more basic, fundamental, lower order skills. An example is teaching addition before multiplication because one way of thinking about multiplication is as repeated addition. Likewise, skills that lead to successful beginning reading performance must be taught and mastered so that a student will be able to use reading as a means to acquire information from print at higher grade levels across subjects. These considerations are another element of an appropriate curriculum focus.

A second reason for this arrangement is that listing the content that is to be taught (i.e., the scope of the curriculum) and the sequence (i.e., the order) will contribute to the establishment of the rate, or pace, at which it is to be taught. These standards—particularly the rate at which students are expected to master skills—will determine which students are at risk for failure and, therefore, need to be provided intensive, remedial instruction. For instance, students who are designated as being either at-risk for failure or eligible to receive special education services are not demonstrating the attainment of targeted learning outcomes in the core curriculum at an expected rate.

Importance of Academic Learning Time

A general education classroom in which high-quality instruction is presented will focus its work on the knowledge and skills that comprise the core curriculum and will do so in a way that affords students maximum academic learning time. Students need to be taught skills that are at their instructional level rather than skills that are significantly beneath or above this level. The latter circumstance may result from a school policy that requires teachers to present prescribed content according to a pacing guide, which results in prescribed curriculum content being taught on a designated day and at a designated time irrespective if this is the content a student should be taught in accordance with his instructional level.

Use of a pacing guide as just described will increase the probability that a student will engage in off-task behavior. Students need to be challenged appropriately so that they expend their efforts engaged in on-task, instructionally relevant behaviors rather than engaged in disruptive behaviors because they are either bored with tasks that they perceive to be too easy or are frustrated and overwhelmed with tasks that they perceive to be too difficult.

Reasons for Addressing Both Academic and School Social Behaviors in a General Education Classroom[21]

Despite research that has documented the desired outcomes that can be attained from simultaneously teaching both academic and school social behaviors,[22] some teachers do not believe they should have to spend time teaching students school social behaviors—nor see a reason for doing so. Rather, these teachers see their role as applying consequences to displays of inappropriate behavior. Historically teachers have applied consequences intended to function as punishment. These consequences include reprimands, loss of privileges, office referrals, afterschool detention, suspension, and expulsion.[23]

Many teachers who do not believe that they should have to spend time teaching school social behaviors contend that their job is to teach students academic content. Their position is supported by the fact that the vast majority of core curriculum state standards address academic content exclusively.

Furthermore, some teachers who do not see a reason for having to teach students school social behaviors believe that students are capable of figuring out, on their own, how to behave appropriately. That is to say, these teachers believe that students can intuit how to behave appropriately simply by observing others do so. Additionally, these teachers surmise that other adults, such as a child's parents, are responsible for teaching their child how to exhibit appropriate school social behaviors while at school.

When appropriate school social behaviors are conceptualized as the behaviors that students are to display for the purpose of sharing both their classroom and non-classroom school space safely with others—and in a manner that allows for the efficient presentation of effective instruction—then teachers can readily identify many of these behaviors that they, in fact, do teach.

Still, a number of teachers need to be made cognizant of some of the reasons why they need to either directly teach students appropriate school social behaviors or steps they can take that will increase the probability that students will engage in these behaviors.[24] These reasons are offered next.

1. Appropriate social behavior is context specific. This means that there is no such thing as generic, appropriate school social behavior. For example, in some schools, students are permitted to use their cell phones in accordance with certain guidelines while in other schools all cell phone use is strictly prohibited. Often, local norms, as referenced previously regarding who develops a curriculum, rather than research result in the identification of the social behaviors to teach. With respect to teaching students how to engage in appropriate school social behaviors, aside from matters that readily pertain to safe schools (e.g., weapons are prohibited on campus), appropriate school social behaviors will be context specific and, therefore, locally defined.

A more efficient use of a teacher's time is to explicitly teach students the social behaviors that are appropriate in their school rather than operating under the assumption that students know which behaviors are appropriate and how to engage in them, and then to only address students' engagement in inappropriate behaviors when students disrupt class by engaging in these behaviors. Teaching appropriate school social behavior, such as how to transition efficiently across activities, can maximize a teacher's use of their allocated time.

2. Many students with disabilities will be in general education classes, and the IEPs for some of these students will require their general educations teachers to provide instruction about appropriate school social behaviors. This matter might be addressed explicitly in a document known as a behavior intervention plan.

3. The presentation of inappropriate academic instruction can set the stage for a student's display of inappropriate school social behavior. This means that inappropriate academic instruction can function as an antecedent for a student's engagement in inappropriate social behavior. A student who becomes frustrated because they cannot complete academic tasks that far exceed their current instructional level is more likely to engage in inappropriate social behavior than is a student who remains engaged in assigned tasks that are challenging but target the student's instructional needs.

Curriculum Focus: Functional Performance Versus Academic Achievement

It is necessary to note, again, how the curriculum for some students with disabilities will differ from their same-age peers' curriculum. These students with disabilities will be expected to master what is referred to in the federal special education law—the Individuals with Disabilities Education Act—as functional content, or activities of daily living.

These activities were not addressed previously because they are rarely the focus of instruction in a typical general education classroom. This topic is addressed in detail in chapter 7 because intensive small group instruction is an appropriate forum for teaching these students these activities.

High-Quality Instruction: Valid, Reliable Assessment

The last component of high-quality instruction is valid, reliable assessment. Specifically, the use of data from assessments to inform instruction. These data are meaningful to the extent that the assessments are aligned with the curriculum and the curriculum has been taught. Of particular importance is progress monitoring.

Progress monitoring assessments produce data regarding students' levels and rates of progress. These assessments are aligned with the curriculum that is taught, provide information about students' attainment of expected learning outcomes, and result in data that informs instruction. This means the data provide the teacher with information that is useful in adjusting instruction, if doing so is necessary.

Progress monitoring contributes to high-quality instruction because it allows a teacher to make data-based decisions concerning both what to teach and how to present instruction. These data increase the probability that a teacher will address content that is at a student's instructional level. The data also may indicate which component of high-quality instruction needs to be modified so that it is effective. This is an important reason why high-quality instruction needs to be operationally defined.

Chapter 6 addresses the topic of assessment as it pertains to intensive small group instruction. Additionally, in this chapter both assessment that is tied to the instruction that is being presented in a general education classroom and that which is quite distinct (e.g., instruction about an activity of daily living, such as independently toileting oneself) are discussed.

CHAPTER 2 COMPREHENSION CHECK

Now that you have finished reading the chapter, you should be able to:

List at least two reasons why the general education classroom and the features of the instruction that is presented in it serve as the reference point for the provision of intensive small group instruction.

Explain what is meant by an operational definition.

Identify the components that comprise high-quality instruction as a multi-dimensional construct with respect to the way that it is explained in this book.

Operationally define high-quality instruction in terms of (a) environmental arrangements, (b) time management, (c) universal and discipline-specific effective instructional strategies, (d) curriculum, and (e) assessment.

Define the term "curriculum."

Discuss a process that is followed to construct a curriculum.

Explain what is meant by a curriculum's scope and sequence.

Differentiate between a curriculum focus on academic content, functional content, and school social behaviors.

NOTES

1. Aaron C. Barnes and Jason E. Harlacher, "Clearing the Confusion: Response-to-Intervention as a Set of Principles," *Education and Treatment of Children* 31, no. 3 (2008): 417–31.

2. Douglas Fuchs and Lynn S. Fuchs, "Introduction to Response to Intervention: What, Why, and How Valid is It?" *Reading Research Quarterly* 41, no. 1 (2006): 93–99.

3. Individuals with Disabilities Education Improvement Act of 2004, 20 U. S. C. § 1400 et seq. (2004); Angela MT Prince, Mitchell L. Yell, and Antonis Katsiyannis, "Endrew F. v. Douglas County School District (2017): The US Supreme Court and Special Education," *Intervention in School and Clinic* 53, no. 5 (2018): 321–24.

4. Douglas Fuchs and Lynn S. Fuchs, "Introduction to Response to Intervention: What, Why, and How Valid is It?" *Reading Research Quarterly* 41, no. 1 (2006): 93–99.

5. R.H. Horner, G. Sugai, A. W. Todd, T. Lewis-Palmer, L. Bambara, and L. Kern, "Individualized Supports for Students with Problem Behaviors: Designing Positive Behavior Plans," (2005); Tam E. O'Shaughnessy, Kathleen L. Lane, Frank M. Gresham, and Margaret E. Beebe-Frankenberger, "Children Placed at Risk for Learning and Behavioral Difficulties: Implementing a School-Wide System of Early Identification and Intervention," *Remedial and Special Education* 24, no. 1 (2003): 27–35; Brandi Simonsen, George Sugai, and Madeline Negron, "Schoolwide Positive Behavior Supports: Primary Systems and Practices," *Teaching Exceptional Children* 40, no. 6 (2008): 32–40; George Sugai and Robert R. Horner, "A Promising Approach for Expanding and Sustaining School-Wide Positive Behavior Support," *School Psychology Review* 35, no. 2 (2006): 245.

6. Rachel M. Stewart, Ronald C. Martella, Nancy E. Marchand-Martella, and Gregory J. Benner, "Three-Tier Models of Reading and Behavior," *Journal of Early and Intensive Behavior Intervention* 2, no. 3 (2005): 115–24.

7. Russell Gersten, David J. Chard, Madhavi Jayanthi, Scott K. Baker, Paul Morphy, and Jonathan Flojo, "Mathematics Instruction for Students with Learning Disabilities: A Meta-Analysis of Instructional Components," *Review of Educational Research* 79, no. 3 (2009): 1202–42.

8. John W. Maag, *Behavior Management: From Theoretical Implications to Practical Applications*, second edition (Belmont, CA: Edith Beard Brady, 2004).

9. Michael S. Rosenberg, Lawrence J. O'Shea, and Dorothy J. O'Shea, *Student Teacher to Master Teacher: A Practical Guide for Educating Students with Special Needs* (New York: Prentice Hall, 2001).

10. Jere E. Brophy, *Teaching*, International Academy of Education and the International Bureau of Education. 1999. www.cklavya.org/edu-practices_01_eng.pdf; Jere Brophy, "Teacher Influences on Student Achievement," *American Psychologist* 41, no. 10 (1986): 1069–77.

11. Jere E. Brophy, *Teaching*, International Academy of Education and the International Bureau of Education. 1999. www.cklavya.org/edu-practices_01_eng.pdf.

12. Ibid.

13. John W. Maag, *Behavior Management: From Theoretical Implications to Practical Applications*, second edition (Belmont, CA: Edith Beard Brady, 2004).

14. Devin Kearns, "Explicit Instruction: Modeling and Practicing to Help Students Reach Academic Goals," National Center on Intensive Intervention, Module 5, 2018; Anita L. Archer and Charles A. Hughes, *Explicit Instruction: Effective and Efficient Teaching* (New York: Guilford Press, 2010).

15. Jere E. Brophy, *Teaching*, International Academy of Education and the International Bureau of Education. 1999. www.cklavya.org/edu-practices_01_eng.pdf.

16. Marilyn J. Adams, "Beginning to Read: Learning and Thinking About Print," *MIT Press*, 1990; National Reading Panel (US), National Institute of Child Health, and Human Development (US), *Teaching Children to Read: An Evidence-Based Assessment of the Scientific Research Literature on Reading and Its Implications for Reading Instruction*, (National Institute of Child Health and Human Development, National Institutes of Health, 2000). http://www.nationalreadingpanel.org/Publications/summary.htm; National Research Council, *Preventing Reading Difficulties in*

Young Children, National Academies Press, 1998, https://doi.org/10.17226/6023; Louisa Cook Moats, *Speech to Print: Language Essentials for Teachers*, second edition (Baltimore, MD: Paul H. Brooks Publishing Company, 2010; Louisa Cook Moats, "Teaching Reading Is Rocket Science: What Expert Teachers of Reading Should Know and Be Able to Do," Washington, DC: American Federation of Teachers, (Item no. 39-0372), (1999).

17. Mary Abbott, Cheryl Walton, and Charles R. Greenwood, "Phonemic Awareness in Kindergarten and First Grade," *Teaching Exceptional Children* 34, no. 4 (2001): 20–26; Robin D. Morris, Karla K. Stuebing, Jack M. Fletcher, Sally E. Shaywitz, G. Reid Lyon, Donald P. Shankweiler, Leonard Katz, David J. Francis, and Bennett A. Shaywitz, "Subtypes of Reading Disability: Variability Around a Phonological Core," *Journal of Educational Psychology* 90, no. 3 (1998): 347.

18. Linnea C. Ehri and Alison G. Soffer, "Graphophonemic Awareness: Development in Elementary Students," *Scientific Studies of Reading* 3, no. 1 (1999): 1–30; Rebecca H. Felton and Pamela P. Pepper, "Early Identification and Intervention of Phonological Deficits in Kindergarten and Early Elementary Children at Risk for Reading Disability," *School Psychology Review* (1995); B. R. Foorman, D. J. Francis, and J. M. Fletcher, "Growth of Phonological Processing Skills in Beginning Reading: The Lag versus Deficit Model Revisited," *Society for Research on Child Development* (1995).

19. Linnea C. Ehri, "Development of the Ability to Read Words," *Handbook of Reading Research* 2 (1991): 383–417.

20. Barbara R. Foorman, David J. Francis, Jack M. Fletcher, Christopher Schatschneider, and Paras Mehta, "The Role of Instruction in Learning to Read: Preventing Reading Failure in At-Risk Children," *Journal of Educational Psychology* 90, no. 1 (1998): 37; David J. Chard and Edward J. Kameenui. "Struggling First-Grade Readers: The Frequency and Progress of Their Reading," *The Journal of Special Education* 34, no. 1 (2000): 28–38. Frank R. Vellutino, Donna M. Scanlon, Edward R. Sipay, Sheila G. Small, Alice Pratt, RuSan Chen, and Martha B. Denckla, "Cognitive Profiles of Difficult-to-Remediate and Readily Remediated Poor Readers: Early Intervention as a Vehicle for Distinguishing Between Cognitive and Experiential Deficits as Basic Causes of Specific Reading Disability," *Journal of Educational Psychology* 88, no. 4 (1996): 601; Mary Abbott, Cheryl Walton, Yolanda Tapia, and Charles R. Greenwood, "Research to Practice: A "Blueprint" for Closing the Gap in Local Schools," *Exceptional Children* 83 (1999): 339–62; Connie Juel, "Learning to Read and Write: A Longitudinal Study of 54 Children from First Through Fourth Grades," *Journal of Educational Psychology* 80, no. 4 (1988): 437.

21. Russell Gersten, David J. Chard, Madhavi Jayanthi, Scott K. Baker, Paul Morphy, and Jonathan Flojo, "Mathematics Instruction for Students with Learning Disabilities: A Meta-Analysis of Instructional Components," *Review of Educational Research* 79, no. 3 (2009): 1202–42.

22. Bob Algozzine, R. Putman, and R. H. Horner, "Support for Teaching Students with Learning Disabilities Academic Skills and Social Behaviors within a Response-to-Intervention Model: Why It Doesn't Matter What Comes First," *Insights on Learning Disabilities* 9, no. 1 (2012): 7–36; Bob Algozzine, Chuang Wang, Richard White,

Nancy Cooke, Mary Beth Marr, Kate Algozzine, Shawnna S. Helf, and Grace Zamora Duran, "Effects of Multi-Tier Academic and Behavior Instruction on Difficult-to-Teach Students," *Exceptional Children* 79, no. 1 (2012): 45–64; Rachel M. Stewart, Ronald C. Martella, Nancy E. Marchand-Martella, and Gregory J. Benner, "Three-Tier Models of Reading and Behavior," *Journal of Early and Intensive Behavior Intervention* 2, no. 3 (2005): 115–24; Rachel M. Stewart, Gregory J. Benner, Ronald C. Martella, and Nancy E. Marchand-Martella, "Three-Tier Models of Reading and Behavior: A Research Review," *Journal of Positive Behavior Interventions* 9, no. 4 (2007): 239–53.

23. Lee Kern and Nathan H. Clemens, "Antecedent Strategies to Promote Appropriate Classroom Behavior," *Psychology in the Schools* 44, no. 1 (2007): 65–75.

24. George Sugai and Robert R. Horner, "A Promising Approach for Expanding and Sustaining School-Wide Positive Behavior Support," *School Psychology Review* 35, no. 2 (2006): 245.

Chapter Three

Features of Intensive Small Group Instruction

OVERVIEW

This chapter identifies and explains numerous aspects of small group instruction that is explicit, teacher-directed, intensive, and remedial. Addressing these aspects in terms of the instructional needs of students who demonstrate long-standing, significant learning challenges ensures that, for the most part, this instruction is not "more of the same" ineffective large group instruction that was presented in a general education classroom.

That is to say, presenting the same type of large group instruction to (a) fewer students, (b) with increased frequency, and (c) for longer periods of time (i.e., increasing the amount of time that a student receives instruction during a school day) is one way to differentiate small group instruction from large group instruction. Yet this differentiation alone most likely will not result in the effective instruction that is hoped for on behalf of students with persistent and significant challenges learning targeted academic content and school social behaviors.

Rather, the type of small group instruction that is the focus of this book seeks to refine the high-quality instruction that is effective for the majority of the students in a general education classroom. This refinement is calculated to make intensive small group instruction markedly different in ways that will enable it to be effective with students who demonstrate ongoing, significant learning challenges.

After detailing how intensive small group instruction can be designed and presented so that it is distinctly different from large group instruction, the chapter addresses how small group instruction can be refined even further in an attempt to meet the needs of students who are described as needing ultra-intensive small group instruction. These students will not have made hoped for progress after initially receiving intensive small group instruction and could be characterized as demonstrating the most significant and persistent challenges learning academic content and school social behaviors.

As you read this chapter and the remainder of this book, remain mindful that the focus of the content that is presented is the teacher who will present intensive small group instruction. Thus, the issues that are discussed are primarily ones a teacher can address exclusively when they design and present intensive small group instruction.

Additionally, note that academic content and school social behaviors are the focus of the central issues that are discussed in this chapter and chapters 4 and 5. Functional content is referenced periodically but the use of intensive small group instruction to address this curriculum content is discussed in detail in chapter 7.

Key points in the chapter include the following:

1. Regarding the relationship between large group instruction in a general education classroom and intensive small group instruction, while intensive small group instruction cannot be "more of the same," there are reasons why it needs to be connected to the high-quality instruction that is presented in a general education classroom. These reasons include the fact that certain components of this high-quality instruction will still be relevant to intensive small group instruction, such as a proper environmental arrangement, successful time management, and the use of universal principles of effective instruction.
2. Certain students who are presented intensive small group instruction will continue to receive related subject matter instruction in a general education classroom while being provided accommodations or modifications. An accommodation is a change of the conditions that are put in place to enable a student to master a targeted learning standard, and a modification involves changing the standard. Typically, the standard is made less complex. The provision of either or both is not to be conflated with the provision of intensive small group instruction.
3. In most instances the purpose of providing intensive small group instruction is to teach students targeted learning outcomes that are at a much lower level in the core academic curriculum than is their age-appropriate, grade-level content. Yet small group instruction can also focus on teaching functional content and school social behaviors.
4. The two primary approaches to presenting small group instruction involve the use of either a standard treatment protocol or a problem-solving protocol.

5. A direct instruction lesson plan is a format that readily allows for the presentation of intensive small group instruction. This lesson plan consists of a collection of evidence-based, behavioral techniques that include teacher modeling and guided practice.
6. Intensive instruction is defined as instruction that allows for more prolonged and individualized student engagement with instructional level content. This prolonged engagement is defined in relative terms, meaning compared to a student's engagement in a general education classroom. This is another example of how intensive small group instruction is connected to the instruction that is presented in a general education classroom.
7. The elements of intensive instruction can be described in terms of two types of changes—quantitative and qualitative—that can differentiate this instruction from high-quality instruction that is presented in the general education classroom.
8. Quantitative changes involve a readily identifiable numerical aspect of an intervention. Examples include the frequency, or number of days per week, that intensive small group instruction is presented and the amount of time each day this instruction is presented.
9. Qualitative changes pertain to descriptions about the characteristics of small group instruction more so than counts or measures of the characteristics. Examples include the heterogeneity of the students in the group and the teacher's qualifications.
10. Intensive small group instruction will not initially prove to be effective for some students who demonstrate ongoing, significant learning challenges. Their small group instruction will need to be made ultra-intensive by changing elements of their initial, intensive small group instruction so that the ultra-intensive instruction allows for even more individualized and prolonged student engagement. Ways elements can be changed include reducing the group's size, increasing the number of days per week intensive small group instruction is presented, and making the group more homogeneous.

WAYS INTENSIVE SMALL GROUP INSTRUCTION IS RELATED TO HIGH-QUALITY INSTRUCTION IN GENERAL EDUCATION CLASSROOMS

Even when all of the components of high-quality instruction are adequately addressed in a general education classroom, there is a relatively high probability that certain students will (a) not attain targeted learning outcomes and (b) acquire the content they are mastering at a very low rate. These students, therefore, will need to receive intensive small group instruction.

This state of affairs does not mean, however, that the type of instruction that was being presented to these students should be completely discounted. In fact, the exact opposite is true. There are a number of reasons why the high-quality instruction that is presented in a general education classroom must serve as a reference point for the intensive small group instruction that will be presented to certain students.

1. Public schools are subject to finite instructional resources. Hence, these schools cannot afford to identify false positives in terms of students who display significant, persistent learning challenges. What this means is that schools cannot mistakenly conclude that a student's learning challenges are the result of circumstances that are innate to the student rather than woefully substandard, large group instruction that is being presented in a general education classroom—and that could be made more effective, thereby rendering additional remedial instruction unnecessary.

   The primary way to prevent this from happening is to clearly, operationally define and monitor the provision of high-quality instruction in general education classrooms. Students who do not respond to this instruction—meaning they do not attain all of the targeted learning outcomes—can then be provided intensive small group instruction that can be calculated to be more effective because it (a) accounted for the high-quality instruction that was presented in a general education classroom and (b) subsequently changed what were considered to be critical instructional variables.

2. Certain components of the high-quality instruction that was described in chapter 2 will still be relevant with respect to the presentation of intensive small group instruction that is calculated to provide the teacher and their students with the highest probability that this instruction will be effective. For instance, some of the principles of an appropriate environmental arrangement, sufficient time management, and the use of universal principles of effective instruction will be relevant.

   In particular, a focus on engaged and academic learning time lies at the heart of intensive small group instruction. In terms of one of the components of high-quality instruction—sufficient time management—this means that the purpose of this instruction is to ensure that students spend every available moment attending to, and cognitively processing, instruction that targets the students' instructional level tasks. In other words, the way that intensive small group instruction is designed and presented should result in the terms engaged and academic learning time becoming nearly synonymous.

3. General education teachers who supplement large group instruction with small group instruction on behalf of "struggling learners" who may be

in the special education eligibility determination process will want to have this small group instruction be something other than "more of the same" large group instruction that has proven to be ineffective with these students. Thus, some type of intensive small group instruction will be appropriate, and needed, in these situations.

This circumstance highlights how certain instructional concepts, such as (a) large and small group instruction and (b) high-quality general education and intensive small group instruction, are interconnected and must be discussed in terms of each other. For example, to be able to settle upon the maximum number of students that meets the pupil:teacher ratio that is put forth in a definition for small group instruction, one must know the corresponding lower limit for the number of students that meets the pupil:teacher ratio that is put forth in a definition for large group instruction.

Likewise, to be able to operationally define and implement intensive small group instruction, one must have a clear understanding of how high-quality instruction has been operationally defined and is being presented in a general education classroom.

4. Some students, including both those who have and have not been determined to be eligible to receive special education services, who receive intensive small group instruction will simultaneously receive large group instruction in a general education classroom. In many instances the large group instruction will address the same subject matter that is being addressed during intensive small group instruction.

However, given the historical challenges these students have demonstrated mastering this content solely through the delivery of large group instruction in a general education classroom, provisions need to be put in place to increase the probability that this instruction will be at least somewhat effective (i.e., the students will acquire some, but not all, of the targeted learning outcomes).

To enhance the probability that this instruction will be effective, these students may be provided accommodations or modifications. These are changes to the typical instruction that is being presented in a general education classroom and are dependent on the features of the current, ongoing instruction.

An accommodation is a change to the conditions under which a student is expected to acquire knowledge or perform a skill. Accommodations may include, but are not necessarily limited to, (a) the manner in which the instruction is presented to the student (e.g., in writing rather than an oral presentation), (b) the arrangement of the setting when instruction is being presented (e.g., the student sits at the front of the room, near the teacher, so that the student's attention to instruction can easily be monitored), (c) the time that a student is given to complete a task (e.g., the student may be permitted 1.5 times as long as his peers to complete an assignment), and (d) the mode of responding that is required from the student (e.g., typewritten rather than handwritten answers).

An important point with respect to the use of accommodations is that the grade-level, targeted learning outcome remains the same for students who do, and do not, receive an accommodation.[1] A change to this outcome is a modification.

A modification is a change of the content a student is expected to master. Generally speaking, in the case of a student who is demonstrating significant, ongoing challenges learning grade-level content, a modification will involve a change that results in a student working to master lower-level content than the other students in the class. For example, if the grade-level learning objective focuses on finding the sum when two three-digit numbers are added and regrouping is required, a modification would be for a student to learn how to find the sum when a single digit number is added to a double-digit number, and no regrouping is required.

In particular, it is important that educators not conflate the provision of accommodations or modifications with the provision of intensive instruction in a small group arrangement as it is explained in this book. Accommodations and modifications are unique constructs that involve a different way of viewing the student and their needs. Importantly this view is to be based on supporting assessment data.

An accommodation is to be provided when the student is viewed as being capable of mastering grade-level content as long as the conditions pertaining to the way teaching and student responding occur in a general education classroom are altered, but not excessively. Conversely, intensive small group instruction is to be provided when a student has demonstrated significant, ongoing challenges mastering targeted learning outcomes.

Consequently, the student needs to be provided instruction that addresses content that is at a lower level than the content that is targeted at their age-appropriate grade level. Additionally, the way the content is taught needs to account for the features of intensive small group instruction that are discussed in this book. A modification that is provided in the general education classroom will not be taught in this manner.

To ensure that all students spend the entire school day in a general education classroom, some educators have advocated solely for the use of accommodations and modifications. In these situations intensive small group instruction is not an option that is available to staff or students. Yet this is the type of instruction some students need to be provided to be able to make meaningful progress in their curriculum.

INTENSIVE SMALL GROUP INSTRUCTION: THE DETAILS

The information that follows expands upon the content that was presented in chapter 1 when a broad overview of small group instruction was presented in the form of limited answers to what, who, where, when, why, and how questions. This additional information addresses more of the details that are involved in the design and implementation of intensive small group instruction.

Students and Staff Involved

Primarily the students who will be provided intensive small group instruction will be the students whose progress monitoring data while being provided high-quality instruction in a general education classroom indicate that they are significantly behind their peers in terms of the amount of expected learning outcomes attained and the rate at which new material is learned. For the purposes of this book, "significantly behind" refers to students who are working to master curriculum content that is at least two years behind what they are expected to master in their current grade.

Another group of students for whom intensive small group instruction will be appropriate is those who have what is characterized as a moderate or more significant disability and receive special education services in a placement, such as a self-contained classroom, that is configured with the expectation that small group instruction will be presented. This configuration involves a pupil:teacher ratio that meets the definition for small group instruction that is put forward in this book. Also, evidence pertaining to how these students' disabilities manifest in terms of the learning outcomes they will attain lends further support to providing them intensive small group instruction.

The staff who might provide intensive small group instruction can vary greatly from school to school and is directly related to the approach taken to provide this instruction. The two approaches to presenting intensive small group instruction—a standard treatment protocol and a problem-solving protocol—are explained subsequently.

Across both protocols the range of personnel who might provide this instruction includes school employees and others who are not employed by the school. School employees may include

1. the student's general education classroom teacher;
2. a special education teacher;
3. an intervention specialist, meaning a teacher who has specialized training in the presentation of academic or school social behavior interventions (i.e., a reading therapist, math coach, or behavior specialist);

4. a general interventionist, meaning a teacher who has been hired to implement remedial academic interventions, school social behavior interventions, or both; and
5. a teacher assistant.

Non-paid personnel may include retired adult volunteers, preservice teachers, or even a high school student who is earning community service hours.

Purpose of Intensive Small Group Instruction

In most instances the purpose of providing intensive small group instruction is to teach students targeted learning outcomes that they have not attained and that are at a much lower level in the core curriculum than is their age-appropriate, grade-level content. The students need to learn the lower-level content because it is critical to the acquisition of higher-level content.

In some cases, the purpose of intensive, remedial instruction will be to teach students functional content. This could include teaching them activities of daily living that the vast majority of their same-age peers have been shown, through research, to already have acquired, such as how to independently toilet oneself.

As was noted previously, it is necessary to remain mindful of the fact that, during the time that most students who need to receive it are provided intensive small group instruction, students will simultaneously receive large group instruction in a general education classroom. For example, during a school day a student will participate in both a general education math lesson as well as intensive small group instruction that addresses remedial math learning objectives. In these instances, several issues may need to be addressed.

1. Students' interest in participating in intensive small group instruction. Some students will exhibit a high level of interest and motivation to participate in intensive small group instruction due to its focus on instructional level content. These students perceive the content that is being taught in the general education class as being beyond their present capacity to learn it and are frustrated by their experiences to master this content.
2. Other students will openly balk at having to participate in intensive small group instruction. Reasons for this circumstance include
    a. being frustrated by repeatedly being tasked to master content they have not attained despite being taught it for an extended period of time;
    b. having a desire for all of their instruction to focus on the content that is being taught in the general education classroom, particularly when mastering it is related to a highly desired outcome (e.g., the student

earns course credit that is necessary for the awarding of a high school diploma); and
   c. receiving ridicule from peers about having to participate in intensive small group instruction.
3. Ensuring the integrity of the intensive small group instruction. During the small group lesson the teacher will have to ensure that they focus on the targeted learning objectives and key instructional strategies rather than respond to some students' requests to "help them" with their general education classwork.
4. As was noted previously, each student's program will need to be examined to make certain that accommodations or modifications are provided strategically in the general education classroom so as not to circumvent intensive small group instruction that is warranted because it has a higher probability to result in students' attainment of targeted learning outcomes.
5. Clearly establishing how the content that is taught during intensive small group instruction is tied to the core curriculum that is being taught in the general education classroom. For example, when multiplication is the focus of instruction in the general education classroom and basic addition facts are the focus of instruction in the small group the teacher can explain to students how multiplication is repeated addition.

When a teacher makes this connection, they must do so in a manner that protects the integrity of the intensive small group instruction. Making this connection is a universal effective teaching practice. Additionally, doing so may adequately address some students' concerns about intensive small group instruction not being relevant to their current general education classroom instruction.

Two Primary Approaches to Intensive Small Group Instruction: Standard Treatment and Problem-Solving Protocols

In general, intensive small group instruction is provided in accordance with one of two approaches: either a standard treatment protocol or a problem-solving protocol. A standard treatment protocol involves the use of a prepackaged, research-validated instructional program that has been designed to address a specific academic or school social behavior deficit (e.g., phonics skills, asking questions appropriately in class). This means that the instructor presents this instruction "as it has been designed" to every student in the small group.

Some have referred to these programs as scripted programs given the fact that a number of them not only provide the teacher with the instructional materials that they are to use but also the dialogue they are to present to the students and the pace of instruction that is to be followed. Among other things, the use of a standard treatment protocol means the small group must be homogeneous with respect to each student's remediation needs.

A problem-solving protocol involves a multi-step process that is employed on behalf of each student who exhibits an academic deficit or is not engaging in appropriate school social behavior. This process begins with the identification of the student's academic achievement or school social behavior deficit followed by an examination of various aspects of the deficit (e.g., what is the extent of the deficit, which interventions have already been used to address it, etc.).

An individualized intervention plan is then designed and implemented, and student performance data are routinely collected and evaluated to determine the plan's effectiveness. Hence, unlike the standard treatment protocol, a problem-solving protocol allows for the use of a variety of interventions that are based on a student's unique deficits and performance data.

When a school-wide protocol is being followed for purposes such as (a) identifying students who need to be evaluated to determine whether they are eligible to receive special education services or (b) ensuring that each student is provided with an appropriate instructional match, a multi-disciplinary team engages in a formal problem-solving process. Examples of these protocols would include the execution of what is referred to as a prereferral-to-placement process[2] or the implementation of a response-to-intervention framework.[3]

At some point, students who display the most significant and persistent learning challenges will have their instruction result from some type of a problem-solving protocol. That is to say, even if a standard treatment protocol was used initially with these students, the fact that they did not master targeted learning outcomes as a result means that school personnel will need to problem solve for the purpose of developing a more intensive, individualized intervention plan.[4]

Given some students' significant and persistent challenges mastering targeted learning outcomes, a reasonable, proactive approach would involve planning for the use of some type of problem-solving approach to intensive small group instruction. Arguably this is the least dangerous assumption because it accounts for any instance when either a standard treatment protocol or problem-solving protocol proves to be ineffective.

Furthermore, considering the distinctions between a standard treatment and problem-solving approach to intensive small group instruction that were just described, it is worth examining how the degree to which a teacher needs to be knowledgeable about the intricacies of intensive small group instruction can be thought of as existing along a continuum.

One end of the continuum would represent the small group arrangements in which a standard treatment protocol is employed. To the extent that this protocol involves a pre-packaged, highly scripted intervention, the instructor will be more inclined to present instruction as they are directed rather than engage in improvisation by manipulating variables that they have reason to believe will make the instruction more effective. In these instances persons without formal teacher training, such as retirees, practicum students, and high school volunteers, may be able to provide effective, intensive small group instruction.

This depiction of a standard treatment protocol is supported by two facts. One is that a wide variety of adults, including individuals who have not received any formal training to be a teacher, can be adequately trained to present some standard treatment protocols. The second is that this protocol is to be used with small groups of homogeneous students, meaning each student in the group needs to learn the content that is taught by the protocol (e.g., decoding skills or basic addition facts).

The other end of the continuum would represent the small group arrangements in which some type of problem-solving protocol is employed. When this approach is used a teacher may have to be prepared to employ a wide variety of instructional strategies across a very diverse, heterogeneous group of students.

Yet, even though problem-solving protocols involve the development and implementation of intervention services that are predicated on a case study approach, this practice does not always mean that the services will look markedly different from those that result from the use of a standard treatment protocol. For instance, in a large school a problem-solving protocol may result in intervention services to a homogeneous group of students, such as the group referenced in the previous discussion about a standard treatment protocol.

Conversely, in a small, rural school a problem-solving protocol may result in services to a very heterogeneous group of students because the options for creating homogeneous groups are limited or even non-existent. In this situation the teacher would need to be well-versed in both the art and science of presenting effective, intensive small group instruction.

Time of the Day When Intensive Small Group Instruction Will be Presented

When it has been determined that a student needs to receive intensive small group instruction, provisions have to be made with respect to when, during the school day, this instruction will be presented. Several possible scenarios include the following:

1. A basic arrangement that is used as a part of a schoolwide multi-tier system of support is to designate a block of time (thirty to forty-five minutes) at the end of the school day during which every student participates in an activity referred to as, "What I Need." During this time some students in

the school would participate in enrichment activities, some would complete unfinished general education classroom work, and some students would receive intensive small group instruction. This arrangement highlights the fact that the latter group of students would receive most of their instruction in a large group arrangement in a general education classroom.
2. During times when subject matter content that is well beyond the student's instructional level and aligns with a student's area of significant and persistent learning challenge (e.g., exponential functions are being taught in an Algebra I class and a student has demonstrated significant and ongoing challenges learning basic math skills), the student will be presented intensive small group instruction. This might occur because it has been decided that the student is performing at a level that is so far behind the level that is being addressed in the general education classroom, there is a much higher probability that effective, appropriate instruction will be presented in a small group arrangement.
3. Essentially throughout the entire school day when a student primarily receives instruction in a setting in which all of the students have been determined to be eligible to receive special education services and are performing in a manner which indicates that they need to be provided intensive small group instruction. This may be the case in a self-contained classroom.

Location Where Intensive Small Group Instruction Will be Presented

Just as there are many ways to schedule the provision of intensive small group instruction, there also are many locations where this instruction can be provided. In some instances the general education teacher provides this instruction—or some variant of it—in their classroom. This might occur when a teacher is trying to remediate a student's academic performance deficit while the student is in the special education eligibility determination process. This also might occur in a school with extremely limited resources and a small total student population.

However, given the need for a general education teacher to focus on the provision of high-quality, large group instruction while also addressing numerous administrative tasks, it is questionable whether this teacher can also effectively present the intensive instruction that is the focus of this book. Thus, for the purposes of this book, this instruction is explained in terms of an instructor other than the student's general education teacher providing it—either in the classroom or elsewhere in the school. These instructors were identified previously.

Outside of the general education classroom, intensive small group instruction may be provided elsewhere in the school or on the school's campus.

These locations include a classroom that has been configured for small group instruction; a dual use location, such as the cafeteria; or a detached building, such as a portable trailer.

EXPLICIT, TEACHER-DIRECTED, INTENSIVE, AND REMEDIAL SMALL GROUP INSTRUCTION

In this and the remaining sections of this chapter the features of explicit, teacher-directed, intensive, remedial instruction are discussed in greater detail, meaning well beyond the definitions for these terms that were presented in chapter 1. The content in this section addresses the ways that this instruction is directly related to, yet different from, the high-quality instruction in a general education classroom that has not proven to be effective with students who present significant, persistent challenges learning targeted outcomes.

Consequently, it is imperative that the characteristics of explicit, teacher-directed, intensive, remedial small group instruction be identified and operationally defined so that one can (a) be sure that students are not getting "more of the same" general education instruction that has been ineffective and (b) have a basis for going about adjusting this instruction if it, too, proves to be ineffective.

A key element of the following discussion is the identification and description of the aspects of a direct instruction lesson plan. This plan serves as the foundation for intensive small group instruction as it is explained in this book. Accordingly, this plan will also be discussed in chapters 4 and 5.

Explicit Instruction and a Direct Instruction Lesson Plan

In this book explicit instruction refers to a type of teacher-directed instruction during which all aspects of it are made known to the learner. Features of explicit instruction include the teacher selecting the learning objective and then designing a structured lesson that, as is appropriate, is comprised of (a) direct explanation and modeling by the teacher, (b) guided practice, (c) independent practice, (d) assessment, and (e) lesson review. Altogether, explicit instruction embodies universal effective teaching practices.

A structured lesson is in keeping with the nature of explicit instruction. Structure, as it pertains to the presentation of instruction, refers to the teacher selecting the learning objective, determining how the student is to go about mastering the objective, and establishing how long each activity within the lesson—as well as the lesson itself—will last.[5] A structured lesson is also systematic in the sense that it is easily replicable.

Others have described a format for the use of a collection of evidence-based, behavioral techniques that have proven to result in the presentation of effective instruction to students with disabilities. This format has been referred to as a direct instruction lesson plan.[6] Considering that many students with disabilities will be in need of intensive small group instruction, a direct instruction lesson plan would be suitable to follow as it allows for the presentation of the explicit instruction that is a key element of the presentation of effective, intensive small group instruction.

A direct instruction lesson plan can account for numerous universal effective teaching practices, including previewing instruction, reviewing previous instruction, pre-teaching key vocabulary, maximizing academic engagement, using appropriate pacing, using wait time after questioning, circulating and scanning the instructional environment, recognizing appropriate behavior, exhibiting enthusiasm, displaying awareness of what is happening in the classroom, and monitoring student performance.[7] Additional evidence-based practices the lesson plan accounts for include explaining the goals and objectives of the lesson, sequencing content, reviewing requisite skills, delivering information, giving clear instructions and explanations and relevant examples, providing guided practice, checking for comprehension, providing quick and specific feedback, provide independent practice, and conducting formative evaluation.[8]

In the following, a series of steps that comprise one version of a direct instruction lesson plan are identified and defined. This lesson plan serves as the basis for the discussion in chapter 5 regarding how to present a lesson in a small group arrangement. This plan's format allows for the presentation of all of the components that comprise explicit, teacher directed, intensive, remedial small group instruction as well as instructional strategies that are uniquely available as a result of a small group arrangement.

1. *Attention directive.* A teacher directive that is intended to communicate to students that they are to display behaviors that will convey to the teacher that the students are attending to their teacher and, therefore, are ready to receive instruction. While the teacher will most often present an attentional directive at the outset of a lesson, this directive can be presented at any point in time when a student is engaging in off-task behavior.

    There are no set components for an attention directive. Rather, its components are determined by the teacher who must then teach their meanings to the students. An example of an attention directive is the phrase "Get ready," which is an abbreviation for the phrase "Get ready to learn."
2. *Attention response.* Behaviors a student is taught to display, in response to the presentation of an attention directive by the teacher, for the purpose of communicating to the teacher that the student is paying attention. There are no set components for an attention response. Rather, its components

are determined by the teacher who must then teach the students how and when to display them.

One possible attention response would be for a student to face the teacher while sitting straight up in their chair with their feet flat on the floor and their hands in his lap. The student also would be expected to remain quiet.

3. *Statement of the learning objective.* The teacher explicitly tells the students the knowledge or skills they will teach the students during the lesson (e.g., "I am going to teach you how to count to seventeen"). The teacher also might display a written version of the objective and refer to it when they review it with the students.
4. *Review of previously mastered, related learning objectives.* Prior to modeling how to perform the behavior that is at the heart of the learning objective (see point 5 below), the teacher will review how to perform one or more behaviors that the students have mastered and are closely related to the learning objective that is the focus of the lesson (e.g., prior to modeling how to count to seventeen, the teacher will review how to count to fifteen and sixteen).
5. *Teacher modeling.* The teacher explicitly demonstrates how to perform the behavior that is at the heart of the learning objective. Teacher modeling may be followed by a role play during which a teacher assistant acts like a student for the purpose of demonstrating to the students how they are to behave in response to the teacher during the guided practice portion of the lesson.
6. *Guided practice, with appropriate feedback.* The student is directed to perform the behavior while receiving support, in the form of prompts, from an instructor to ensure that the student responds correctly. Any support that is provided by the teacher after they present the task directive is a prompt. After the student responds correctly, they are provided immediate, behavior-specific praise.
7. *Independent practice.* Independent practice consists of the student engaging, on their own, in the behavior that is the focus of the learning objective. However, it may involve having the student only complete activities that pertain to previously mastered material (e.g., read CVC words) if the student would exhibit a high rate of errors on the new material. In some instances, this component of the direct instruction lesson plan would be omitted.
8. *Lesson review.* The teacher reviews the lesson by reiterating the activities that occurred during the lesson.
9. *Preview of the next lesson.* The teacher tells the students the topics that will be addressed in the next lesson in this content area, and notes when that lesson will occur (e.g., "Later this morning . . .; "Tomorrow at this time . . .").

It is important to note that the elements that comprise this direct instruction lesson plan can be omitted altogether or modified to meet students' needs. For instance, independent practice may be omitted if the students participating in the lesson have not learned how to work independently.

Likewise, the teacher may decide to forego reviewing the topics that were addressed during the lesson if they have reason to believe that doing so may confuse the students. Some students may employ a visual support, much like a to-do list, that enables them to better understand all of the work they will do, the order in which it will be done, and when a task is finished (e.g., by crossing a line through its written representation). Reviewing the lesson may confuse the students who have come to conclude that once they have crossed through all of the items the lesson is over.

Finally, the lesson plan also can be modified with the addition of appropriate tasks. One task would be conducting a probe, which is a type of formative assessment, after the presentation of the attention directive but before stating the learning objective for the lesson.

Teacher-Directed Instruction

A type of instruction that involves the teacher taking the lead in a number of ways, which include selecting a curriculum standard, writing a relevant learning objective, modeling how to successfully perform the activity that is the focus of the learning objective, and supporting students in their initial attempts to do the same. This support involves the use of prompts and the delivery of immediate, descriptive, behavior-specific feedback.

Intensive Instruction

Intensive instruction refers to strategically designed interventions that consist of a number of elements that allow for more individualized and prolonged student engagement. Prolonged student engagement results from actions that keep the student cognitively processing the content that is the focus of instruction. Examples of these actions include

1. repeatedly directing the student to attend to activities that are at, or only slightly above, their instructional level;
2. having the student respond more often than they typically do in large group arrangements—both directly via a mode of active student responding or indirectly through active participation in a way that sets the occasion for observational and incidental learning; and

3. providing the student with feedback that is immediate, descriptive, and specific to both their correct and incorrect responses.

The goal is for this individualized and prolonged student engagement to result in both a higher level and rate of student attainment of the targeted learning outcomes than was the case when less intensive large group instruction was presented in a general education classroom. The elements of intensive instruction can be described in terms of the types of changes that can differentiate this instruction from high-quality instruction that is presented in a general education classroom. The two types of changes have been classified as either quantitative or qualitative changes.

Quantitative Changes

Quantitative changes involve a readily identifiable numerical aspect of an intervention. Examples of these changes include, but are not limited to, decreasing group size, increasing the frequency and duration of the intervention, increasing the rate of active student responding as well as the use of prompts during a lesson, providing immediate and descriptive feedback following each student's response, and upping the frequency of progress monitoring. Information about each of these quantitative changes is presented in the following.

1. *Decreasing group size.* The first element of intensive instruction that sets the stage for more individualized and prolonged student engagement is the use of a small group arrangement. For the purposes of this book, this arrangement is defined as a pupil:teacher ratio that involves two to eight students per instructor. Because the term "small group instruction" is used quite often to refer the delivery of instruction using these arrangements, throughout this book this term is used interchangeably with the term "small group arrangement."

    A small group arrangement allows for the unique implementation of a number of the elements described here and that have been shown to permit students to attain targeted learning outcomes that were not realized under the conditions in place in a general education classroom. In chapter 5 the way that these elements can be manipulated so that relatively more or less intensive, small group instruction is presented is discussed.
2. *Increasing the frequency and duration of instruction.* This element of intensive instruction pertains to how often and how long students will receive it. With respect to the intensive, remedial instruction that some

students are provided, the central issue is that the increased frequency and duration pertains to the targeted learning outcomes they have not mastered (i.e., they are allocated more time to receive instruction that pertains to the subject matter area in which they have not attained targeted learning outcomes—such as reading, math, and writing—or the school social behavior they have not attained).

However, several scenarios need to be considered when this element of intensive instruction is addressed. The questions that must be addressed with respect to these scenarios are

a. how long will a student participate in small group instruction exclusively, meaning that this is the only instruction a student will receive during the school day that addresses the subject matter area that is the focus of small group instruction;

b. how long during the school day will a student receive both large group instruction in a general education classroom as well as intensive small group instruction that addresses the same subject matter area; and

c. irrespective of whether a student is a member of a large or small group, how much engaged and academic learning time will a student experience.

3. *Increasing active student responding.* Active student responding refers to students' displays of overt behaviors to indicate their responses to a teacher's questions that are posed for the purpose of gauging how well students are comprehending the lesson. Requiring active student responding is one strategy for keeping students engaged in a lesson by getting them to cognitively process the instructional content. As you now know, this behavior is one component of the definition for the term "intensive intervention" that is used in this book.

There are many forms of active student responding, and a number of them can be used similarly in large and small group arrangements. For instance, a teacher can pose a true/false question and direct all of the students to respond at the same time by showing a thumbs up if they believe the correct answer is true or a thumbs down if they believe the correct answer is false.

This type of simultaneous responding is called unison, or choral, responding. In most instances when a general education teacher requires this type of response, they intend to get a general idea regarding whether the class, as a whole, is comprehending the instruction rather than closely assess the responses of individual students.

In small group arrangements the teacher can present more opportunities for active student responding as well as closely assess the responses of individual students. The teacher can do both because, due to its size, they will spend less time scanning the group and will have to keep track of fewer responses. This is particularly the case when the pupil:teacher ratio is 2–4:1 as opposed to 5–8:1. Also, when the pupil:teacher ratio is 2–4:1 the teacher can require individual rather than choral responding.

4. *Increasing prompting for desirable behavior.* A prompt is defined as additional information that a teacher presents, after delivering the task directive, to increase the probability that a student will emit a correct response. For example, when a teacher is instructing students about reading consonant-vowel-consonant words, they might show a student an index card on which the word "cat" is written and simultaneously present the task directive, "Read this word." To increase the probability that the student will read the word correctly, the teacher says the first two sounds of the word that are represented by the letters c and a.

The information that is presented after the task directive is a prompt. Relative to the large group arrangement that exists in a general education classroom, a small group arrangement will enable the teacher to provide more prompts as well as individualize the prompts to meet each student's needs.

Increasing the frequency of immediate, descriptive, behavior-specific feedback.[9] The information that a teacher presents to students after they provide a response is referred to as feedback. Among other things, it lets the student know whether their response was correct. Feedback can be described in terms of a number of features, including whether it is (a) immediate or delayed, (b) pertains to a correct or incorrect response, (c) is descriptive or not (i.e., references the behavior that is the focus of the learning objective), and (d) is general ("Good reading") or specific ("Correct, you read the word cat").

A small group arrangement will enable the teacher to provide more immediate, descriptive, behavior-specific feedback. By its very nature, this feedback is individualized.

5. *Increasing the frequency of progress monitoring.* Because students who need to be provided intensive, remedial instruction are demonstrating noteworthy achievement deficits, they cannot be permitted to spend relatively long periods of time engaging in additional ineffective interventions. Hence, a specific type of progress monitoring—formative assessment probes—can be presented as often as is deemed appropriate, including daily.

Probes are short assessments (i.e., they are intended to take students about one to three minutes to complete) that consist of items that directly and extensively measure a student's performance on a targeted learning objective. "Extensively" means that the assessment is comprised of a relatively large number of items that address the targeted learning objective. The resulting data are intended to be used to readily inform instruction. This means that changes to the way that a lesson is conducted in terms of teacher or student behaviors, or both, can be made as a result of the information that is obtained.

Qualitative Changes

Qualitative changes pertain to descriptions about the characteristics of intensive small group instruction more so than counts or measures of the characteristics of this instruction. Yet these qualitative changes compliment quantitative changes and contribute to the learning outcomes attained. Interestingly, these outcomes also can be described in terms of quantitative and qualitative changes.

Examples of qualitative changes to small group instruction are listed and explained in the following. These include decreasing the heterogeneity among the students who comprise a small group; arranging the environment so that it allows for teaching and learning that is somewhat unique to small group arrangements; employing interventions that specifically account for the students' characteristics of thinking and learning; defining learning objectives that are more precisely aligned with students' instructional needs; presenting individualized, descriptive, behavior-specific feedback; and improving the instructor's knowledge and skills.

Again, as you read the explanations for each description it is important that you remember that the point of reference for each qualitative change is the manner in which instruction is being provided in large group arrangements in a general education classroom. References to this high-quality, large group instruction are provided to enhance your understanding of the types of qualitative changes that can be made to intensive small group instruction.

1. *Decreasing the heterogeneity among the students who comprise a small group.* A homogeneous group refers to one in which the students are similar in a number of key respects, whereas a heterogeneous group is one in which the students are dissimilar. Homogeneity and heterogeneity can, therefore, be thought of as opposite sides of the same coin.

    In most public schools, students are randomly assigned to general education classrooms, which often results in significant diversity among the students in terms of their levels of performance and rates of learning. Thus, one way to differentiate small group instruction from typical large group instruction in a general education classroom is to reduce the diversity among the students who are assembled together for small group instruction.

The creation of small group arrangements gives teachers some flexibility—which is not available to them when general education classrooms are constructed—regarding which students will be in a group. Teachers of small groups can take full advantage of this opportunity by exercising great care in selecting which students will receive instruction at the same time in the small group. The reason for doing so is because small group instruction will be more efficient and effective when the students in the group have more in common with respect to the content they need to learn and how they go about processing information and indicating their understanding of it.

2. *Arranging the environment so that it allows for teaching and learning that is somewhat unique to small group arrangements.* The physical arrangement for small group instruction can set the occasion for the use of instructional strategies that are more easily employed in this arrangement because of the relatively close proximity of the teacher and students as compared to their proximity in a general education classroom.

For instance, if the environment is arranged so that every student in the group can readily observe all of the other students in the group, this arrangement will increase the probability that observational learning will occur—provided the teacher is aware of this possibility and systematically plans for it. Observational learning occurs when a student attains a targeted learning outcome that has been established for another student in the group after the first student observes the second student correctly perform the task and receive reinforcement for doing so. A related type of learning, incidental learning, is also possible. Incidental learning is described in subsequent sections in this book.

3. *Employing interventions that specifically account for the students' characteristics of thinking and learning.* Being able to determine which students will be in a small group enables teachers to decide upon, and use, interventions that can address the characteristics of thinking and learning that are exhibited by the students. This opportunity exists more so than is the case in a general education classroom. For instance, if the students in the group are prone to distractions, challenged to process oral language, and respond optimally to an exceedingly structured environment, the teacher could account for these characteristics of thinking and learning as described subsequently.

   a. *Prone to distractions.* If small group instruction is conducted within the general education classroom the teacher could seat the students who are in the small group such that their backs are facing their classmates.

Additionally, the teacher could position portable dividers to block anything that might be seen in front of, or to the sides of, the students and serve as a distraction.
b. *Processing oral language.* The teacher could provide single step, rather than multi-step, directives as well as intentional pauses to give students extra time to process their oral language.
c. *Structure.* Structure refers to a teacher systematically directing all instructional activities, including deciding the tasks students will perform, how they will perform them, and for how long. Elements of structure could include requiring students to execute routines for entering and exiting the small group, and the use of a lesson plan that is based upon the tenets of explicit instruction (such as the direct instruction lesson plan described previously).
d. *Defining learning objectives that are more precisely aligned with students' instructional needs.* Remedial instruction is designed to address the specific learning outcomes a student has not mastered and provide the student with the repetition—both in terms of receiving instruction that consistently follows a particular protocol as well as repeatedly practicing targeted learning outcomes—that they need to attain these outcomes.

This state of affairs means the curriculum that is addressed during intensive small group instruction is to be much narrower in scope than is the curriculum that is being taught in a general education classroom. In general education classrooms students work to attain rather broadly stated learning outcomes from a curriculum whose scope and sequence, along with its pacing guide, results in the presentation of instruction at a rate that is not well aligned with some students' characteristics of thinking and learning.

e. *Presenting individualized, descriptive, behavior-specific feedback.* During small group instruction the teacher is in a more tenable position to provide individualized, descriptive, behavior-specific feedback following student responses to questions that a teacher poses to assess the students' understanding of a lesson than is the case in a large group arrangement. This is so whether the students who comprise a small group respond in unison or individually.

Given the pupil:teacher ratio in a general education classroom, a teacher will be challenged to provide feedback that is specific to each student's response. More often than not, the teacher will provide general feedback, or feedback that is specific to one student's response, such as the student who was called upon to solve a math problem on the whiteboard that is at the front of the class.

f. *Improving the instructor's knowledge and skills.* Whenever intensive small group instruction is being designed and subsequently implemented there are a number of variables specific to the instructor that can be addressed in an attempt to improve the quality of the instruction (i.e., its efficiency and effectiveness) that is presented—both in its own right and relative to the high-quality instruction that is being presented in a general education classroom.

These variables include an instructor's knowledge and teaching skills with respect to the academic content being taught, use of interventions that are particularly suited for small group instruction (e.g., prompting, active student responding, individualized feedback, conditions that set the occasion for observational and incidental learning), behavior management, and diagnostic assessment.[10]

Remedial Instruction

Remedial instruction targets learning outcomes that have not been attained by a student but were expected to have been attained at a much earlier point in time. Students who need to receive remedial instruction are said to present significant learning challenges. Among other things, this characterization means there is a need to operationally define the meaning of the term "significant."

Like many terms in the field of education, there is not a universally agreed upon definition for the term "significant learning challenge." In this book, the term refers to students who are performing at least two years behind their age-appropriate grade level. Most likely the small percentage of students who are identified as needing intensive, remedial small group instruction will be performing closer to three or more years behind.

In many instances the content these students need to master are foundational, or basic, skills that lead to the acquisition of higher order skills. However, be careful not to equate basic with easy. Both teaching and mastering foundational skills can prove to be formidable. Similarly, do not mistakenly conclude that students who are struggling mightily to master basic skills are not able to develop higher-order thinking skills.

PROVIDING ULTRA-INTENSIVE TIER 2 SERVICES

In some instances, a student's performance data will indicate that there is little to no change in their level or rate of learning despite the intensive small group instruction they are receiving. In these cases substantive quantitative and qualitative changes to this instruction may have to be made. Essentially this student's intensive small group instruction will have to be changed in ways that afford the student even more of an opportunity to receive strategically designed interventions that consist of a number of elements that allow for more individualized and prolonged student engagement. Some ways of making these changes are as follows.

1. *Size of the instructional group.* The size of the group can be made as small as possible such that it still meets the definition for group instruction. This would mean that the pupil:teacher ratio is no more than 2–3:1. A 2:1 ratio is the smallest allowable to meet the definition for a small group arrangement.

    Resources permitting a 1:1 arrangement could be used, and some of the small group instructional strategies that are discussed in this book—such as providing the student with an attention directive, prompts, and specific feedback—could be employed. However, other strategies, such as those that address observational learning, could not.
2. *Frequency of progress monitoring.* Progress monitoring may be conducted daily through the use of probes. As was noted previously, probes are short assessments that consist of items that directly and extensively measure a student's performance on a targeted learning objective. The resulting data are intended to be used to readily inform instruction. This means, with respect to the way that small group instruction is presented, changes in a teacher's or student's behavior, or both, can be made as a result of the information that is obtained.

    Even if daily probes are not conducted, some type of appropriate progress monitoring assessment could be conducted more often than was the case previously, but for the same reasons. For instance, progress monitoring could be conducted three, rather than two, times per week. Overall, teachers need to balance the need to gather assessment information that both documents student progress and informs instruction against performing assessment activities that take away from a student's academic learning time.
3. *Duration of the intervention.* The duration of each instructional session could be extended. For instance, instead of a thirty- to forty-five-minute session, each session could be increased to sixty to seventy-five minutes of instruction.
4. *Frequency with which the intervention is delivered.* Likewise, the number of days per week or the number of sessions per day when intensive small group instruction is provided could be extended. This instruction could be extended to four to five days per week if it was previously being delivered

two to three days per week. Or, if this instruction is being presented during one session every day of the week that school is in session, it could be extended to two sessions every day or two sessions on a fewer number of select days each week, such as every Monday, Wednesday, and Friday.
5. *Focus on the content or skills.* The instruction will continue to address the specific academic knowledge and skills, or school social behaviors, a student has not mastered, but only fewer of them. Also, the learning objectives will become as precise as possible through the use of diagnostic assessments and will be established to increase the probability that the student will demonstrate not only skill mastery but also maintenance.

   For instance, a learning objective may be revised to indicate that a student's response is considered to be correct if it is made after an increased period of latency (e.g., instead of saying, "After being shown an index card with a numeral, the student will state the numeral's name," the learning objective will be changed to say, "After being shown an index card with a numeral, the student will state the numeral's name within five seconds").
6. *Teacher or specialist training.* It is as important as ever that the instructor who presents intensive small group instruction should have specialized training, and a wealth of experience, pertaining to both teaching the content that is the focus of the student's instruction and directing this type of small group arrangement. If this type of instructor had not been providing intensive small group instruction previously, this is one way that a qualitative change to it could be made.

CHAPTER 3 COMPREHENSION CHECK

Now that you have finished reading the chapter, you should be able to:

Explain why intensive small group instruction needs to be connected to the high-quality instruction that is presented in a general education classroom.
Differentiate between an accommodation and a modification.
Discuss how programming that involves the provision of accommodations in general education classrooms differs from intensive small group instruction.
Explain the two primary approaches to intensive small group instruction: standard treatment protocol and problem-solving approach.
List and describe the behavioral techniques that comprise a direct instruction lesson plan.
Identify and describe the quantitative and qualitative changes that can be made to various instructional components so that intensive small group

instruction can be markedly different from the high-quality instruction that is presented in a general education classroom.

Discuss how intensive small group instruction can be made ultra-intensive for the purpose of calculating how to provide effective small group instruction to students for whom previous intensive small group instruction has been ineffective.

NOTES

1. The IRIS Center, "Providing Instructional Supports: Facilitating Mastery of New Skills," https://iris.peabody.vanderbilt.edu/module/sca/#content. (2005).

2. The IRIS Center, The Pre-Referral Process: Procedures for Supporting Students with Academic and Behavioral Concerns, last modified 2008. https://iris.peabody.vanderbilt.edu/module/preref/.

3. Aaron C. Barnes and Jason E. Harlacher, "Clearing the Confusion: Response-to-Intervention as a Set of Principles," *Education and Treatment of Children* 31, no. 3 (2008): 417–31; Lynn S. Fuchs, Douglas Fuchs, and Donald L. Compton, "Rethinking Response to Intervention at Middle and High School," *School Psychology Review* 39, no. 1 (2010): 22; Barbara R. Foorman, David J. Francis, Jack M. Fletcher, Christopher Schatschneider, and Paras Mehta, "The Role of Instruction in Learning to Read: Preventing Reading Failure in At-Risk Children," *Journal of Educational Psychology* 90, no. 1 (1998): 37.

4. The IRIS Center, Evidence-Based Practices (Part 2): Implementing a Practice of Program with Fidelity, last modified 2014. https://iris.peabody.vanderbilt.edu/module/ebp_02.

5. Gary B. Mesibov, Victoria Shea, and Eric Schopler, *The TEACCH Approach to Autism Spectrum Disorders* (New York: Springer Science & Business Media, 2005).

6. John W. Maag, *Behavior Management: From Theoretical Implications to Practical Applications*, second edition (Belmont, CA: Edith Beard Brady, 2004).

7. Caroline Torres, Cynthia A. Farley, and Bryan G. Cook, "A Special Educator's Guide to Successfully Implementing Evidence-Based Practices," *Teaching Exceptional Children* 47, no. 2 (2014): 85–93; Frederick J. Brigham, Thomas E. Scruggs, and Margo A. Mastropieri, "Teacher Enthusiasm in Learning Disabilities Classrooms: Effects on Learning and Behavior," *Learning Disabilities Research & Practice*, (1992); Jere Brophy, "Teacher Influences on Student Achievement," *American Psychologist* 41, no. 10 (1986): 1069–77; Bryan G. Cook, Melody Tankersley, and Sanna Harjusola-Webb, "Evidence-Based Special Education and Professional Wisdom: Putting It All Together," *Intervention in School and Clinic* 44, no. 2 (2008): 105–11; Melody Tankersley, Sanna Harjusola-Webb, and Timothy J. Landrum, "Using Single-Subject Research to Establish the Evidence Base of Special Education," *Intervention in School and Clinic* 44, no. 2 (2008): 83–90.

8. John W. Maag, *Behavior Management: From Theoretical Implications to Practical Applications*, second edition (Belmont, CA: Edith Beard Brady, 2004).

9. National Center on Intensive Intervention (NCII) at American Institutes for Research, *Data-Based Individualization: A Framework for Intensive Intervention*, ERIC Clearinghouse, 2013.

10. Daryl F. Mellard and Evelyn S. Johnson, editors, *RTI: A Practitioner's Guide to Implementing Response to Intervention* (Thousand Oaks, CA: Corwin Press, 2007); National Center on Intensive Intervention (NCII) at American Institutes for Research, *Data-Based Individualization: A Framework for Intensive Intervention*, ERIC Clearinghouse, 2013.

Chapter Four

Preparing for Small Group Instruction

OVERVIEW

In this chapter, you will learn about the issues that teachers must address as they prepare for the presentation of intensive small group instruction. Specifically, this chapter focuses on topics such as the arrangement of the location where small group instruction will be presented, the group's composition, and efficient routines that include teaching students how to enter, participate in, and transition out of a small group.

As you read this chapter and the two that follow, you need to remain mindful of the fact that the majority of the features of high-quality instruction that were discussed in chapter 2 are relevant to the design and presentation of small group instruction. Yet these features need to be employed in ways that account for the unique attributes of intensive small group instruction. These relationships are identified in the text.

While presenting this information in a book necessitates the use of a linear format, be sure to note that many—if not most—of the issues that are addressed in this chapter are interdependent and, therefore, must be considered and addressed simultaneously.

Key points from the chapter include the following:

1. Key preparation considerations for the presentation of intensive small group instruction include the environmental arrangement, the group's composition, appropriate group participation behaviors, and the teacher's organizational strategy for the group.
2. A number of the environmental arrangement principles that apply to a general education classroom (and were discussed in chapter 2) are relevant to the location where intensive small group instruction will be presented.

However, these principles need to be applied with a consideration of the ways this instruction will differ from the large group instruction that is presented in a general education classroom.
3. Group composition refers to determining which students will comprise a small group. Relative to the composition of large groups in general education classrooms, teachers will have more say regarding which students will be placed in a particular small group.
4. Factors that teachers need to consider when they compose a group include the number of students, the students' ages, the students' instructional levels, the students' targeted learning outcomes, the instructional materials that will be used with each student, the students' repertoires of school social behaviors, and, to the extent that they are relevant, the students' categories of disability.
5. When preparing for intensive small group instruction the teacher will have to decide how they will go about teaching students appropriate school social behaviors with the aim of maximizing their engaged and academic learning time. These behaviors include an appropriate attention response and engaging in efficient protocols for entering and exiting a small group.
6. The teacher's organizational strategy for small group instruction refers to how they will present instruction to each student while remaining mindful of the instructional needs of all of the students. The two main organizational strategies are intra-sequential (involving no student interactions) and inter-sequential (involving some type of student interaction).

PREPARATION CONSIDERATIONS FOR INTENSIVE SMALL GROUP INSTRUCTION[1]

There are a number of issues that teachers must address as they prepare for the presentation of intensive small group instruction. These include matters such as the arrangement of the location where small group instruction will be presented, the group's composition, and efficient routines that include teaching students how to enter, participate in, and transition out of a group.

From the outset when considering how to arrange the environment where the teacher will present small group instruction, a teacher's two primary concerns will be its physical arrangement and teaching the group's students the appropriate school social behaviors they are to perform along with the protocols that will be used to indicate when they will be expected to perform them.

When a teacher addresses these issues, they need to be cognizant of the fact that the majority of the features of high-quality instruction that were discussed in chapter 2 are relevant to the design and presentation of intensive small group instruction. However, these features are relevant in ways that account for the unique features of this type of instruction. These matters are highlighted in the following text.

Preparation Consideration: Environmental Arrangement

Although most students who will receive small group instruction will receive the majority of their instruction in a general education classroom, other students will receive small group instruction throughout the school day in a location that essentially serves as their classroom. Consequently, one reason for spending time addressing the appropriate arrangement of this location is that it is where teachers and students will spend most of their time together.

A second reason is because the safe, orderly arrangement of the location in which small group instruction will be presented allows for the highest probability that effective, efficient instruction will occur. That is to say, there exists a notable relationship between learning academic content and students' displays of appropriate school social behaviors. Whereas a student's inability to master a targeted learning outcome may lead to their display of inappropriate behavior, it is highly likely that a student who engages in high rates of disruptive behavior, or is exposed to this type of behavior by their peers, will not master targeted learning outcomes.

Hence, one of the first orders of business in preparing for small group instruction is to plan for an environmental arrangement that supports the aims of the instruction and allows for the highest probability that it will be successful. As was noted in chapters 1 and 3, small group instruction can be presented in a variety of locations on school grounds, including a general education classroom, a room that is designed for small group instruction, part of a commons area (e.g., a table in the cafeteria), or a portable building. Thus, teachers must be knowledgeable about general small group environmental arrangement principles that they will need to apply to their particular circumstance.

In general, the same environmental arrangement principles that were discussed in chapter 2 will apply to the arrangement of the environment in which small group instruction will be presented. However, these principles need to be applied with a consideration of the ways that intensive small group instruction, as it is discussed in this book, will differ from the large group instruction that is presented in the general education classroom.

Specifically, the application of these principles should support, as much as possible, the instructional strategies that permit intensive small group instruction to be distinctive from the large group instruction that is presented in a general education classroom. A few of these strategies include massed trials; immediate, descriptive, behavior-specific feedback; and random responding. Chapter 5 presents a detailed discussion of these strategies.

An appropriate environmental arrangement for intensive small group instruction also needs to enable students to maximize their engaged time. This means that the setup of the physical location needs to ensure that each student is supported in attending to all aspects of instruction. This includes both the times when the teacher is working directly with a particular student as well as when the teacher is working with another student but has designed the instruction such that every student in the group can benefit from their interaction with the student with whom they are working.

In this latter instance the teacher may have designed the lesson such that the students who are attending to their interaction with one student will have opportunities to benefit from different types of learning. Some of these types are discussed subsequently.

1. For a student who already has demonstrated mastery of the targeted learning outcome, the interaction between the teacher and another student may serve to promote the maintenance of the knowledge or skill that is being taught.
2. The interaction may serve as a proxy acquisition trial for a student who has not mastered the knowledge or skill that is being taught. This may be the case when the student demonstrates mastery through observational learning.
3. The students who are attending to the interaction may further their understanding of the construct of "learning how to learn" by seeing the way that the teacher presents the instructional sequence that consists of (a) presenting a task directive, (b) providing various prompts to support a student's correct responding, and (c) following a student's response with feedback that, at a minimum, informs them as to whether their response is correct or incorrect.

    Similarly, the students who are attending to the instruction can learn about important aspects of their response, such as ensuring that it is deliberate and matches the behavior that is indicated in the task directive. This topic is addressed in more detail in chapter 6.
4. All students can benefit from attending to the repeated opportunities the teacher will have to either teach them appropriate school social behaviors for group participation or provide feedback regarding their displays of these behaviors. One behavior of particular import is the students' development of a wait response while they are appropriately attending to, or directly participating in, instruction.

With all of the aforementioned in mind, basic considerations for the physical design of the location where intensive small group instruction will be presented and the operation of this location are discussed next.

1. *Group cohesion.* The environmental arrangement needs to set the stage for group cohesion, which means that each student sees themselves as being an active, participating member of the group. This viewpoint is important because it sets the stage for the instruction to be more efficient as a result of the students learning from one another and their environment, such as when observational and incidental learning occur.

    Reportedly, students who are positioned such that they are offset more than one foot behind their peers do not consider themselves to be a member of the group.[2] Likewise, some students, as a condition of their disability, are predisposed to being disconnected from the group. For instance, this may be the case for some students with autism spectrum disorder who display what has been termed "autistic aloneness." This means that while they are physically present in the group, they may not be mindful of what is most important to all of the members of the group.[3]

    A small group arrangement provides an opportunity for the teacher to be in close proximity to each student. Similarly, each of the students can be in close proximity to one another. Consequently, the teacher needs to arrange and manage the environment in a way that will enhance the effectiveness and efficiency of the instruction that is presented because this proximity provides opportunities for doing so while the teacher also accounts for some potential pitfalls, such as the two described previously.

    These circumstances highlight the need to address, at the outset of the creation of a small group, the appropriate behaviors for participation and the reason for having to engage in certain behaviors (e.g., a student needs to observe their peers so that they can learn from what they are doing—whether it be displays of appropriate academic skills or social behaviors). A number of these behaviors are identified and described in the following.

2. *Lines of sight.* Clear lines of sight must be established so that the teacher can readily see each student and their instructional materials. In the same way, each student must be able to easily see the teacher and their presentation materials. Furthermore, to be able to take advantage of strategies unique to small group instruction, students should be able to readily observe their peers.

    From the teacher's perspective a small group arrangement allows more closely observation of each student they instruct. Among other things, this circumstance will enable the teacher to (a) monitor and respond to each student's displays of social behavior that both contributes to the group's cohesion and complies with class rules and (b) gauge how well each student is processing the content that is to be learned. From the student's perspective, the small group arrangement not only enables them to easily see the teacher and any instructional materials that are the focus of the lesson but also see every other student such that there is an enhanced probability that observational and incidental learning will occur.

Observational learning was defined previously. Incidental learning refers to learning that occurs when a student acquires information that is presented during a lesson but is not directly tied to any instructional strategy. For instance, after a teacher provides immediate, descriptive, behavior-specific feedback by telling a student that they correctly read the word "cat," the teacher may simply spell the word and later assess whether the student learned its spelling.

To realize the potential benefits of clear lines of sight to both the teacher and the students, the students should sit in a semi-circle facing the teacher, who will be seated or will stand near the midpoint. Horseshoe- and kidney-shaped tables are configured for this purpose. Similarly, students can be seated around a circular table such that their positions form a semi-circle with the teacher in the middle. Chairs and desks also can be positioned in this manner, or several rectangular tables can be connected to form a u-shape with the teacher positioned in the middle.

While creating clear lines of sight and accounting for the close proximity that small group arrangements allow set the occasion for benefiting from these potentially advantageous aspects of small group arrangements, there are a number of potential downsides to the close proximity that is afforded by these arrangements. One is that students might more easily come into physical contact with each other, leading to an escalation of the situation when a student who has been inadvertently touched responds in kind.

Another is that the close proximity might result in an increase in the number of potentially distracting stimuli in the area where the group is being instructed. A third is that the close proximity makes it easier to dishonestly claim credit for a classmate's answer.

3. *Having instructional materials nearby and ready to use.* Having instructional materials nearby allows a teacher to stay engaged with students in multiple ways that would not be possible if they were to have to leave the group repeatedly to get these materials from another location within the classroom. One way to stay engaged is to consistently scan the group every one to two minutes as an effective behavior management technique. The teacher can also remain engaged in this way when they do not have to leave the group to get materials ready to use, as

would be the case if they forgot to make copies of worksheets before the start of the lesson.

Having instructional materials nearby and ready to use is critically important to the effective and efficient operation of small group instruction because, depending on the characteristics of the students who comprise the group and whether a standard treatment or problem-solving protocol is being followed, managing these materials can present the teacher with a significant challenge relative to performing this task in a large group arrangement in a general education classroom.

If the group is homogeneous in terms of the content the students are learning, and a standard treatment protocol is used, then the teacher can plan for managing the use of the materials in much the same way as would be done in a general education classroom. Yet, if the group is heterogeneous, particularly with respect to the content that the students are learning to master, and a problem-solving protocol is used, then managing instructional materials can present a newfound challenge.

For example, if the students are working to master two beginning literacy skills—reading high frequency words and the sound-symbol relationship (i.e., phonics) for short vowel sounds encoded with a single letter—but each student needs to learn a slightly different set of words as well as slightly different phonics skills, then the teacher may have to plan for the use of similar yet different materials during one part of the lesson and then transition to another set of materials (which are likewise similar yet different) during another part of the lesson.

Additionally, the teacher will have to plan for how to distribute, collect, and store the materials so that they do not serve as a distraction when they are not being used. The teacher also does not want to slow the pace of the lesson when performing these tasks.

4. *Classroom aesthetics.* As is the case for a general education classroom, the overall aesthetics of the location where small group instruction will be presented needs to be addressed as the aesthetics might function as an antecedent to the students' engagement in appropriate behaviors. In other words, if the climate of the location is inviting, this circumstance will increase the probability that the student will want to come to this location and engage in displays of appropriate behaviors: both academic and school social.

This issue may take on even more importance in the case of a student who is displeased with having to participate in intensive small group instruction. This student's perceived unpleasant situation could be made even worse if they were required to go to a location that they considered to be drab and uninviting.

5. *Routines.* With respect to the presentation of intensive small group instruction, routines can serve four purposes: (a) allow for the proper use of allocated time, (b) set the stage for displays of appropriate student behavior, (c) enable students to "learn how to learn," and (d) address certain students' characteristics of thinking and learning (e.g., some students with autism who are predisposed to following routines).

   To properly use the time that has been allocated for intensive small group instruction, the teacher will need to establish routines for a number of pertinent activities. These include, but are not necessarily limited to, movement from one spot to another in the same classroom, movement from one classroom to another, starting and ending a small group lesson, and transitioning from one activity to another within a lesson.

   When students are taught, and then properly execute, routines, they will have displayed appropriate behavior. This circumstance provides the teacher with the opportunity to use the students' behavioral momentum to address subsequent behaviors that are disrupting the lesson. This topic is explained more fully in chapter 5.

   When a teacher presents intensive small group instruction, a prescribed routine can be followed when a lesson is presented so that students can assimilate a process for learning. This phenomenon has been referred to as "learning how to learn."

   An example of how this could occur would be when a student realizes that during a direct instruction lesson the teacher is first going to model the behavior the student is supposed to display and then will provide the necessary amount of support until the student finally can perform the behavior independently. The student might learn how to advocate for the type of support they need, and they may be able to more readily attend to instruction because their anxiety has been reduced due to the fact that they have a clear set of expectations for how the lesson will unfold.

   Another use of routines is to address certain students' characteristics of thinking and learning in a way that will increase the probability that these students will behave appropriately. For example, a characteristic of thinking and learning that is demonstrated by some students with autism is responding more appropriately when clear routines are established and followed than when they are not.

6. *Limit potential distractions.* When small group instruction is presented in a classroom that has been designed exclusively for this type of arrangement, the instructor will need to account for potential distracting stimuli similar to the way a general education teacher does. However, when this instruction is presented within a general education classroom or a setting outside of this classroom that is prone to many potentially distracting

stimuli, the teacher will need to take steps to configure the location to mediate the impact of these stimuli. The discussion that follows focuses on how to address potentially distracting visual and auditory stimuli when small group instruction is presented within a general education classroom.

To address potentially distracting visual stimuli, the students who are in the small group should be seated so that their backs are facing their classmates who are not in the group. Portable dividers could be situated to block anything that might be seen in front, or to the sides, of the students in the small group. If the general education teacher is tasked to present the small group instruction, they will have to position themselves so that they can supervise the students in the small group as well as the other students in the classroom.

To address potentially distracting auditory stimuli, the students who are in the small group should be seated as far away as possible from sources of sound (e.g., high traffic areas, keyboards, printers, other instructional activities), and protocols will need to be established to address the overall noise level in the classroom. For instance, students in the small group will need to learn how loud they need to project their voice so that it can be heard within the group but not throughout the entire classroom. Similarly, students who are not in the group will need to learn how loud they can talk and what they need to do to manage other noise they make so that it does not disrupt the small group.

7. *Effective use of wall space.* When small group instruction is presented in a classroom that has been designed exclusively for this type of arrangement, the instructor will need to account for the effective use of wall space in a manner that is similar to the way a general education teacher does. If small group instruction is conducted within a general education classroom and portable dividers are used to establish the location where this instruction will be presented, the teacher may configure the dividers so that they function as additional wall space on which relevant items, such as progress monitoring graphs and visual supports (e.g., a turn taking graphic, work activity list, or a timer) can be placed.

Preparation Consideration: Group Composition

Group composition refers to which students will comprise a small group. The composition that is settled upon will result from the consideration of a number of factors that are discussed subsequently. The overarching issue with respect to group composition will be its homogeneity or, conversely, its heterogeneity. This feature refers to the type and amount of diversity that exists within a small group arrangement. Simply stated, a homogeneous group is one in which there is relatively little diversity whereas a heterogeneous group is one in which there is noteworthy diversity.

Relative to the composition of large groups in general education classrooms, teachers most likely will have more input regarding which students will be put in a specific small group. In a general education classroom the teacher focuses on teaching students a broad range of content from the core curriculum. This content is taught to students who, in most situations, have been randomly assigned to the various general education classrooms in one grade level.

Intensive small group instruction is provided to students who demonstrate significant, ongoing challenges mastering targeted learning outcomes. Therefore, teachers most likely will have more input regarding which students will be put in a specific small group because a primary reason for a student's inclusion in a group will be their need to master a targeted learning outcome that has been identified by the student's teachers.

The planning considerations that are discussed in the following extend from the ideal scenario to what are many times more realistic, demanding scenarios. Ideally, homogeneous small groups will be configured such that the students have many key characteristics in common: the students are the exact same age, need to master the same learning objective, learn at the same rate, exhibit nearly identical characteristics of thinking and learning, profit equally from observational learning, and exhibit similar school social behaviors (e.g., each student is equally respectful of the other students' needs).

The reality, however, can be markedly different. It is possible that the students who comprise a small group differ on a number of the key characteristics identified previously, resulting in what would be called a heterogeneous group. Perhaps what is most important is that a teacher can be made aware of the kinds of diversity that can exist and be addressed in a small group arrangement. Then, instead of contending that not much can be accomplished when a group is heterogeneous, a teacher can readily identify all that might be accomplished when they are confronted with this situation.

Regarding the intensity of the instruction that can be presented in a small group arrangement, a group's diversity certainly will affect it. The less diverse the group, the more intense the instruction can be. Thinking about intensity in terms of a continuum, the more instances in which similar quantitative and qualitative changes can be applied to every student in the group, the more intense the instruction will be. More intense instruction is synonymous with instruction that involves higher intensity.

For example, if a quantitative change involves providing students with more time receiving small group instruction and more opportunities to practice target skills during this instruction, then if every student in the group is working to master the same targeted learning objective, such as skip counting by four to forty-eight and by five to one hundred, then each student will maximize the number of times this skill is practiced. Conversely, if one student needs to learn the names for the letters d and b, another student the names for m and n, and a third student the names for t and f, then each student's opportunities for practice would be diffused. Therefore, their small group instruction would be less intense (i.e., less prolonged and focused on individualized instruction).

The following factors are to be considered when determining the composition of a small group.

1. *Number of students.* In order for an instructional arrangement to be characterized as small group instruction, the pupil:teacher ratio must be 2–8:1. Ideally, in order for the instructional strategies that are explained in this book to have the highest probability of being effective, the pupil:teacher ratio would always be 2–5:1. This situation highlights the fact that the smaller the pupil:teacher ratio the greater the probability that a homogeneous group—as opposed to heterogeneous one—can be created.
2. *Age.* Students who need to receive remedial instruction that addresses the same targeted learning outcomes may vary considerably in age. It is reasonable to expect a "natural difference" of one to two years in age that will be the result of differences in the students' ages when they first enrolled in school and differences that evolved thereafter when students were either promoted or retained.

    Yet some schools may place students who are separated in age by several or more years but need to master the same targeted learning outcome in the same small group because the school is sparsely populated and has very limited resources. This may be the situation that is faced by a school in a rural location.

    In these instances, factors such as the students' dispositions (e.g., does an older student care that they are working with a much younger student) and physical sizes (e.g., an older student who is much larger than the younger students may not care to be grouped with them for this reason) can be determining factors in terms of their placement in a small group. Because the older students would be demonstrating the most significant learning challenge in terms of the targeted learning outcome, their response to this potential arrangement will require thoughtful consideration.
3. *Performance level.* Students' performance levels refer to the grade-level content from the core curriculum that they have mastered—irrespective of the students' current grade-level placement. Students who demonstrate significant, ongoing learning challenges and need intensive small group

instruction will have demonstrated a need to master targeted learning outcomes for some subject matter content that is at a grade level that is significantly lower than their grade-level placement. Further, these students' performance levels call attention to their relatively slow rates of progress in terms of the amount of new content they are able to learn in a designated period of time.

Ideally, the students placed in a small group will work to master the same grade-level content irrespective of their grade-level placement. However, factors such as the students' ages may necessitate different groupings.

Students' differing rates of learning may dictate the instructional strategies a teacher uses in a small group session. For instance, a teacher may present more massed trials to a student in the group who demonstrates a slower rate of learning. These strategies are explained in chapter 5.

4. *Same or different targeted learning outcomes.* Most of the time each of the students who comprise a small group will need to master a different targeted learning outcome. However, a teacher will be able to describe the differences between these outcomes in terms of degrees rather than as absolutes.

For instance, five students who comprise a small group may have in common the fact that they need to master basic reading skills. Specifically, the students may share the need to learn how to decode consonant-vowel-consonant words. However, two of the students may need to learn how to read words that have a short e sound, two other students may need to learn to read words that have short a and u sounds, and one student may need to learn to read words that have a short i sound. This situation stands in stark contrast to a small group in which two students need to learn how to name lowercase letters of the alphabet while three other students need to learn how to count from one to ten.

The point to be made is that it is highly likely that some variance will exist in each small group in terms of the students' targeted learning outcomes. The type and amount of this variance will impact how a teacher designs and implements their instruction.

5. *Same or different instructional materials.* A teacher may need to use the same or different instructional materials with each of the students in a group when they are addressing the same targeted learning outcome. For example, a common practice in math is to follow a concrete-representational-abstract sequence when teaching new concepts. This means that when students first learn how to add two numbers, they manipulate concrete items such as counting blocks. Next, representational items, such as pictures, replace the blocks. Finally, students add two numbers solely on the basis of the abstract numerals that represent them.

In a small group in which each student's targeted learning outcome is the acquisition of basic addition facts, the students may demonstrate different needs in terms of the concrete-representational-abstract sequence. Further, at some point in time certain students may be learning how to find the sum of an addition problem that is presented horizontally whereas other students are learning how to find the sums of these problems when they are presented vertically.

Another example of when the same or different instructional materials may be used to teach the same targeted learning outcome is when students are learning to decode consonant-vowel-consonant words. At the early stages of instruction students may focus on identifying the phonemes that comprise a word and move a block each time they say one of the phonemes. Eventually, when instruction focuses on the alphabetic principle, students will produce the sound that is represented by each letter they see.

The situations described in this section emphasize the details that must be attended to when presenting intensive small group instruction. Even when the students who comprise a group are working to master nearly identical targeted learning outcomes a teacher likely will have to address nuances that pertain to each student's instructional needs, and that will ultimately impact the effectiveness and efficiency of the instruction that is presented.

6. *Students' social behaviors.* Two types of school social behaviors warrant a teacher's consideration when they prepare to present intensive small group instruction. One type are the social behaviors the teacher will expect the students to demonstrate throughout the time that has been allocated for intensive small group instruction so that the group is safe and orderly, and an environment for effective instruction is established. The other type of school social behaviors are those that a student is expected to exhibit across all school environments.

At the outset, school staff will have to determine the primary purpose of a small group. This purpose will be determined by the students' targeted learning outcomes. If these outcomes involve academic content, then the school social behaviors that a teacher will have to prepare for are those that pertain to the operation of the small group.

If these outcomes primarily involve teaching students a wide range of appropriate school social behaviors, then the focus of the intensive small group lesson will be these behaviors. In such a group the teacher likely will be challenged by the facts that each student is prone to exhibiting disruptive behaviors and there is an absence of role models. In a small group with an academic focus a teacher may conclude that they can have one student in it who exhibits high rates of challenging behaviors, but no more than that.

7. *Category of disability.* For students with disabilities who are receiving special education services, knowledge about the way their disability manifests may assist a teacher in preparing for small group instruction. For instance, from the outset it may be prudent for a teacher to plan for how they will use routines to address the needs of students with autism, or arrange the environment in a way that accounts for potential distractions that are likely to be an issue for a student with an other health impairment, such as attention deficit hyperactivity disorder.

While caution needs to be taken not to overgeneralize, one could also argue that it would be irresponsible to completely ignore general information about certain disabilities and effective evidence-based practices that are based upon them.

Preparation Consideration: Appropriate School Social Behaviors Specific to Intensive Small Group Instruction

As is the case any time instruction is presented at school, there is a higher probability that this instruction will be effective when it is presented in a safe, orderly environment. This environment will result from a proper environmental arrangement and students' displays of suitable school social behaviors.

The students who need to be provided intensive small group instruction will need to receive explicit instruction pertaining to the appropriate school social behaviors they are expected to display while participating in the group. Teachers need to be proactive in deciding upon these behaviors as well as the instructional strategies they will use to teach them. A teacher cannot assume students will intuit these behaviors. In the same way, a teacher cannot assume that they can simply apply an aversive consequence to a student's display of an inappropriate behavior that, in turn, will forevermore result in the student only engaging in displays of school social behaviors that are proper for small group instructional sessions.

What follows is a list and description of some school social behaviors that a teacher may want students to engage in during an intensive small group instructional session for the purposes of (a) establishing and maintaining a safe, orderly environment; (b) promoting proper time management, particularly allocated, engaged, and academic learning time; and (c) maximizing students' active responding. Note that, although the majority of the behaviors are overt, students also can be directed to engage in covert behaviors that contribute to the creation of a safe, orderly environment and allow for maximum active student responding.

Also, chapter 5 identifies and describes numerous interventions a teacher can use to set the stage for students' displays of appropriate school social behaviors that are specific to small group instruction. It may be useful to refer to the section in chapter 5 that is titled "Small Group Behavior Management Strategies" in tandem with the following information.

1. *Transition routines.* For the purposes of this book, a transition refers to any time students experience a change at school. Hence, with respect to the provision of intensive small group instruction, there are at least three types of transitions for which a teacher will have to plan: the transition into the group, the transition out of the group, and changing from one activity to another within a session, or even from one trial to another within a session.
2. *Choral responding.* Students will need to be taught to identify the moment when they are to make their response so that it occurs in unison with their peers. They also will need to be taught how to make this response so that a unison response occurs (e.g., a discrete remark that is of an appropriate volume rather than an elongated response, using a relatively loud voice, that is out of sync with the others).
3. *Appropriate behaviors specific to a visual support.* While visual supports can enhance students' understanding and direct their displays of appropriate behaviors, the meaning and use of every visual must be taught explicitly. For example, a teacher may employ the use of a talking stick during small group instruction, after teaching their students that (a) only the person who is holding the stick is permitted to talk and (b) any group member who is not holding the stick must look at and listen to the person who is holding the stick.
4. *Using "the voice in one's head" as a mode of active student responding.* Many times when a teacher is engaged with only one student, they will want the other students to be as actively involved as possible in that student's trial. In addition to having the other students observe the 1:1 interaction, the teacher can instruct the students to "use the voice in your head" and generate a response at the same time the student who is receiving instruction makes an overt response.

    The students who use the "voice in their head" do not make an audible response and may be required to move their lips to indicate to their teacher that they are engaged in an active response. This procedure results in a form of covert choral response that keeps all student appropriately, actively engaged in the lesson.
5. *Observational learning.* Students need to be taught the meaning of observational learning and that the teacher has an expectation for them to demonstrate it (to some degree). To set the occasion for observational learning to occur, students will have to be taught the behaviors they are to exhibit when they watch a teacher instruct a peer.

One behavior pertains to group cohesion, which means the student must remain within physical proximity (i.e., one foot) of all of the members of the group.[4] Likewise, each student will have to orient themselves so that they can see and hear all aspects of the instruction while remaining quiet and engaging in covert active student responding, as is appropriate.

6. *Responding to feedback.* The teacher will have to inform the students about the various ways they will respond to either a correct or incorrect response. An incorrect response would include no response.

   The teacher also will have to teach the students how they are to behave following the presentation of feedback. For instance, when a student responds correctly, they may only be required to listen to the teacher's feedback or else listen plus quickly consume an edible reinforcer or engage with a tangible reinforcer (e.g., play with a spinner). When a student responds incorrectly, they may be expected to continue to engage in appropriate in-seat behavior (as opposed to throw tantrums) plus listen to the teacher's feedback, which may include the re-presentation of the task directive, and subsequently respond accordingly.

7. *Acknowledging incidental information.* The behaviors students are taught to exhibit in order to profit from a teacher's effort to establish observational learning are the same behaviors they need to exhibit to profit from a teacher's effort to establish incidental learning. Incidental learning refers to learning that occurs when a student acquires information that is presented during a lesson but is not directly tied to any instructional strategy. For instance, after a teacher provides immediate, descriptive, behavior-specific feedback by telling a student that they correctly read the word "car," the teacher may simply tell the student that a car is one type of vehicle, as is a bus, in an attempt to teach how to categorize a car.

8. *Delineating personal space.* The teacher may use one of various strategies to clearly define each student's personal space. This is the boundary that is created around a student that other students are not to cross, and the student is not to exceed. Establishing each student's personal space is one strategy a teacher can use to assist students in maintaining their emotional regulation. Techniques for establishing this space include tape on the floor that surrounds each student's desk and tape that partitions a rectangular, horseshoe-, or kidney-shaped table into sections that are aligned across from each student's chair.

9. *Modes of active student responding.* The teacher will have to teach the student how to exhibit the modes of active student responding they will be directed to use during an instructional session. In addition to speech, students may be directed to show a thumbs up for true or agree and a

thumbs down for false or disagree, write a response on a dry erase board, select and then show the teacher the response card that has the student's answer choice, use their computerized augmentative communication device, or tap on their answer choice that is displayed on a static low-tech communication board.[5]

10. *Probe/skill check behaviors.* Chapter 6 presents information about assessment, including general information about a school's assessment milieu and specific information about assessment that pertains to small group instruction. One type of assessment is the use of probes, which also are referred to as skill checks.

    Chapter 6 discusses the need to identify and teach students how to demonstrate key behaviors during probes that enhance the validity of the information that is obtained from this type of assessment. Also, students may have to be taught how to self-regulate their behaviors while peers are completing probes.

11. *Wait response.* Students need to be taught the behaviors they are to exhibit when they are waiting. When students are required to wait, they must endure a delay between two points in time (i.e., the present moment and some point in time in the future). Two ways students can exhibit an appropriate wait response are to continue to engage appropriately in an activity they are involved with (e.g., responding to a math app) or pass the time by remaining in a passive or non-committal position—neither engaging in an appropriate or inappropriate activity.

    If a student is waiting for their turn to complete a trial, then an appropriate wait response might be the same behavior they are to exhibit for the purpose of enabling them to benefit from observational learning. Similarly, if the teacher wants a student to consider their response to a task directive during a probe—meaning the teacher wants the student to wait for two or three seconds before making a response—the teacher might teach a "Get ready to respond" behavior that is appropriate for the context (e.g., feet on the floor, eyes scanning their response options, sitting up in their chair, remaining quiet, and isolating their index finger for a point or touch response).

12. *Demonstrate deliberate responses.* Students will need to be taught the difference between impulsive, indiscernible responses and those that are deliberate, purposeful, and discernable. The latter type of response increases a teacher's confidence that the student's response is a valid representation of his acquisition of knowledge or a skill in terms of the targeted learning outcome.

    A deliberate response is defined as one in which a student behaves in a purposeful manner, demonstrating behavior called for by the teacher,

without any undue hesitation, misdirection, or some other behavior (e.g., touching two response options at the same time) that disallows the teacher from confidently interpreting the student's response.
13. *Active peer engagement.* Even during a teacher-directed lesson, as it is defined in this book, students may be expected to actively engage with their peers in the group. Examples of this type of engagement include handing a talking stick to another student and showing one's response card to peers so that they, in turn, can indicate to the teacher whether they agree or disagree with the response. The students will need to be taught these engagement behaviors.
14. *Group cohesion.* To enable the students to remain within an appropriate proximity to the other students in the group, the teacher will have to employ some mechanism that enables each student to easily determine that they are remaining within the appropriate proximity (i.e., one foot). Examples include placing carpet squares under each student's seat, a strip of tape behind the perimeter of the students' seating area, and positioning the students in front of a wall such that they cannot push themselves backwards and more than one foot away from the group.
15. *Handling instructional materials.* So that their engagement with instructional materials is not inappropriate, thereby resulting in damage to an item (e.g., a tablet computer), disruptive behavior, or injury to a peer (e.g., from an item being thrown or used inappropriately, which would be the case when a student uses a pencil to poke a peer), students will need to be taught both when and how to engage with instructional materials.

For example, as one part of learning how to find the sum of basic addition facts, when it is time to write their answer on their paper students might be taught that they are to get their pencil from their pencil well when the teacher tells them to write their answer, immediately write their answer on their paper, and then promptly return their pencil to their pencil well.

Preparation Considerations: Organizational Strategies

A teacher also must consider how they will organize the small group instruction to be presented. Two organizational strategies pertain exclusively to small group instruction as it is defined in this book. Two other organizational strategies involve 1:1 pupil:teacher ratios in addition to small group arrangements. These strategies may be necessary when the students who comprise the group present needs that dictate that a 1:1 arrangement also be used. This might be the case when a small group will be comprised of two students who, previously, were only provided instruction in a 1:1 arrangement.

These latter organizational strategies highlight the fact that many of the features of the presentation of small group instruction can be used in a 1:1 instructional arrangement. However, for an arrangement to be considered a small group the pupil:teacher ratio, at a minimum, must be 2:1.

Exclusive Small Group Organizational Strategies

1. *Intra-sequential.* The teacher presents instruction to each student in the group but does not have any interaction between the students. This organizational strategy may be appropriate when each student is working to master a unique targeted learning outcome.
2. *Inter-sequential.* The teacher presents instruction to each student in the group and plans for, and reinforces, interaction between the students. For instance, students can present the attention cue and tell a peer whether their answer was correct or incorrect. This organizational strategy may be appropriate when each student is working to master the same targeted learning outcome.

Small Group Organizational Strategies with 1:1 Components

1. *Tandem.* The teacher begins with a 1:1 arrangement and gradually increases the size of the group. As was noted previously, this organizational strategy may be used when the students who will comprise the small group previously have received instruction only in a 1:1 arrangement.
2. *1:1 supplement.* The teacher uses either the intra-sequential or inter-sequential strategy and then works 1:1 with one or more students after the end of the session. An example of when this organizational strategy may be used is when the teacher decides that one or more students needs to be provided more opportunities to engage in active student responding than they were when an intra-sequential strategy was in effect.

CHAPTER 4 COMPREHENSION CHECK

Now that you have finished reading the chapter, you should be able to:

List key preparation considerations for the presentation of intensive small group instruction.

Discuss how the environmental arrangement principles that apply to the provision of high-quality instruction in a general education classroom can be applied to the location where intensive small group instruction will be presented so that it can be markedly different from the general education classroom instruction.

Identify the factors a teacher needs to consider with respect to group composition for intensive small group instruction.

List appropriate school social behaviors that the students who comprise a small group may need to be taught for the purpose of maximizing their engaged and academic learning time.

Explain four small group organizational strategies.

NOTES

1. Belva C. Collins, David L. Gast, Melinda J. Ault, and Mark Wolery, "Small Group Instruction: Guidelines for Teachers and Students with Moderate to Severe Handicaps," *Education & Training in Mental Retardation* 26, no. 1 (1991): 1–18.

2. Cecil D. Mercer and Ann R. Mercer, *Students with Learning Disabilities*, third edition (Princeton, NC: Merrill, 1997).

3. Leo Kanner, "Autistic Disturbances of Affective Contact," *Nervous Child* 2, no. 3 (1943): 217–50.

4. Cecil D. Mercer and Ann R. Mercer, *Students with Learning Disabilities*, third edition (Princeton, NC: Merrill, 1997).

5. Howard C. Shane, Emily Laubscher, Ralf W. Schlosser, Holly L. Fadie, J. F. Source, Jennifer S. Abramson, Suzanne Flynn, and Kara Corley, *Enhancing Communication for Individuals with Autism: A Guide to the Visual Immersion System* (Baltimore, MD: Paul H. Brookes Publishing Co, 2015).

Chapter Five

Small Group Instructional Strategies

OVERVIEW

This chapter addresses issues that pertain to the actual presentation of instruction in a small group arrangement. Specifically, the content focuses on instructional strategies that allow the small group instruction to not only be intensive but also as intensive as is necessary for it to be effective with each student.

These instructional strategies that enable small group instruction to be more intense and result in more effective and efficient instruction are, arguably, closely aligned with universal effective teaching practices. Hence, like universal effective teaching practices these small group instructional strategies will need to be employed with, and account for, other types of instructional strategies. One particular type of instructional strategy they will need to account for are the effective strategies that have been identified to teach subject matter content.

For instance, these small group strategies would be used with evidence-based beginning reading instructional strategies.[1] In the same way, they would be used along with a multi-component intervention that consists of multiple evidence-based practices for students with autism. This might involve using small group strategies along with visual supports, constant time delay, and response-interruption-redirection to teach counting skills. This process has been referred to as informed eclecticism.[2]

Overall, three broad topics are addressed in this chapter.

1. Instructional strategies specific to intensive small group instruction that make it markedly different from the high-quality instruction that is presented in a general education classroom.

2. *Interventions and strategies that can be employed to address students' appropriate displays of school social behaviors while intensive small group instruction is being presented.*
3. *The direct instruction lesson plan as one example of a lesson plan format that allows for the incorporation of the content that is presented in this chapter so that effective and efficient intensive small group instruction is realized.*

Key points from the chapter include the following:

1. An organizational framework that consists of four categories of instructional strategies can be used to explain how intensive small group instruction can be designed and presented such that it is markedly different from the high-quality instruction that is presented in a large group arrangement in a general education classroom. The four categories are (a) trial presentation strategies, (b) student response strategies, (c) feedback strategies, and (d) instructional efficiency strategies.
2. Within the direct instruction lesson plan format these strategies are employed most often when guided practice is presented.
3. Given the definition for an instructional strategy, which is the planned actions a teacher executes to impart knowledge or skills to their students, arguably there are four rudimentary instructional strategies a teacher can employ—either singularly or in combination—when they present instruction. These instructional strategies include oral instruction, modeling, written instruction, and physical prompting.
4. Trial presentation strategies address how many opportunities all of the students in the group will be given to engage in the behavior that is stipulated in their learning objective, as well as how many opportunities each student will be presented. Examples of trial presentation strategies include massed, spaced, and distributed trials.
5. Student response strategies address the response modes students will employ, as well as when students will be provided opportunities to respond. These strategies are designed to maximize active student responding throughout a small group session. Examples of response modes include hand gestures (e.g., thumbs up or thumbs down) and response cards. Regarding student opportunities to respond, examples include sequential and random responding, as well as individual and choral responding.
6. Instructional efficiency strategies include the planned actions a teacher employs to solicit the greatest amount of student learning relative to factors such as the time, effort, and cost involved in both planning for and presenting instruction. Examples of instructional efficiency strategies,

such directing student attending and providing additional information in the antecedent and consequence phases of instruction, include those that increase the probability that observational and incidental learning will occur.
7. Feedback strategies involve actions a teacher can engage in after a student has an opportunity to demonstrate the behavior that is stipulated in their learning objective. Key features of feedback are that it is descriptive, immediate, and behavior specific.
8. A teacher will have to plan for interventions, or strategies, they will put into practice to manage the display of appropriate school social behaviors during intensive small group instruction. These strategies include those that set the occasion for displays of appropriate school social behaviors (i.e., antecedent-based interventions) and those that follow students' opportunities to respond (i.e., contingency-based strategies).
9. Examples of antecedent-based interventions include visual supports, prompting, and environmental arrangements.
10. The primary contingency-based strategy that is discussed in this book is teacher feedback.

INTRODUCTION

A point that has been highlighted throughout this book is that, although intensive small group instruction needs to employ relevant features of high-quality, large group instruction, this type of small group instruction needs to be markedly different such that it is not simply "more of the same" general education classroom instruction that has proven to be ineffective. This means that the intensive small group instruction is not essentially large group, general education instruction that is presented for a longer period of time. A student might receive this instruction for a longer period of time because the time spent in the small group session is added to the time spent in the general education classroom session.

Although the focus of this chapter is on instructional strategies that enable intensive small group instruction to be unique, it must be noted that some of the instructional strategies that are explained can be employed in a general education classroom. Two examples are the strategies that set the occasion for observational learning and involve the use of immediate, descriptive, behavior-specific feedback.

However, what enables these instructional strategies to contribute to the presentation of intensive small group instruction that is unique is that their use is thoughtfully calculated to address the significant, ongoing challenges certain students demonstrate with respect to mastering targeted learning outcomes. During large group instruction in a general education classroom these instructional strategies are employed with the broader, more general intent to advance the learning of the entire group rather than target an individual student's instructional needs.

As you consider the use of these instructional strategies remain mindful of the fact that you most likely will have twenty to forty minutes allocated for a small group session. This includes time transitioning into and out of the location where the session will be conducted as well as time to transition from one major activity to another during the lesson you will present during the session. This fact highlights why successful time management is one of the key elements of high-quality instruction.

REVIEW OF KEY CONCEPTS

To enhance your understanding of the content that is presented in this chapter, two topics that were discussed previously are reviewed. One topic is the definition for an instructional strategy. The second topic is the way that certain instructional strategies can be characterized. Specifically, the distinction between universal effective teaching practices and subject matter practices is reviewed.

An instructional strategy refers to the planned actions a teacher executes when they present a lesson. With respect to these actions, most people probably readily think of teacher behaviors including modeling, prompting, and questioning when they consider the meaning of this definition. However, it also refers to more subtle, less obvious planned actions such as teaching a student the name of the letter m well apart from the name of the letter n because the letters are visually similar and, therefore, easy to confuse.

This latter aspect of an instructional strategy leads to the second topic that was referred to previously, which is the way that certain instructional strategies can be characterized. The characterization scheme that is the focus of this discussion is one that identifies some instructional strategies as universal effective teaching practices and other strategies as subject matter, or academic discipline, strategies.

Universal effective teaching practices can be applied to any subject matter lesson. These strategies involve teacher behaviors that keep the student informed about what is being taught, provide the student with feedback about their understanding of the content, ensure that the lesson moves along at an appropriately brisk pace, and allows the student to participate (i.e., engage in active student responding).

Subject matter, or academic discipline, instructional strategies apply to particular academic content. For example, beginning reading instruction needs to address topics such as phonemic awareness (identification of the sounds that comprise a word) and phonics (letter-sound relationships). Likewise, mathematics instruction is to employ a concrete-representational-abstract sequence when new concepts are taught. Essentially this involves having students first use tangible manipulatives (e.g., base ten counting blocks), then pictorial representations (e.g., pictures of objects), and, finally, numerals in the process of mastering targeted learning outcomes.

The small group instructional strategies that are the focus of the content that is presented in this chapter are more closely aligned to universal effective teaching practices than subject matter practices. In fact, some of the small group strategies have been identified as universal effective teaching practices. However, the way that they are described here as being put into practice during small group instruction is what makes this instruction unique from the large group instruction that is presented in a general education classroom.

Among other things, this assertion means that many (if not all) of the subject matter practices will remain constant across small and large groups. When beginning reading instruction is presented, phonemic awareness and phonics will be taught, and when basic math skills are taught the concrete-representational-abstract sequence will be followed—regardless whether instruction is presented to students in a small or large group arrangement.

Additionally, two other matters, which are new to the discussion about instructional strategies, are important to your understanding of the content that is presented in this chapter. One matter is that most of these strategies will be implemented during the guided practice section of the direct instruction lesson plan. The second matter is that the strategies are predicated on what is known as the A-B-C paradigm.

The A-B-C paradigm is a depiction of the relationship of the events that occur in an instructional exchange.[3] In the middle of the exchange is the learner's observable behavior, which is represented by the letter B. Specifically, this is the behavior a teacher wants a student to exhibit for the purpose of demonstrating that they have mastered the targeted learning outcome. Examples of these behaviors include writing the sum for an addition problem, saying the phoneme that is encoded by the letter d in isolation, and raising one's hand to request permission to answer a teacher's question.

The conditions that precede the student's behavior are called antecedents, which are represented by the letter A. Antecedents are wide-ranging and, in general, teachers design them to establish the highest probability possible that a student will demonstrate the behavior for the targeted learning outcome.

The term "antecedent-based interventions" refers to interventions that are employed to increase the probability that a student will engage in a target behavior.[4] The goal may be for a student to increase their performance of the target behavior (e.g., the number of sight words read) or decrease their performance (e.g., frequency of instances of out-of-seat behavior). Examples of antecedent-based interventions include:

1. The teacher's use of concise language;
2. Visual supports (e.g., picture prompt sequences and social narratives);
3. Prompting;
4. Behavioral momentum strategies; and
5. Environmental arrangements.

The third component of the A-B-C paradigm is the consequence, or conditions, that follows a student's behavior. This component is represented by the letter C. For the purposes of this book and its explanation of intensive small group instruction, the feedback a teacher provides to a student is the focus of this component of the A-B-C paradigm.

It is important to note that a student's behavior may be characterized in one of three ways: a correct response, an incorrect response, and no response. A correct response would be a behavior that met the operational definition for the behavior set forth in the targeted learning objective (e.g., the learner wrote the sum for an addition problem comprised of two single-digit addends). An incorrect response would be an observable behavior that did not meet the operational definition set forth in the targeted learning objective (e.g., the learner wrote an incorrect sum for an addition problem comprised of two single-digit addends).

What would be considered a "no response" by a student would be the absence of any behavior that met the operational definition for a correct or incorrect response. For example, if a student was presented with a worksheet on which was written three addition problems, each of which consisted of two single-digit addends, and was given the task directive, "Write the sums for each problem," a no response would be recorded for any problem to which the student did not write either a correct or incorrect response.

The consequence to each behavior has multiple dimensions and corresponding characterizations. In terms of dimensions, one dimension is whether the consequence is designed to either increase or decrease the probability that the student will exhibit the behavior in future pending similar circumstances. A consequence that is designed to increase the probability that the behavior will be displayed in the future under similar circumstances is called a reinforcer or reinforcement. A consequence that decreases the probability that the student will exhibit the behavior in the future under similar circumstances is called a punisher or punishment.

Consequences can be characterized in terms of the type of feedback that students have been provided. Feedback can be:

1. immediate (follows a student's correct or incorrect response, or no response, without a delay) or delayed (is provided at a time removed from the phase of the lesson when a student response was solicited);
2. general or descriptive (e.g., Good job!" [general] or "That's right, c-a-t is cat" [specific]);
3. behavior-specific or not ("That's correct, you wrote that 5 is the sum of 3+2" instead of "That's correct, 5 is the answer.");
4. uni- or multi-modal (The mode refers to how the feedback was encoded, meaning whether the teacher used speech, text, hand gestures, facial expression, tone of voice—or some combination of two or more modes. It is important for a student to be able to demonstrate comprehension of the mode the teacher uses.);
5. massed, spaced, or distributed (e.g., is feedback presented after every trial or less often, such as at the end of the lesson only); and
6. calculated to promote observational or incidental learning, or neither (is the teacher cognizant of this type of learning and, if so, what strategies will they put in place for the purpose of creating a high probability that this type of learning will occur).

As it has been explained here, the A-B-C paradigm is a viable framework for designing, implementing, and assessing instruction irrespective of one's overarching theoretical perspective pertaining to teaching and learning. The three-part paradigm allows for the consideration of the relative positioning of events that occur during an instructional exchange and a systematic investigation of their impact on students' attainment of targeted learning outcomes.

BASIC INSTRUCTIONAL STRATEGIES

Given the definition for an instructional strategy, which is the planned actions a teacher executes to impart knowledge or skills to students, it may be argued that there are four fundamental instructional strategies a teacher can make use of, either singularly or in combination, when they present instruction.

1. *Oral.* The teacher can use speech. For instance, if a student does not know the name of an object, the teacher can tell its name. If a student does not

know the steps to perform to wash their hands, the teacher can lead the student through the task by telling each step to perform.
2. *Modeling.* The teacher can demonstrate how to do something. For example, if a student cannot spell the word "cat" the teacher can demonstrate how to write each letter as well as the correct order for doing so.
3. *Writing.* The teacher uses written words, phrases, or sentences. When a student first learns how to use a calculator to check their answers on an addition worksheet the teacher might provide a set of written instructions to teach the student how to perform this task.
4. *Physical prompting.* The teacher can provide hand-over-hand guidance, or some variation of this type of support, to enable the student to learn how to do an activity. For example, a teacher may use this instructional strategy when teaching a student how to put on a coat.

As was noted previously, teachers can use these strategies either singularly or in combination. Most times teachers combine oral strategies with modeling. To a lesser degree, teachers of very young students combine oral strategies with some degree of physical prompting.

INSTRUCTIONAL STRATEGIES UNIQUE TO SMALL GROUP ARRANGEMENTS

In this section numerous instructional strategies that can be uniquely employed in small group arrangements are identified and explained. What permits the strategies to be unique are their contributions to intensive instruction which, by definition, allows for more individualized instruction that enables a student to engage with instructional-level content (i.e., cognitively process it) for a relatively longer period of time. Altogether this means that the teacher will still use evidence-based universal instructional strategies and those specific to the subject matter area, and embellish them with the strategies described in the following to produce intensive small group instruction that is distinct from large group, general education classroom instruction.

As you read the following content, it is important that you know the meanings of two key terms: session and trial. A session refers to the total amount of time when intensive small group instruction is presented. For example, a session could be twenty, thirty, or forty-five minutes long.

A trial refers to an opportunity that a student is given to respond to a teacher directive that pertains to the targeted learning objective. For example, if the learning objective states that the student will name the numerals 0 to 3 when directed to do so by the teacher, then a trial could consist of the following steps: (a) the teacher holds up an index card with the numeral 2 written on it; (b) the teacher presents the task directive, "Name this numeral"; (c) the teacher immediately provides a prompt, which is the first phoneme in the word "two"; (d) the student says, "Two"; and (e) the teacher presents immediate, descriptive, behavior-specific feedback: "Good job, you said the name of this numeral, which is two."

The following framework is presented as one way to think about the various small group instructional strategies a teacher can employ. The framework consists of four categories: (a) opportunities to respond, (b) types of active student responding, (c) feedback/contingency strategies, and (d) efficiency strategies. Additionally, a fifth category—behavior management—is discussed in terms of being a category of support strategies that will result in the establishment of an atmosphere that will allow for the effective and efficient use of the strategies that comprise the other four categories.

When a teacher considers each strategy, they will need to remain mindful of factors such as the amount of time they will have to present small group instruction plus students' needs and their characteristics of thinking and learning. One constraint on the employment of the strategies discussed subsequently is the amount of time that has been allocated for small group instruction. Simply stated, if a teacher has been allocated thirty minutes to transition into, conduct, and then transition out of a small group lesson in which four students participate, these conditions will influence how the strategies below are employed.

Similarly, the students' needs and characteristics of thinking and learning will influence how the strategies are employed. On the one hand, a student's learning history may indicate they need to be provided a relatively high number of opportunities to respond when they are acquiring a new skill in order to meet the criterion for mastery. Yet the same student may have demonstrated that they require a relatively longer duration of time to not only process the teacher's instruction and task directive but also to produce a response. These characteristics of thinking and learning may counterbalance a student's needs but also will have to be accounted for when a teacher plans for how they will present instruction.

Trial Presentation Strategies

One way that small group instruction can differ markedly from the large group instruction that is presented in a general education classroom is in terms of the number of opportunities students are given to respond. Specifically, this refers to the number of times a student is given to engage in the behavior that is the focus of the targeted learning objective. Considerations that a teacher will need to address include the total number of trials that will be presented during the time allocated for small group instruction and the way that these trials will be presented. This second consideration refers to the order in which trials will be presented and the way they will be presented.

Regarding the total number of trials the teacher will present during a session, the teacher will have to figure out how they will incorporate the number of trials that are appropriate for each student relative to the total number of trials that will be presented during the session. Further, as was recounted in chapter 1, a student may advocate that they need to engage in a relatively large number of trials (e.g., eighteen as compared to four). Ongoing progress monitoring data, students' anecdotal reports, and students' characteristics of thinking and learning are some of the factors that will influence a teacher's decision in this regard.

In addition to settling upon the total number of trials they will present, the teacher will have to decide upon the way they will present the trials. This consideration involves the order and manner of trial presentation.

With respect to the order of trial presentation, it can be sequential or random. Sequential trial presentation refers to a situation that involves presenting trials in an arranged manner that is based upon pre-determined criteria. The criteria might be the students' ages (e.g., youngest to oldest), the seating arrangement in the group (e.g., from the teacher's left to right), or the instructional level of the material (e.g., lower grade-level material to higher grade-level material).

Random trial presentation refers to when trials are presented in an order that is predicated on the teacher's discretion, meaning the trials are not presented in accordance with clearly pre-set criteria. For example, the teacher may decide to present trials to students at a point in time when they believe that the students' externalizing behavior indicates there is a relatively high probability that they will profit from the trial presentation.

One possible advantage of presenting trials sequentially is that students can be prepared to engage in behaviors that result in observational and incidental learning. This is because sequential trial presentation enables students to clearly define their roles: one role is that of active student responder and another role would be as an active observer.

A second advantage of presenting trials sequentially would be affording students the time they need to process the teacher's presentation of information. As the teacher gets ready to move to the next student, they could present, to that student, some sort of introduction to the task directive that will be presented, thereby providing the student with additional time to process the teacher's instruction.

For example, the lesson's learning objective may be that the student will state the most common phoneme that is represented by three consonants: b, m, and s. A trial might consist of the teacher showing the student an index card on which is written one of the letters and then presenting the task directive, "Say the sound this letter stands for. If you do not know the sound, wait and I will help you." If the student waited for help, the help would be a prompt in the form of /eh/, the first of two sounds in the name for the letter. This instructional strategy, which involves the teacher providing a prompt after a short period of time when a student does not respond, is known as constant time delay.

When using sequential trial presentation, as the teacher moves from one student to the next, they might say to the second student in line, "Remember, I am going to show you a letter and tell you to say what sound it stands for. Think about the sound that the letter s stands for." This introduction would enable the student to have additional time to process the teacher's instruction and prepare for the trial.

A disadvantage of sequential trial presentation would be students not attending to the teacher during the times that the teacher is interacting with other students in the group. The likelihood of the student not attending would be greatest right after the student completed a trial because they would not be called upon again until all of the other students had completed trials with the teacher. This potential situation highlights the need for teachers to be knowledgeable about the various instructional strategies that can be employed in small groups.

Knowing about this potential disadvantage of sequential trial presentation, as well as the possibility for both observational and incidental learning to occur,[5] the teacher could plan for the simultaneous use of a visual support (e.g., a symbol that depicts a set of eyeballs that is used to direct where students are to look), a talking stick, and the presentation of a directive (e.g., "Look here") to ensure that students were attending to the lesson when it was not their turn. This multi-component strategy would be an antecedent-based intervention designed to increase the probability that students would display attending, on-task behaviors when it was not their turn to work with the teacher.

An advantage of random trial presentation would be that it would increase the probability that every student would remain attentive throughout a lesson because they would not know when the teacher would call upon them to complete a trial. Disadvantages of random trial presentation include:

1. not being able to use strategies that give students additional time to process the teacher's instruction, as can be done with sequential trial presentation;

2. the pre-planning that is required so that the teacher knows when they will call on particular students, and that they do so for the number of trials that they want each student to complete; and
3. managing the use of instructional materials, including data collection sheets, especially when the students in the group are working to master different learning objectives using different instructional materials.

As for the manner in which students can be provided opportunities to respond, meaning how many trials are presented with respect to one another, the teacher can use one of three methods: massed, spaced, and distributed trial presentation.

1. Massed trial presentation refers to when one trial is presented immediately after another. Once the teacher presents the student feedback the teacher initiates the next trial to the same student. The teacher continues in this manner until they have presented the number of trials intended for the student to perform under these conditions.
2. Spaced trial presentation refers to trials that are separated in time during the small group instructional session. Essentially this means that, in between the presentation of two trials to a student, the teacher presents one or more trials to one or more other students in the group.
3. Distributed trial presentation refers to trials that are presented outside of the small group instructional session and, therefore, can be separated by a relatively lengthy period of time between the instructional session and the next time a trial is presented. An example of a distributed trial would be when a student was being taught to read community signs (e.g., Enter, Exit, Stop, Boys Restroom) and was presented trials for reading the word "Exit" during a small group instructional session that was conducted at the beginning of the school day. Later, around midday as the student was leaving the building to go outside for recess, the teacher would conduct a trial by using the exit sign located above the door of the building.

The main advantage of massed trials is that they enable a student to get the large number of repetitions needed. The main disadvantage is keeping the other students in the group engaged while one student is receiving the majority of the teacher's attention.

Spaced trials resemble how trials are typically presented in a general education classroom, so their use fosters generalization. They also increase the probability that students will remain engaged throughout the entire lesson because spaced trials can be presented quickly and efficiently regardless of whether trials are being presented sequentially or randomly. Thus, they can be combined with strategies for promoting observational and incidental learning.

Distributed trials can be used to assess a student's maintenance and generalization of targeted learning outcomes. When a student successfully completes trials that are separated by not only time but also by engagement in other activities during the break between trials, this provides some evidence that the student is maintaining the targeted learning objective.

Similarly, information about a student's generalization of a targeted learning objective can be attained when the trials are performed under different conditions. The conditions can include different materials, locations/settings, and people.

Finally, the type of knowledge being taught will dictate, to some degree, the way that trials are presented. For instance, trials that involve the mastery of declarative knowledge (i.e., discrete pieces of information, such as the names of objects or stating a synonym for a word) will be more amenable to the presentation of massed trials than will trials that involve the mastery of procedural knowledge (i.e., involves the completion of several or more interconnected steps, such as performing the algorithm to divide a three digit number by a single digit number).

Student Response Strategies

The type of responding that a teacher has students use is another way that small group instruction can differ markedly from large group instruction. A noteworthy difference will be realized to the extent that student responding is individualized and allows for the presentation—and receipt—of feedback in a way that either is not possible or as likely to occur in a general education classroom.

The term "active student responding" is commonly used to refer to how a student responds to the task directive for a trial. In terms of this discussion, relevant aspects of active student responding include the following:

1. Its alignment with the behavior called for in the targeted learning objective. Learning objectives will contain action verbs that stipulate the observable behaviors a student must exhibit to demonstrate mastery of the targeted learning objective. Hence, during trials the teacher must require the student to engage in this behavior when responding.

    A central issue is whether the learning objective calls for a recognition/recall or generative/production response. For example, if the learning objective notes that a student will "identify" all twenty-six lowercase letters of the alphabet, then an appropriate active student response during a trial would be for a student to point to the target letter after it and two other letters are presented on index cards that are positioned in front of the student.

Conversely, if the learning objective notes that the student will "name" all twenty-six lowercase letters of the alphabet, then during a trial the student will have to generate a response to the task directive. Typically a student would say the name of the letter upon being shown it and given a task directive, such as "Name this letter." However, some students who use a speech generating augmentative communication device will be required to activate it to generate their response.

2. It allows for descriptive, behavior-specific feedback. Regardless of the mode of active student responding that is used by the students who comprise the group, the size of the group should allow for the provision of immediate, descriptive, behavior-specific feedback to each student because the teacher will be able to monitor each student's response. This type of feedback is explained later (see the section titled, "Feedback Strategies.")

In terms of group participation, two types of active student responding can be required: choral or individual. Choral responding involves every student in the group responding simultaneously. Thus, it is also referred to as unison, group, and whole group responding.

To ensure that the students do respond at the exact same time the teacher may present a visual directive in addition to an oral directive. For instance, the teacher may hold her right hand in the air with her palm facing outward toward the students while she states the directive, "Name the numeral." She then pauses for a second and subsequently slowly—but deliberately—lowers her hand with her palm facing the ground. This communicates to the students that it is now time for them to respond altogether.

The pause between the oral directive and visual/gestural directive not only allows the students to think about how they will respond but it also increases the chances that the students will respond altogether. In particular, when a student has to formulate a response using an augmentative communication device this pause increases the chances they will be able to state a response at the same time as their peers.

Another type of choral responding is semi-choral responding. It involves having some of the students in the group respond in unison while others do not. For example, two of the five students in a group may respond to a particular task directive while three do not. Afterwards, these three students may respond to a different task directive while the other two students do not. This strategy could be used when students are working to master the same general targeted learning outcome (e.g., naming uppercase letters), but different specific content (e.g., N or F).

Individual responding refers to when only one student responds at a time. This type of responding clearly allows for the provision of immediate, descriptive, behavior-specific feedback.

Providing this type of feedback when choral responding is required is more or less challenging based on a number of factors, including:

1. The size of the small group. When two or three students are in the group the teacher should be able to easily monitor and react to each student's response. When four to eight students are in the group the teacher will face more of a challenge in this regard but still should be able to react, as necessary, to each student's response.

   The main point is for a teacher to be able to react to each student in a way that is not happening in a large group arrangement in a general education classroom. Thus, if two students in a small group respond, in unison, with either the same or different incorrect responses, then the way that these students' small group instruction is designed and implemented should be different in terms of the teacher's reaction. The teacher being able to react will be enhanced by establishing an environmental arrangement that allows for clear lines of sight.
2. The type of active student responding being exhibited by the students. Regardless of the group's size, a teacher will be able to provide feedback more easily to student responses that are visual (e.g., showing their response cards, presenting a thumbs up/thumbs down) as opposed to oral.
3. Whether the teacher needs to explore the reason for the student's response. One instance when this may occur is when a student is directed to demonstrate, by using a self-talk strategy, how to complete a three-step arithmetic algorithm. When the student is finished, the teacher asks the other students to present a thumbs up if they believe that the student performed the algorithm correctly or a thumbs down if they believe otherwise. The teacher may then ask the students who raised their hands to explain why they responded as they did before the teacher presents descriptive, behavior-specific feedback.
4. How easily a teacher can present prompts so that the student can emit the required response. Single-step, recognition responses tend to lend themselves more easily to teacher prompts than multi-step, generative responses. For instance, a teacher can readily present gestural or positional/proximity prompts when a student is required to point to the correct answer that is displayed among a field of three possible answers. When a student is required to write an answer on a response card and needs

prompting to produce either the correct answer or legible text, the teacher will be more challenged to provide these prompts for no other reason than they will have to assume a new position among the group each time this type of prompt is provided.
5. Whether it allows for engagement in behaviors that could result in observational and incidental learning by peers. For a student to be able to engage in observational and incidental learning, two aspects of active student responding must be addressed appropriately. First, every student must be able to see and hear the response of each of their peers to whom the teacher reacts. Second, every student must be able to see and hear all of the features of the teachers' feedback (e.g., both see the letters and hear the teacher's naming of them when the word's spelling is the incidental knowledge the teacher intends for the students to acquire).

As was noted in chapter 4, there are many types of active student responding, including those listed in the following. Further, many students will have to receive explicit, systematic instruction regarding how to emit some of the responses (e.g., The student will have to be taught the difference between pointing versus touching, or how an examiner can present two different directives that mean the same thing, such as "Show me the 5" and "Find the 5.").

1. Oral (the student states a response aloud or uses an augmentative communication device to make the remark);
2. Gestural (the student raises their hand to indicate agreement with a teacher's statement, shows either a thumbs up to indicate agreement or a thumbs down to indicate disagreement, or shows an "Okay" gesture to indicate that they are ready for the teacher to present the next trial);
3. Written responses on a dry erase board;
4. Response cards (cards on which answer choices are displayed; the student holds up the card with the response of their choice); and
5. Electronic responses (use of handheld devices, such as a remote control that has four answer choice buttons, to submit responses that are viewed and compiled by the teacher on a central unit).

Feedback Strategies

A third way that small group instruction can be made markedly different from large group, general education classroom instruction is with respect to how a teacher behaves in the consequence phase of the A-B-C paradigm. As was noted previously, in an instructional sequence the B represents the student's behavior. The focus is the behavior a student is learning that indicates they have mastered the targeted outcome. References to the student's behavior in this context are synonymous with references to their responses.

There are three types of student responses during a trial: correct, incorrect, and no response. The events that follow a student's response comprise the C, or consequence, component of the A-B-C paradigm. One such event is how a teacher reacts to the three types of student responses. A way that a teacher can react to a student's response is to provide information to the student that is known as feedback.

Feedback refers to the information, or message, that the teacher communicates to the student during the consequence component of the A-B-C paradigm. While a teacher's feedback should be based on a student's specific type of response, feedback also must be calculated to address three key features:

1. the timing of the presentation of the feedback (is it provided immediately after a student response or at some more distant point in time in the future; in terms of timing, feedback can be immediate or delayed);
2. whether the feedback is a general statement about the student's behavior ("Good job") or is descriptive in terms of the behavior ("Good job, the numeral is seven"); and
3. the relationship of the feedback to the behavior that is stated in the learning objective (does the teacher, in their feedback, clearly identify the student's performance of this behavior or not; for example, in their feedback does the teacher only make a general statement regarding the student's behavior ["Good job"] or do they characterize it in a way that references the verb in the targeted learning objective [e.g., "Good job, you said the name of the letter. It is a."]; in terms of its relationship to the behavior that is stated in the learning objective, feedback can be behavior-specific or not).

An example of how the last type of feedback could be applied to an incorrect response would be when the teacher characterizes the student's behavior relative to the behavior that is stated in the learning objective. For instance, after a student incorrectly names a numeral the teacher might say, "No, you said six but the name of this numeral is nine. Say nine."

Several types of feedback that pertain specifically to each of the three types of student responses are identified and explained in the following.

1. Teacher feedback for correct student responses.
    a. The teacher only presents verbal/oral feedback ("Good job. You spelled the word dog correctly: d-o-g").
    b. The teacher presents feedback that mirrors the student's response. For example, if the student correctly spelled the word "dog" then the

teacher would do the same. In addition, the teacher could simultaneously present verbal feedback by using self-talk as a means of explaining what they were doing.

The present discussion does not address the presentation of what would be characterized as reinforcement following correct student responses. The verbal feedback that was explained previously, as well as the teacher attention that is presented simultaneously, can, by definition, both function as reinforcement. This topic is addressed in the following section that deals with strategies for behavior management during small group instruction.

2. Teacher feedback for incorrect student responses, or no response by the student. Each type of feedback that is identified and explained in the following can follow an instance of either an incorrect student response or no response by the student.
    a. The teacher ignores the error (i.e., says nothing). This approach may be used with a student who is prone to exhibit disruptive behaviors when it is made known that they have emitted an incorrect response.
    b. Indicate that the response was incorrect (i.e., say, "No" or "Incorrect").
    c. Either (a) or (b) and then:
        1) Model the correct response and, with appropriate prompting, have the student repeat it;
        2) Model the correct response and have the student complete massed trials with appropriate prompting;
        3) Model the correct response and have the entire group repeat it using choral responding, or independent responding with either sequential or random presentation of the trials; or
        4) Conduct a brief in-seat time out (e.g., the teacher avoids looking directly at the student for five to ten seconds) if teacher attention functions as reinforcement.

Note that the teacher may use a combination of these consequences during a session.

Instructional Efficiency Strategies

A teacher's ultimate goal is to present effective instruction, which is defined as instruction that results in a student demonstrating mastery of the targeted learning objective. As the teacher strives to achieve this goal on behalf of each student in a small group, they will want to use strategies that, at the same time, also result in the most efficient instruction possible.

Efficient instruction is effective instruction that, relative to one or more other means of presenting effective instruction, requires less teacher effort, time, or money, and fewer tangible resources (e.g., fewer instructional materials). Simply stated, instructional efficiency results in a teacher "getting more for less" in terms of students' mastery of targeted learning outcomes through less of the teacher's effort than might otherwise be required.

A student may learn more content per trial. This could occur when incidental information is presented in either the antecedent or consequence phase of the A-B-C paradigm. For instance, if the targeted learning objective is for the student to learn how to read consonant-vowel-consonant words, during a trial the teacher could spell the words in either the antecedent or consequence phase. As a result, if the student learned how to both read and spell the words, this instruction would be more efficient than two separate instructional approaches: one that only resulted in students learning how to read the words and another that only resulted in them learning how to spell the words.

Likewise, a student may learn more content per session through observational learning. For example, they may learn to read not only their set of vocabulary words but also the set being taught to a peer. This outcome would be more efficient than having to teach the student the two sets of vocabulary words across different sessions.

Some of the strategies that are listed and described in the following can be used during intensive small group instruction to increase efficiency. As you consider these strategies it is important to note how they can address different aspects of students' learning, including their acquisition and maintenance of targeted learning outcomes.

1. *Planning for observational learning.* Observational learning is defined as a student's acquisition of a targeted learning outcome for a peer. The student acquires this content as a result of attending to the peer while they are receiving instruction that concerns the targeted outcome. A key component of this instruction is the provision of feedback that informs the peer, as well as the student who is observing the peer, about whether a response is correct or incorrect.

    With respect to presenting the most efficient instruction possible, a teacher needs to plan for the possibility that the students in a small group will demonstrate observational learning rather than just discover that it happened. To be able to plan for observational learning the teacher needs to know (a) the curriculum's scope and sequence, and (b) each student's learning profile (i.e., the curriculum content each student has mastered and has yet to learn).

Even when observational learning does not occur, designing and implementing instruction in a manner that establishes a relatively high probability that it will occur can still result in some type of instructional efficiency. This can be the case when a student requires less intensive instruction than would otherwise be the case because the student has been exposed to the content—by watching a peer learn it—that has been targeted for the student to master at a later point in time.

When a teacher plans for observational learning to occur, they will have to decide how to conduct relevant assessments. Options include always assessing the observational content at the same time as the instructional content; assessing the observational content routinely, but not as often as the instructional content (e.g., assessing the observational content every third probe when instructional content is assessed); and assessing the observational content when a student enters intensive small group instruction to confirm that they have not mastered it, and then again just prior to the time when it is scheduled to be taught.

2. *Planning for incidental learning.* Incidental learning refers to a student's acquisition of curriculum content that is presented during a trial but is not acted upon by either the teacher or the student. An example would be when a teacher is focusing instruction on teaching students how to read words that begin with the consonant digraph ch, and the teacher spells each word prior to presenting the task directive, "Read the word." If, during a probe, the student demonstrates that they can spell each word, incidental learning will have occurred.

Subsequently, the teacher would provide feedback about the student's reading of the word but would say no more about its spelling. Neither would the student be required to perform any action with respect to the word's spelling.

Planning for incidental learning can involve curriculum content that is presented during a student's trial as well as content that is presented in a peer's trial. The presentation of the content only requires that a student attend to it. Unlike observational learning, the student does not have to discern anything from the teacher's feedback to a peer's behavior.

As is the case with respect to observational learning, to be able to plan for incidental learning the teacher needs to know the curriculum's scope and sequence, and each student's learning profile (i.e., the curriculum content each student has mastered and has yet to learn). Challenges to planning for incidental learning include when to present the curriculum content and how much content to present.

Regarding when to present the content, most often it is either presented in the antecedent phase, as was the case in the earlier example, or in the consequence phase of the A-B-C paradigm. In terms of the earlier example, instead of presenting the word's spelling before the task directive the teacher could have spelled the word after they provided the student with feedback about the response.

As for how much content to present as incidental information, the amount will depend on the student's learning characteristics. If the student learns new information at an extremely low rate, then the teacher may decide that adding incidental information in the instructional exchange may result in a situation in which there is too much information for the student to cognitively process.

Even when incidental learning does not occur, designing and implementing instruction in a manner that allows for it to happen may still result in some type of instructional efficiency. This might occur when a student requires less intensive instruction than would otherwise be the case because the student has been exposed to content that has been targeted for the student to master at a later point in time.

When a teacher plans for incidental learning to occur, they will have to decide how to conduct relevant assessments. Options include always assessing the incidental content at the same time as the instructional content; assessing the incidental content routinely, but not as often as the instructional content; and assessing the incidental content when a student enters intensive small group instruction to confirm that they have not mastered it, and then again at the conclusion of all of the sessions when it was presented.

3. *Directing student attending.* A student will have the highest probability of demonstrating observational or incidental learning when they attend to the instruction a teacher presents to others. Strategies a teacher can use to direct a student to attend to others include the use of visual supports (e.g., a talking stick) and explicit teaching of a relevant attention directive and response.

4. *Priming.* Priming refers to previewing upcoming instruction. It can occur to varying degrees, ranging from making a student aware of what will take place during an upcoming instructional session to presenting some type of instruction that is related to the upcoming instructional session. For instance, if, during the upcoming session a student will be taught the multiplication facts that have seven as one of the factors, a student's priming activity might include a quick review of multiplication facts that have factors less than seven.

For priming to be effective, the teacher must be knowledgeable about the curriculum's scope and sequence, the content a student has mastered and still needs to learn, and how any of this matter can be addressed during

priming. Priming can contribute to efficient instruction when a student requires less intensive instruction than would otherwise be the case because the student has been exposed to the content that has been targeted for them to master.
5. *Maintenance.* Maintaining learned content often presents a challenge to students with significant, ongoing learning challenges. Thus having these students attend to content that is being taught to peers but that the students have already mastered increases the probability that the students will demonstrate maintenance. This result would mitigate the time and effort that would have been required to reteach the content had the students not maintained it.
6. *Transition strategies.* Seamless transitions result in more time being available to present instruction during a session than would otherwise be the case if transitions were disjointed. This circumstance can result in a student needing fewer total sessions to master a targeted learning outcome.
7. *Prompting.* The identification of what is called a controlling prompt can result in more efficient instruction by reducing the amount of time it takes a student to attain a targeted learning outcome. A controlling prompt is one that nearly always results in a student making a correct response. This prompt can be systematically faded as quickly as possible so that the student demonstrates that they can perform the targeted learning outcome independently.

SMALL GROUP BEHAVIOR MANAGEMENT STRATEGIES

When a teacher presents small group instruction, they also will have to ensure that students exhibit school social behaviors that allow for the safe and orderly functioning of a session. The term "behavior management" refers to the teacher's actions in this regard. Addressing students' displays of appropriate school social behaviors during a session is a bit different from using a small group arrangement to teach students a broad array of school social behaviors.

This latter circumstance is akin to a student needing to receive explicit, intensive small group instruction to learn the content that comprises a wide-ranging curriculum pertaining to school social behaviors. The student would need to receive this intensive instruction because they have demonstrated ongoing, significant challenges acquiring these behaviors.

The school social behaviors the student is expected to demonstrate during small group instruction may be a subset of this larger curriculum. However, for the purpose of this discussion the focus is on actions a teacher can take to manage displays of appropriate school social behaviors that students need to demonstrate consistently while they participate in the group. This discussion is not an example of how to use explicit, intensive small group instruction to teach these behaviors.

Small group behavior management can include what a teacher does before and after students perform behaviors that are the focus of the targeted learning objective. This means that the teacher actions occur in either the antecedent (A) or consequence (C) phase, or both, of the A-B-C paradigm.

Historically, teachers have focused more on what they could do in the consequence phase. Specifically, they have used strategies that were thought to be punitive in nature, such as afterschool detention, suspension, and expulsion with the expectation that students' displays of inappropriate behaviors would decrease because the students wanted to avoid these types of consequences.[6]

Further, emphasis was placed on the consequence phase as opposed to the antecedent phase due to certain, near universally held assumptions by teachers: Students were able to intuit how to engage in, and display, appropriate school social behaviors simply by watching their peers. In other words, teachers did not need to directly teach school social behaviors and if, or when, these behaviors needed to be taught it was someone other than a teacher who was responsible for doing so. Specifically, a parent was the person who was responsible.

Presently there is a recognition that school personnel need to teach students appropriate school social behaviors and can be effective in this regard.[7] Moreover, in terms of the A-B-C paradigm, this means that teacher actions need to occur in both the antecedent and consequence phases.[8] This focus is particularly relevant to a teacher's use of behavior management in small group instruction. This matter is addressed next.

First, the discussion focuses on a teacher's use of what are referred to as antecedent-based interventions. Next, the discussion addresses what are referred to as contingency strategies. These are actions a teacher employs following student engagement in a behavior. Therefore, they occur in the consequence phase of the three-term paradigm.

As the name implies, antecedent-based interventions are employed during the antecedent phase of the three-phase paradigm. Their purpose is to set the stage for a student's engagement in desired behavior. With respect to their relationship to certain school social behaviors, it is important to explain the meaning of the term "intervention."

For the purpose of this discussion, "intervention" refers to a change of the environment. In an educational context an intervention is designed and implemented to meet an instructional need.

For example, if two students engage in high rates of disruptive, off-task behavior when they are seated next to each other a teacher may decide to seat them on opposite sides of the room. This change to the environment is an intervention. To determine whether the intervention was effective in meeting an instructional need, which was to decrease the students' rates of disruptive, off-task behavior, the teacher would need to compare pre- and post-intervention data.

An intervention is synonymous with the term instructional strategy in the sense that both terms refer to planned actions that a teacher executes for the purpose of affecting student behavior. However, the term instructional strategy is, more often than the term intervention, used interchangeably with the terms teaching strategy and teaching methodology.

Thus, when these latter terms are used they imply that the teacher will plan for, and execute, a number of actions that will lead students to the mastery of targeted learning outcomes, whether they involve academic or functional content, or school social behaviors. Intervention can refer to less complex actions, such as the one described earlier, and these actions may serve to support teacher behaviors that are more readily and commonly viewed as academic instruction.

Accordingly, in this section of the book the term "intervention" is used to refer to changes of the environment that address an instructional need with respect to behavior management during small group instruction. Specifically, antecedent-based interventions are identified and discussed in terms of how they can establish a high probability that students will demonstrate appropriate school social behaviors during small group instruction.

1. *Visual supports.* A visual support is anything that a student can see, and which is intended to enhance understanding of what a teacher says (whether through speech or sign language). One's understanding can be enhanced by affording the student more time to process the teacher's fleeting remark; clarifying known possibilities for misunderstandings, such as not knowing classmates' names; and enhancing the short-term memory capabilities of students who are challenged in this regard. Generally speaking, during small group instruction visual supports are used to provide answers to students' who, what, where, when, why, and how questions before the students have a reason to pose them aloud—either through speech or challenging behaviors.

    The use of visual supports further highlights the complexities involved with the presentation of intensive small group instruction. As is stated elsewhere in this book, although what are considered to be basic skills will be the focus of what is taught and learned during this instruction, it should not be equated with an easy undertaking for either the staff or students who are involved.

Regarding the use of visual supports, at a minimum a teacher most likely will have to create at least some of the ones that they will use, employ explicit instruction to teach students the meaning and appropriate usage of each support, and manage their application in real time. In some instances the use of visual supports can serve a dual purpose.

For example, the display and use of a work list can both address behavior management and contribute to emergent literacy instruction when a teacher highlights to the students that they are conducting a visual scan from left-to-right or top-to-bottom to progress through the list, deriving meaning from each symbol in the list (i.e., developing graphic literacy), and learning that symbols—whether they be letters, line drawings, or color photographs—stand for something.

Examples of these types of visual supports are presented in the following. The information in parentheses is related to a question a student may pose if the visual support was not available. When a visual support provides an answer to one or more of these questions, a student's anxiety about what is to happen may be reduced or eliminated. In turn, this reduces or eliminates any probability that a student will act out because they are confused and anxious about their situation.

a. *Look here.* A support that directs the student where to look. One type of this kind of support, a talking stick, can serve a dual purpose in terms of behavior management by not only informing a student who they are to look at but also who is—and is not—allowed to talk. Other types of this kind of support, such as a graphic symbol that depicts a set of open eyes or a teacher's use of a hand gesture that involves moving two of their fingers from a student's eyes to where the student is supposed to look, can serve a singular purpose by indicating to the student where he is to look. ("Who am I supposed to look at?" "Where am I supposed to look?")

b. *Work list.* This is a visual representation of the activities that will take place during a session. Essentially, it is a "To Do" list. During a math lesson a work list might depict rote counting beginning at one, counting on from a number other than one, and answering basic addition facts. ("What are we going to do while we're at the table?" "What will we do next?" "How many activities are we going to do?")

c. *Trial flip ring.* Number cards can be placed on a flip ring and then displayed in ascending or descending order to communicate to students how many of the total number of trials have been completed, or how

many more trials remain to be completed. ("How many have I done already?" "How many more do I have left to do?")
d. *Timer.* Multiple devices, including egg timers, hour glasses, and digital stop watches, can be used to display the amount of time the session, or an activity within a session, will last. ("How much longer do we have to do this?" "When will we get to do something else?")
e. *Green and red arrows.* These arrows depict where to begin and end a task, such as counting from three to nine, reading a sentence from left-to-right, writing the numeral 3, and adding a two-digit addition problem that is displayed vertically. ("Where do I begin reading?" "How do I start writing the numeral 3?")
f. *Attention response.* This visual support contains some type of graphic (i.e., a symbol or photograph) that depicts the behaviors a student must exhibit in order to demonstrate an attention response. ("What am I supposed to do with my hands and my feet to show the teacher that I am paying attention?")
g. *Group rules.* A short listing of the rules for appropriate school social behaviors a student is to engage in while they participate in a small group. The rules may be displayed using a single mode of representation (e.g., only text) or multiple modes (e.g., text and symbols or photographs). ("How am I supposed to behave while I am in the group?")
h. *Finished pocket, bucket, or folder.* The teacher should design a mechanism for communicating to the students that an activity is finished and that the entire session is finished. One such mechanism would be to place the graphics that comprise the work list in a container or a folder with pockets when each activity that is represented by the graphic has been completed. Another would be to place a checkmark next to the graphic for each completed activity, or to draw a line through the graphic. ("How many more activities are we going to do?" "Is this our last activity?")
i. *Whose turn?* Using a mode of representation that the students understand, the teacher can depict the student whose turn it is. Depending on the ways that trials are being presented, the student can use this support to figure out how many, and which, students will take a turn before they do. When students do not know each other's names, this support further enhances their understanding of what the teacher says. ("When is it going to be my turn?" "Who gets to go next?")
j. *Available reinforcers.* Using an appropriate mode of representation, the teacher can depict the reinforcers that are available to the students. Note that a student's reinforcer preference can change quickly, so the closer the opportunity to select a reinforcer is to its presentation to the student,

the more likely it will be that a student will not change his mind. ("What do I get if I complete all of my work?" "What do I get if my answers are correct?")
2. *Presentation of instructional level tasks.*[9] When students perceive that the targeted learning outcome is something they can attain by putting forth a reasonable, as opposed to an extraordinary, amount of effort, there is a higher probability that they will remain emotionally regulated and engaged in displays of appropriate behavior—both academic and social. Yet, if the targeted learning outcome is too easy or too difficult, the probability that students will engage in inappropriate behavior is relatively high.
3. *Sequencing low probability behaviors after high probability behaviors.* A low probability behavior is one for which there is a small chance that a student will engage in it at a given point in time, whereas a high probability behavior is one for which there is a considerable chance that the student will engage in it. To increase the chances that a student will engage in a low probability behavior it can be placed in a pre-determined sequence so that this behavior is solicited after the student has successfully been directed to engage in several high probability behaviors.

For instance, because the student is just learning how to do so, there may be a low probability that a student will state the correct answers to basic addition facts that consist of two single-digit addends—each of which is either four, five, six, or seven—if this is the first activity that is presented in an instructional session. Additionally, if this is the arrangement the teacher had settled upon there is a relatively high chance that the student will engage in an inappropriate behavior that will enable them to escape this activity, such as pushing their chair back and away from the place at a table. Instead, if the teacher were to arrange the sequencing of activities as follows, there will be a greater chance that the student will remain emotionally regulated while working to learn the sums for the addition problems.

   a. Rote counting from one to fifteen. This is a task that the student has mastered and performs correctly nearly every time. Therefore, it is a high probability task because chances are great that the student will engage in it when directed to do so.
   b. Counting from two, three, four, and five to fifteen. Like the previous task, the student has mastered this one and performs it correctly nearly every time. It, too, is a high probability task.
   c. States the sums of ten addition problems in which there are two one-digit addends, each of which is either four, five, six, or seven. Because the student is working to acquire this skill, at times they are experiencing frustration while doing so. Lessons that have started with this task

have resulted in the student exhibiting challenging behaviors, including attempting to escape the work area. In these instances, this has been a low probability task because there is a very small chance they will engage in it when directed to do so.

However, in the current scenario the student has successfully completed two high probability tasks. Further, these tasks are directly related to learning how to add the numbers that are the focus of the learning objective. Thus, the student has established behavioral momentum in terms of complying with teacher directives. This circumstance increases the probability that they will engage in this low probability task when directed to do so.

4. *Controlling the distribution and use of instructional materials.* Teachers have noted that some students become distracted when they are given certain instructional materials, such as a pencil, because they pay more attention to those items than they do the teacher. To set the stage for student displays of appropriate behavior throughout a small group instructional session, a teacher must plan for how and when they will distribute certain items, as well as how they will direct their use.

Some items, such as response cards and pencils, will be distributed shortly before students need to use them and then retrieved right after students finish using them. When the items are in the students' possession the teacher may direct when and how students use them. For instance, a teacher may tell the students when to retrieve their pencil from the pencil well that is on their desk as well as when to return it to this location.

Note that there is a difference between directing the distribution and use of these materials and those that are used by students to maintain their emotional regulation (e.g., Thera-putty). The latter items may be one aspect of a calming strategy for a student.

5. *"Get ready" attention directive.* The teacher can instruct students as to what behaviors they are to exhibit after the teacher presents a directive that communicates to the students that they are about to begin presenting instruction that they need to attend to. The behaviors the students exhibit constitute what is referred to as their attention response. An example of an attention response would be for the students to simultaneously look at the teacher, remain quiet, sit upright in their chairs, place their feet flat on the floor, and place their hands flat on either their lap or their desk.

Student displays of these behaviors not only indicate to the teacher that they are prepared to attend to the instruction, but they also are physically incompatible with inappropriate, potentially disruptive behaviors. For instance, when a student's feet are flat on the floor, they are not using them to kick one of the desk's legs or tap the ground with their toes. Likewise, if the student remains quiet, they are not humming or talking out loud.

6. *Use of appropriate language.* The multiple ways that a teacher can use language during small group instruction can increase the probability that students will engage in appropriate school social behaviors during this instruction. The teacher can (a) monitor the number of directions they present at any one time as well as allow students relatively more time to process, and then respond to, the directions; (b) keep remarks as short and concise as possible; (c) focus on telling students what to do as opposed to what not to do; and (d) be certain to use vocabulary that students understand.
7. *Employ meaningful and purposeful routines.* When students know how they are to behave when they enter a group, work throughout the session, and then transition out of the group there is a high probability that they will exhibit appropriate behaviors. Hence, a key behavior management intervention is to establish and teach students meaningful and purposeful routines that address all aspects of the small group session.

A second category of strategies that a teacher can use to manage students' behaviors during small group instruction are contingency-based strategies. These involve the event(s) that occur immediately after a student displays a behavior or exhibits a no response during the time they have been given to respond. These events are referred to as contingency-based because the strategy that the teacher actually employs is contingent upon, meaning based upon, the type of behavior a student exhibits.

It is important to note that contingency-based strategies can be used throughout a lesson. That is, they can be used every time a student completes a trial; following the completion of each activity, or subcomponent, within a session; and at the very end of the session. Also, the strategies can be based on the behavior of an individual student, two or more students, or the entire group.

Examples of the types of contingencies that can be presented by the teacher were explained previously during the discussion about feedback. Examples of the ways that these strategies can be employed are identified and explained in the following.

1. *Individual.* Each student's contingency is based on their type of response (i.e., correct, incorrect, or no response) or the teacher's evaluation of the student's effort. That is to say, to increase the probability that a student will engage in appropriate behavior a contingency can be based on how the teacher views the student's effort rather than whether the response is correct or incorrect.
2. *Interdependent.* All of the students in the group receive the contingency based on a specified level of group performance.

3. *Sub-group dependent.* All of the students in the group receive a contingency, such as a tangible reinforcer, based on the performance of one or two students.
4. *Individualized behavior intervention plan.* For some students who receive special education services, their contingencies will be applied in accordance with the relevant content in their individualized behavior intervention plans.

PUTTING IT ALL TOGETHER: DIRECT INSTRUCTION LESSON PLAN

In chapter 2, the elements that comprise a direct instruction lesson plan were identified and discussed. This lesson plan is one format that allows for the presentation of intensive small group instruction, particularly the strategies that have been explained in this chapter. In the following, the elements of this lesson plan are presented, again, along with examples of how some of these strategies can be incorporated in them. In some instances references are also made to aspects of high-quality instruction. Overall, the number of examples that are presented are meant to be representative rather than exhaustive.

1. *Attention directive and attention response.* An attention directive is a teacher directive that is intended to communicate to students that they are to display behaviors that will convey to the teacher that the students are attending to the teacher and, therefore, are ready to receive instruction. An attention response consists of the behaviors a student is taught to display, in response to the presentation of an attention directive by the teacher, for the purpose of communicating to the teacher that the student is attending to the instruction.

    Some of the group behavior management strategies can be used during this part of the lesson. For instance, visual supports can be used to direct where a student is to look and the behaviors they are to display to indicate that they are ready to attend to the teacher's instruction. (e.g., visual supports).

2. *Statement of the learning objective.* During this part of the lesson the teacher tells the students the knowledge or skills that will be taught during the lesson (e.g., "I am going to teach you the names of four items of clothing.").

    When a teacher clearly states the learning objective for the lesson, they are making the instruction explicit. The students will know the targeted learning outcome they are expected to master as a result of participating in intensive small group instruction. Also, the teacher's statement of the targeted learning objective addresses one of the elements of high-quality instruction: maintaining a clear curriculum focus.

Visual supports can be used to supplement the teacher's remarks. The teacher might display a written version of the objective and refer to it when they review it with the students. Additionally, the teacher could employ a work list as a visual support to enhance the students' understanding of the targeted learning outcome.

3. *Review of previously mastered, related learning objectives.* Prior to modeling how to perform the behavior that is at the heart of the learning objective (see subsequent discussion), the teacher will review how to perform one or more behaviors that the students have mastered and are closely related to the learning objective that is the focus of the lesson (e.g., prior to modeling how to count to five the teacher will review how to count to three and four).

Aside from increasing the probability that a student will master the new content because they can connect it to related content they have mastered, conducting at least a brief review of previously mastered material sets the occasion for behavioral momentum because this activity will most likely involve high probability behaviors and increases instructional efficiency by ensuring that the previously learned content is maintained. Thus, it is less likely that allotted time will need to be spent reteaching this previously mastered content.

4. *Teacher modeling.* The teacher explicitly demonstrates how to perform the behavior that is at the heart of the learning objective. Moreover, the teacher shows the students what they are to do during the guided practice portion of the lesson.

Teacher modeling affords the teacher the opportunity to make explicit all of the instructional strategies that comprise the multicomponent intervention to teach the targeted learning outcome. The teacher's modeling will be enhanced if they have someone assist with role play, meaning someone else needs to play the role of the student. Options for this arrangement include a teacher assistant, a colleague whose role play has been pre-recorded, or a student who is a member of the small group.

Time permitting, the teacher should model examples and non-examples of the instructional exchange. In other words, some modeling should demonstrate how the teacher intends the instructional exchange to proceed while some modeling should demonstrate how the teacher does not intend the instructional exchange to proceed, and what will occur if this were to happen.

A relevant instructional strategy—think aloud—is often a key aspect of this part of the lesson. A think aloud involves the teacher telling students what they are thinking as they engage in an activity.

5. *Guided practice, with appropriate feedback.* The student is directed to perform the behavior while receiving support, in the form of prompts, from an instructor to ensure that the student responds correctly. After the student responds correctly, they are provided immediate, behavior-specific praise.

   This is the point in time during a direct instruction lesson when the teacher will put into practice most of the small group instructional strategies that were described previously in this chapter. For example, if the learning objective states that, when the teacher presents the student a picture of one type of fruit, the student will state its name, and will do so for a total of ten different fruits (e.g., apple, orange, grape, banana, strawberry, etc.), the teacher might decide to use the following strategies.
   a. Present the trials sequentially.
   b. Employ simultaneous prompting during each trial as the evidence-based practice.
   c. When it is the student's turn, present massed trials (i.e., three) to each student for the picture of a fruit that they are learning to name.
   d. Implement strategies that are intended to result in observational learning. For instance, each student will demonstrate observational learning by mastering the names for fruits that they did not know but that were taught to a peer. Strategies the teacher might employ include the use of visual supports, such as a talking stick, and presenting an attention directive routinely.
   e. Provide each student with immediate, descriptive, behavior-specific feedback following each of their three trials per picture.
   f. At the end of the session provide each student with tangible reinforcement for attending throughout the session and demonstrating an appropriate effort to learn.
6. *Independent practice.* Independent practice consists of the student engaging, on their own, in the behavior that is the focus of the learning objective. In some instances, this component of the direct instruction lesson plan would be omitted. This might be the case if the students have not mastered self-regulation behaviors.

   One way a form of independent practice could be included in terms of this lesson's learning objective would be to have the students engage in semi-choral responding that involves them independently practicing (i.e., without teacher modeling or prompting) saying the names of the pictures of fruit that they know already.
7. *Lesson review.* The teacher reviews the lesson by reiterating the activities that occurred during the lesson. When the teacher states, explicitly, the activities that were performed during a lesson they are reminding students

of the sequence they follow in a direct instruction lesson to "learn how to learn." Additionally, the teacher is addressing one element of high-quality instruction, which is maintaining a clear curriculum focus.
8. *Preview of the next lesson.* The teacher tells the students the topics that will be addressed in the next related lesson, and notes when that lesson will occur (e.g., "Later this morning . . .; "Tomorrow at this time . . ."). When the teacher previews the next lesson, they are implementing some form of priming. Additionally, the teacher is addressing one element of high-quality instruction, which is to maintain a clear curriculum focus.

CHAPTER 5 COMPREHENSION CHECK

Now that you have finished reading the chapter, you should be able to:

Discuss four fundamental instructional strategies for teaching academic content, functional content, and school social behavior.

List the four categories of instructional strategies that comprise an organizational framework that can be used to explain how the presentation of intensive small group instruction can be markedly different from the high-quality instruction that is presented in large group arrangements in general education classrooms.

When using a direct instruction lesson plan, identify the point in time when the instructional strategies referred to in the previous list are most often employed.

Explain each of the following categories of intensive small group instructional strategies and list several examples of each: trial presentation strategies, student response strategies, feedback strategies, and instructional efficiency strategies.

Differentiate between sequential and random trial presentation.

Define the terms observational learning and incidental learning.

List five types of active student responding.

Explain what is meant by "immediate, descriptive, behavior-specific feedback."

Discuss the difference between a teacher engaging in behavior management strategies during small group instruction and teaching school social behaviors during this instruction.

Explain the difference between antecedent-based interventions and contingency-based strategies in terms of small group behavior management.

List and discuss three antecedent-based interventions for small group behavior management.

List and discuss two contingency-based strategies for small group behavior management.

NOTES

1. Debra M. Kamps and Charles R. Greenwood, "Formulating Secondary-Level Reading Interventions," *Journal of Learning Disabilities* 38, no. 6 (November/December 2005): 500–09.

2. Connie Wong, Samuel L. Odom, Kara Hume, Ann W. Cox, Angel Fettig, Suzanne Kucharczyk, and T. R. Schultz, *Evidence-Based Practices for Children, Youth, and Young Adults with Autism Spectrum Disorder* (Chapel Hill: The University of North Carolina, (Frank Porter Graham Child Development Institute, Autism Evidence-Based Practice Review Group, 2014).

3. John O. Cooper, Timothy E. Heron, and William L. Heward, "Applied Behavior Analysis," Pearson, (2007); Paul Alberto and Anne C. Troutman, *Applied Behavior Analysis for Teachers*, ninth edition (Pearson: 2007); Mark Wolery, Donald B. Bailey, and George M. Sugai, *Effective Teaching: Principles and Procedures of Applied Behavior Analysis with Exceptional Students* (Boston, MA: Allyn and Bacon, Inc., 1988).

4. Samuel L. Odom, Lana Collet-Klingenberg, Sally J. Rogers, and Deborah D. Hatton, "Evidence-Based Practices in Interventions for Children and Youth with Autism Spectrum Disorders," *Preventing School Failure: Alternative Education for Children and Youth* 54, no. 4 (2010): 275–82.

5. Jennifer R. Ledford, David L. Gast, Deanna Luscre, and Kevin M. Ayres, "Observational and Incidental Learning by Children with Autism During Small Group Instruction," *Journal of Autism and Developmental Disorders* 38, no. 1 (2008): 86.

6. Lee Kern and Nathan H. Clemens, "Antecedent Strategies to Promote Appropriate Classroom Behavior," *Psychology in the Schools* 44, no. 1 (2007): 65–75.

7. R. H. Horner, G. Sugai, A. W. Todd, T. Lewis-Palmer, L. Bambara, and L. Kern, "Individualized Supports for Students with Problem Behaviors: Designing Positive Behavior Plans," (2005); Brandi Simonsen, J. Freeman, S. Goodman, B. Mitchell, J. Swain-Bradway, B. Flannery, and B. Putman, "Supporting and Responding to Behavior: Evidence-Based Classroom Strategies for Teachers," *USA: US Office of Special Education Programs* (2015).

8. Lee Kern and Nathan H. Clemens, "Antecedent Strategies to Promote Appropriate Classroom Behavior," *Psychology in the Schools* 44, no. 1 (2007): 65–75.

9. John W. Maag, *Behavior Management: From Theoretical Implications to Practical Applications*, second edition (Belmont, CA: Edith Beard Brady, 2004).

Chapter Six

Assessment and Small Group Instruction

OVERVIEW

In this chapter both overarching information about the topic of educational assessment and information about assessment as it applies to small group instruction is presented. This approach to the topic is in keeping with the approach throughout the book whereby a small group instruction issue is interconnected to the way that matter is addressed school-wide.

At the outset of the chapter key assessment terminology are identified and defined. Next, assessment matters that pertain to intensive small group instruction are explained. Afterwards, school-wide educational assessment issues are discussed.

Key points from the chapter include the following:

1. Although the terms "assessment," "testing," and "evaluation" are often used and thought about interchangeably, they have distinct yet interconnected meanings.
2. Just like its instruction component, the assessment that pertains to small group instruction is tied to the assessment that is conducted in a general education classroom as well as a school's assessment milieu. Hence, a teacher needs to be knowledgeable about key terms and concepts, including formal and informal assessment and criterion- and norm-referenced assessment.
3. A key purpose of assessment is to inform instruction. This means that the information is used to make decisions about how a teacher is to proceed with their work on behalf of the students in a small group. Given the achievement deficits that are being demonstrated by the students who are receiving intensive small group instruction, it is important that assessments

be conducted often enough and are strategic in terms of producing meaningful information.
4. Assessment is more pronounced when small group instruction is presented than when large group instruction is presented. Pronounced means that assessment occurs more often and for different, multiple purposes (e.g., as a progress monitoring measure and for diagnostic purposes).
5. General outcome measures address an entire curriculum. These measures—which include standardized, norm-referenced assessments—generally consist of a very small number of items that have been correlated with students' mastery of the related targeted learning outcome. For example, to evaluate a student's mastery of basic addition facts only three such problems may be presented on a test.
6. Assessments that are employed with intensive small group instruction must be closely aligned to students' targeted learning objectives. A type of assessment that is well suited in this regard is a probe, or skill check.
7. A probe is a type of assessment that is designed to obtain data about the student's performance in terms of a learning objective. Generally speaking, probes that are used in conjunction with intensive small group instruction are short, easy to administer and score, and criterion-referenced.
8. Some students may need to be taught a test-taking curriculum, meaning they need to learn knowledge and skills that pertain to participating in an assessment so that the information obtained is valid.
9. Aspects of student learning that are important to assess include one's rate and level of learning and their maintenance and generalization of mastered learning outcomes.
10. Testing accommodations allow for changes to the conditions under which a student is expected to perform an academic skill or school social behavior, rather than an alteration of the standard that has been set for the performance of the task (which is a modification). Categories of these accommodations include time, input, student response, and setting.

INTRODUCTION

The content presented in this chapter progresses from a discussion of universal assessment topics to those that are specific to intensive small group instruction. General terms, concepts, and issues that pertain to assessment and evaluation are discussed at the outset of the chapter. Next, these same matters are discussed with respect to their relevance to small group instruction.

Moreover, in this chapter basic concepts about assessment are discussed as opposed to intricate details about the design and administration of what are commonly referred to as assessment instruments. You may think of these as the actual tests that are administered to students. Each test either specifies who is qualified to administer it based upon their prior training and current credentials (e.g., a board licensed psychologist) or who can become qualified to administer it (e.g., a special education teacher who receives training from a certified teacher who has at least two years experience administering the test).

In most instances a school district or an individual school will select the assessment instruments they will use, determine the training requirements for those who will administer the tests, and then ensure that the training is provided. Further, most instruments are administered to obtain a global understanding of how the general student population is performing. Because the focus of this book is students with intensive instructional needs, your knowledge about these instruments is relevant to the extent that it is consistent with the book's premise that teachers who provide intensive small group instruction to students with significant, persistent learning challenges have to remain cognizant of the relationship of their work to the general population.

Therefore, it is important that you have a conceptual understanding of assessment rather than detailed knowledge about particular assessment instruments or topics. You will acquire this information at the time you need to do so as well as in the school where you need to do so. For now you need to know about the relevance of the assessments described earlier to reports of students' levels of performance and maintaining everyone's focus on the students' ultimate attainment of grade-level standards.

For purposes with respect to the students who are the focus of this book, you need to learn about the ways in which assessment is directly related to intensive small group instruction. These matters are the focus of the content that is presented in this chapter. The chapter's discussion centers on how the data that are obtained from assessments can guide you in presenting instruction. Another way of saying this is that you will learn how assessment informs instruction.

Teachers who instruct students who exhibit significant learning challenges and need intensive instruction can leave nothing left to chance—which is why the numerous details that are involved with this type of instruction are addressed in this book. Some have described this approach as the micro analysis of teaching. Therefore, to increase the probability that these students' assessment data are valid, they probably will need to be provided explicit instruction about how to complete the assessment.

The time and effort that is spent teaching test taking is worthwhile when valid data are obtained. These students cannot afford for the limited instructional time that is available to them to be spent on skills they already have mastered.

KEY TERMS: ASSESSMENT, TESTING, AND EVALUATION

Oftentimes the terms "assessment," "test," and "evaluation" are used interchangeably, as if they were synonymous. Although their meanings are related in that they pertain to information about students' performances in terms of their attainment of academic knowledge and skills and school social behaviors, their meanings are distinct. Understanding the different definitions for these terms will further your understanding of assessment as it pertains to intensive small group instruction.

Assessment is defined as the collection of information. One type of assessment is informal assessment, which refers to the collection of information that is not governed by established procedures. Some of these types of assessment occur without the teacher giving much thought about the fact that they are conducting this type of assessment. Yet the data (i.e., information) the teacher collects readily informs the instruction.

For example, a teacher may observe that when two students are seated next to each other they engage in more instances of disruptive behavior than when they are seated far apart. Consequently, the teacher accounts for this when they arrange the classroom seating chart so as to produce a safe and orderly environment that sets the stage for effective instruction.

Likewise, the teacher might observe a student who quickly becomes frustrated when they do not know how to complete an assignment. When the student becomes frustrated, they just sit quietly at the desk but waste valuable academic learning time. In response to this behavior the teacher adjusts the routine so that after the class is given a task to perform, the teacher follows up with this student shortly afterwards to provide needed support. The teacher also allows for the student to ask a nearby peer, who typically knows what to do, for assistance if the teacher is not available.

Testing is the means by which the presence of something is determined. In schools, tests determine the presence of things such as a student's academic knowledge and skills, or a student's ability to perform either a school social behavior or functional task.

Mostly, a test consists of the presentation of a stimulus, or some type of directive, to which a student must independently provide a response. Examples include a teacher presenting the directive (e.g., "Spell the word coat"), the written instruction (e.g., "Compare and contrast Nakisha and JaQuan's reactions to the loss of their beloved pet dog" on an English test), the written statement (e.g., "Simplify $2X + 6X - 4$" on an Algebra test), or the remark "Wash your hands."

When most people refer to taking a test, they are describing a situation during which a student, sitting at a desk with a pencil in hand, makes independent responses to questions or similar items, such as task directives, that are posed. In other words, a student is required to demonstrate their knowledge or skill in response to a task directive. The student's responses provide information, which is assessment, and when a grade is assigned this is evaluation.

Evaluation refers to placing a value on the merits, or meaning, of the information, or data, obtained through assessment. For example, a student who answers 65 percent of the questions correctly on a final exam may have their performance characterized as satisfactory whereas a classmate who answers 97 percent of the questions correctly has their performance characterized as superior.

A FEW MORE KEY ASSESSMENT TERMS AND CONCEPTS

To round out your basic understanding of assessment, testing, and evaluation, some additional topics are identified and explained subsequently.

Formal and Informal Assessment

The terms "formal" and "informal assessment" refer to whether there are specific, prescribed ways to conduct the assessment. Formal assessments are prescribed ways of finding out what a student has learned, or how much they have improved, during the instructional period. These assessments have standardized methods of administration and grading. Likewise, they have a formal method of interpreting grades, thereby allowing for a succinct evaluation of a student. An example of a formal assessment is an academic achievement test.

Informal assessments refer to various ways of collecting data without the use of standardized, formal methods. Examples of these assessments are teacher observations, student daily classwork, and pop quizzes. Informal assessments are what teachers use every day to evaluate their students' performance and progress. Thus, they immediately inform instruction.

Formative and Summative Assessment

The terms "formative" and "summative assessment" refer to when, meaning how often, assessments are administered. Formative assessments are administered often; think of the "f" in formative as also being the "f" in the word frequent.

Formative assessment is an integral part of intensive intervention, with these assessments being administered as often as two or three times per week, or even daily. Formative assessments are generally low stakes and consist of probes (which are also referred to as skill checks). A probe is a short, easy to administer assessment that consists of a small number of items that are exclusively and directly tied to the content that is being addressed during instruction. Examples of probes include having a student read ten high frequency words, answer ten multiplication facts, and spell ten consonant-vowel-consonant words.

The goal of formative assessment is to monitor student learning by providing ongoing feedback that can be used by students to improve their learning and instructors to improve their teaching. Formative assessments help students identify their strengths and weaknesses and target areas that need work, and help instructors recognize where students are struggling and address problems immediately. Instructors can do this by revising the instructional strategies that have been used to teach skills students are not mastering or making progress toward mastering.

Summative assessments are administered periodically, most often following weeks of instruction. In most instances the goal of a summative assessment is to evaluate student learning at the end of an instructional unit by comparing the student's performance against some standard or benchmark.

Examples of summative assessments include, but certainly are not limited to, final and mid-term exams, and unit tests. Summative assessments also include high stakes tests. Information from summative assessments can be used to inform instruction when students or instructors use it to guide their subsequent efforts and activities, such as when a teacher teaches a unit again in the future or immediately reteaches some or all of a unit based on the results from a summative assessment.

Criterion- and Norm-Referenced Assessment

The terms "criterion-" and "norm-referenced assessment" address the standards that are used to evaluate a student's performance on an assessment. A criterion-referenced assessment compares a student's performance to a predetermined performance level on a targeted learning outcome, such as whether a student is able to name all twenty-six lowercase letters of the alphabet. Criterion-referenced assessments are a mainstay of intensive small group instruction. A norm-referenced assessment compares a student's assessment results to an appropriate target group (e.g., other students the same grade), such as whether a student's score met or exceeded the scores of 75 percent or more of the students in their grade.

Progress Monitoring and Students' Levels and Rates of Learning

Progress monitoring involves an assessment of all of the skills that a student is to learn during the school year. Progress monitoring assessments address all of the skills a student must master and not just the skills that are covered in the current unit of instruction. Additionally, these assessments are conducted to determine a student's level and rate of learning. A progress monitoring assessment is also referred to as a general outcome measure. As is the case with other assessments, data obtained from progress monitoring are used to evaluate a teacher's instructional effectiveness and to inform instruction.

A student's level of learning can be thought of as the amount, or scope, of a curriculum that they have learned, whereas their rate of learning refers to how quickly the student learns new content. To the extent that a curriculum is vertically or horizontally sequenced, the level of learning refers to an arrangement where the learning of certain skills is to precede the learning of others. Thinking in terms of grade levels, at the end of the school year when a fourth grade student shows, on an assessment, that they have mastered only first-grade math skills, the student would be said to be performing at a lower level than a classmate who has demonstrated mastery of the fourth-grade math skills.

One's rate of learning refers to the ratio of the number of new skills learned per unit of time. For example, if twelve new skills were learned in six weeks, then the rate of learning would be two skills per week (twelve skills:six weeks is two skills:one week).

Quantitative, Qualitative, and Anecdotal Data

Quantitative data is information about quantities; that is, information that can be measured and written down with numbers. Some examples of quantitative data are one's height and weight. Quantitative assessment involves data that are mathematically computed and summarized, such as the mean, median, and mode for a set of scores that concern a class's history exam.

Qualitative assessments generate descriptive, non-numerical information about things. This information pertains to features and attributes of a phenomenon, such as whether a person's outward disposition appears to be confident or bewildered. Because this type of information cannot actually be measured, qualitative assessments provide descriptions that tend not to be as precise as quantitative data.

Finally, anecdotal assessment essentially involves the telling of a story. Quite often teachers are encouraged to record anecdotal data, which means they are to write a narrative in which they document the events they observed about a phenomenon of interest.

RATIONALE FOR ASSESSMENT: INFORMING INSTRUCTION OR ACTING AS A BARRIER

There are two basic purposes of assessment, which can exist separately or in combination. One purpose is to inform instruction, whereas the other is to serve as a barrier, or function as a gatekeeper, in terms of the outcomes some entity does or does not receive based on the results of an assessment.

When assessment informs instruction, it means that the assessment data are used by the teacher when they make decisions about how to present instruction differently from how they previously did with the expectation that the new way will be more effective and efficient.[1] Assessments can inform instruction in one of two ways. One way is by providing information about students' behaviors. The other way is providing information about the teacher's behavior.

When assessment serves as a barrier, or gate keeper, it means that the data are used to determine whether either an advantageous or adverse consequence—for either a student, teacher, or a school—will be applied. Examples for a student would be promotion to the next grade versus retention in the current grade, and the awarding, or not, of a standard high school diploma. An example for a school might be receiving a designation that would allow for financial rewards to be paid to the staff versus the reassignment or removal of administrators and other staff.

Although it is important for you to be aware of the many issues that pertain to the assessment of students, the primary focus of assessment that is specific to intensive small group instruction is as a tool to inform instruction. This issue is central to the following discussion about assessment that is most relevant to intensive small group instruction.

ASSESSMENTS SPECIFIC TO INTENSIVE SMALL GROUP INSTRUCTION

Two types of assessment that would be appropriate for students who are being provided intensive small group instruction are general outcome measures and assessments that are directly aligned with targeted learning objectives that address a subcomponent of a Common Core State Standard. Often these assessments are probes.

General Outcome Measures

General outcome measures address an entire curriculum. They provide meaningful data but may not be the most ideal type of assessment for students with significant, persistent learning challenges. Reasons why this may prove to the case include the following.

1. General outcome measures probably are not sensitive to the micro growth of students with intensive instructional needs.
2. The data obtained from these measures may not accurately inform instruction. For example, if a student incorrectly answers two of the three basic addition facts that are presented on the measure, then a teacher probably can conclude that the student needs to receive instruction that addresses this academic task. However, the teacher does not know which facts that student does not know, and does not want to spend valuable academic learning time presenting instruction that pertains to targeted learning outcomes that a student has mastered.
3. These measures most likely do not address functional tasks.
4. The time students spend completing these measures is time that cannot be used to present instruction. If the measures do not appreciably inform instruction, this trade off may not be worthwhile.
5. For some students who have participated in a relatively high number of assessment activities, having to complete a general outcome measure may serve as an aversive antecedent event for the subsequent display of inappropriate behavior.

Although general outcome measures may not be the most ideal type of assessments for students with significant, persistent learning challenges, this does not mean that they have no value for these students. Rather, the information presented previously is an attempt to put the use of these measures with these students in proper perspective. Doing so once again highlights the need for a teacher to be cognizant about how their individual work fits into a school's work scope.

General outcome measures are useful in the following ways for students who exhibit significant, persistent learning challenges.

1. These measures are useful to parents who readily comprehend data that are reported in terms of grade-level equivalents.

2. With respect to a student's level and rate of learning, general outcome measures provide information about one's level of learning.
3. Use of a general outcome measure keeps everyone—students, parents, and staff—focused on the level at which we want students to perform. Their use helps guard against setting low expectations for students who have a history of being challenged to master grade-level content.

Assessments Directly Aligned to Targeted Learning Objectives

These assessments cover less curriculum content than a general outcome measure, but the content is covered in more depth in that more items per learning objective are presented. This circumstance increases a teacher's confidence in the validity of the data that are obtained from the assessment.

Additionally, these assessments only address the content that a student is working to master by way of intensive small group instruction. This means that a student will not spend time engaged in assessment activities that are not related to the instruction they are receiving. Instead, the time can be spent in instruction. Hence, two advantages of these types of assessment are that

1. the resulting data readily informs instruction because it is directly tied to the content that is being taught; and
2. these assessments present students who most likely have experienced noteworthy, repeated failures on tests with a relatively high probability that they will experience some amount of success. This situation might enhance a student's self-esteem and result in them beginning to see themselves as capable. Further, if, as is discussed in the following, a probe is conducted at the outset of a small group session, the probe could function as an antecedent-based intervention for a student to enter the location where small group instruction is presented with a "can do, will do" attitude.

Probes

A probe is a type of assessment that is based on an alignment with a student's targeted learning objectives. Thus, probes, which are also referred to as skill checks, are particularly useful as a component of intensive small group instruction.

What Is a Probe?

A probe is a type of assessment that is designed to obtain data (i.e., information) about a student's performance in terms of a learning objective. For example, if the learning objective stipulates that the student will rote count from one to five, a probe would be designed so as to require the student to exhibit this behavior (or as much of the behavior that he has acquired). To conduct the probe, the teacher could simply present the task directive, "Start at one and count to five."

Features of Probes

Generally speaking, probes that are used in conjunction with intensive small group instruction have the following features.

1. They are short, which means they have relatively few items and can be administered in several minutes or less.
2. They are easy to administer and score.
3. They have a representative number of items that are directly aligned to a learning objective as opposed to a curriculum standard that is stated in more encompassing terms with respect to the content it covers,[2] which means it is a curriculum-based measurement.
4. To allow for a determination of a student's mastery of the targeted learning outcome, a probe is criterion-referenced rather than norm-referenced. Often this criterion must be met across multiple days or sessions (e.g., across three consecutive sessions or four out of five consecutive school days).
5. This aspect of the criterion increases confidence in the reliability and validity of the data obtained.
6. Additionally, this aspect of the criterion is a measure of task maintenance.
7. A probe has its task directive align with the observable, measurable behavior that is stated in the learning objective (e.g., state, spell, read, identify). Hence, during guided practice the task directive should match how the task has been modeled by the teacher.
8. Probes can be, and many times are, teacher-made and individualized in terms of the content covered and how the probe is administered.
9. Their administration often involves providing students reinforcement for their effort rather than feedback about correct or incorrect responding so that the same probe can be repeatedly administered to the same student.
10. The teacher employs simple, concise language in the directive or directions.
11. Probes can incorporate measures of task generalization with the use of controlled variance. Controlled variance is a strategy that involves systematically modifying one or two aspects of the instructional or assessment setting each day with the intent of having a student either learn or perform a task across different persons, conditions, or locations/settings.

An example would be having a student practice reading high frequency words using a different font style and font size across two different days.

When to Administer Probes

As a result of these features, probes are particularly well suited for use as one part of intensive small group instruction. They can be administered at a point in time when a session is conducted, or at another time outside of the scheduled session. The following considerations need to be taken into account when deciding upon the point in time to administer a probe.

1. How the task directive is to be presented. If the teacher needs to orally repeat a directive at the start of each trial (e.g., the teacher presents a picture of a clothing item and says, "Name this picture"), then the probe probably will be administered outside of the small group session. Reasons for this include the fact that administering this type of probe would be distracting to the other students in the group and having to administer several types of these probes in one session would take too much time away from instruction.
2. If the directive consists of one simple oral directive or written directions (that the teacher may have to read aloud to the students), then this situation increases the chances that the probe can be administered during the time allocated for intensive small group instruction.
3. The type of student response that is required. If a student is required to say each response out loud, then this increases the chances that the probe will need to be administered at a point in time outside of the small group session for reasons akin to those noted previously. Likewise, if the student needs to respond using a mode that must be observed by the teacher, then there is an increased likelihood that the probe will need to be administered outside of the time allocated for the session.

    This may be the case for a student who demonstrates limited speech and is not proficient at using an augmentative communication system. To indicate their knowledge of the names for numerals, the student may be shown three numeral cards simultaneously and directed to touch the card with the target numeral.
4. If independent, written responses are required or a student must circle an answer on a multiple choice assessment, then there is a higher probability that the probe can be administered during the time allocated for intensive small group instruction.
5. The configuration of the location where intensive small group instruction is being presented. In some instances, the confines of the location will

be prohibitive to conducting probes. There will not be enough space to position needed materials and conduct two activities simultaneously such that they would not be disruptive to each other. For instance, the teacher could not conduct a probe with one student while two other students completed an assignment independently.
6. The timing of the probe relative to when relevant small group instruction has been presented. If a probe is conducted at some point during the time that has been allocated for the small group session, the teacher will have to decide when to conduct the probe relative to the instruction presented.
7. If the teacher conducts the probe near, or at, the end of the lesson, it is possible that a student will attain a relatively high score because they have been able to retain the content in short-term memory. Conversely, if the teacher conducts the probe near, or at, the very outset of the session—before any instruction has been presented—then they can be more confident that the student's performance reflects mastery and retention of the targeted learning outcome. This confidence would be related to the fact that the student has been one or more days removed from the presentation of instruction (if, in fact, this is the case).
8. When a probe is conducted outside of the time that has been allocated for small group instruction, the teacher will need to consider how to address any variable that could impact the validity of the assessment. That is to say, the teacher needs to present the probe under conditions that are similar to the conditions that have been in place while the student is working to master the targeted learning outcome. Everything from the environmental arrangement to the use of materials and the way that the task is presented should not differ markedly.
9. While a teacher wants to account for a student's ability to demonstrate task generalization, generalizing one's performance is a matter of degree. Unless noteworthy task generalization is what is being assessed, conducting probes outside of the time allocated for small group instruction, and perhaps in a new location, needs to ensure that the data obtained are not more attributable to the unique circumstances of the probe than they are to the student's actual ability to demonstrate behavior that is indicative of mastery—or lack thereof—of the targeted learning outcome. This topic was addressed during the discussion of controlled variance.

Individualizing Probes

Probes are to be individualized. This means that they are to reflect the unique circumstances of each student who is a member of the small group. Accordingly, the following issues may be relevant.

1. If the group is heterogeneous the teacher will be challenged to schedule the time they will need to appropriately conduct the probes. Aside from the targeted learning objectives they address, the probes can differ on a wide range of variables, including how the teacher presents the task directive, each student's mode of responding, the types of materials that are used, the type of data that are being recorded in accordance with the dimension of behavior that is being assessed (e.g., frequency, rate, latency, duration, locus, topography, force/intensity), and the total number of items that comprise the assessment.[3]
2. Introducing the probe in a way that is consistent with the other elements that comprise the lesson plan that is being used. For instance, the elements of a direct instruction lesson plan were introduced in chapter 3 and were revisited in chapter 5. If a probe was added to this lesson plan format, introducing and conducting the probe would need to be consistent with all of the other elements of the lesson plan.
3. Hence, probes could be introduced in a manner similar to a teacher's statement of the learning objective for the lesson. The teacher could say, "Now you are going to show me what you know about adding two numbers. I am going to give you a piece of paper that has twenty addition problems (single-digit addend plus single-digit addend) and you are to write the sum for each problem."
4. Further, the teacher could explain the contingencies that will be employed for the student's behaviors. As was noted previously, the teacher could elect to not present any consequence that pertains to whether a student's answer is correct or incorrect. Rather, the teacher will present a consequence (e.g., a reinforcer) based upon the teacher's evaluation of the effort a student put forth.

TANGENTIAL MEASURES OF STUDENT PROGRESS

Until now, this discussion about assessment has focused, primarily, on attaining data specific to a student's mastery of targeted learning outcomes. This means that the focus has been on a student's acquisition of academic knowledge or skills, or school social behaviors.

However, a teacher needs to consider the merit of collecting data about other features of a student's progress. Three of these features—rate of learning, maintenance, and generalization—are discussed next.

Rate

As has been noted previously, a student's level of achievement and rate of learning may be assessed. Rate of learning is defined as the quantifiable amount of content mastered during a unit of time (e.g., learning to read ten high frequency words in twenty instructional days, or one word every two days). Small group instructional arrangements allow for a more detailed analysis of students' rates of learning. For instance, to assess a student's rate of learning, one or more of the following dimensions of instruction may be measured:

1. Number of sessions to criterion;
2. Number of trials to criterion;
3. Number/percent of errors to criterion;
4. Minutes of instructional time to criterion; and
5. Other: Dimensions of behavior, such as response latency (i.e., the amount of time between the presentation of the task directive and when the student makes a response).

These measures highlight the necessity for teachers to remain mindful of the need to continually question why they are collecting data through assessments. Collecting data to address the preceding items will involve a labor-intensive process that might cause teachers to question why they should collect it.

However, if the resulting data confirm that a student requires many trials and sessions to master a remedial targeted learning outcome, then these data may inform the student's individualized education program team that they need to expend much time and effort deciding upon the curriculum that should be taught to the student. An individualized education program team must be mindful about the upper limit that is set to the time that is available to present instruction. The length of the school year and each school day combine to establish this limit. A student's relatively low rate of learning will serve to highlight the fact that a curriculum can delineate more content students should be taught than there is time to teach it.

Maintenance

Periodically, data must be collected to verify that students are maintaining the knowledge and skills they acquired by meeting the criterion for mastery of a targeted learning outcome. Maintenance could be measured by having students complete a portion of a general outcome measure that assesses content they have mastered.

Generalization

A key measure of the effectiveness of small group instruction is the extent to which a student is able to perform a task in settings aside from the small group. Aspects of generalization include performing the task across different persons, settings, materials, or some combination of these three facets of task performance. Generalization also involves performing the same skill across subtopics within a subject matter area (e.g., generalizing regrouping from addition and subtraction problems to multiplication and division problems).

In terms of academic content, acquiring the ability to generalize one's performance permits a student to participate in a more typical instructional setting, such as a large group arrangement in a general education classroom. For example, the primary reason for providing what are referred to as Tier 2 and Tier 3 services in a small group arrangement in a multi-tier system of support is to teach a student skills that will enable them to return to the general education classroom—a setting with a large group arrangement. Here, the student is expected to learn, forevermore, at an expected rate from the high-quality instruction that is presented by the general education teacher.

Regarding functional content, the purpose of instruction is to enable a student to perform the tasks and activities in settings outside of what is considered to be school grounds. These non-school locations might include a personal residence, place of employment, commercial location (e.g., a grocery store), or a public facility, such as the local post office.

ENSURING VALID INFORMATION IS OBTAINED FROM ASSESSMENTS

When a teacher administers an assessment, they will want to do their utmost to obtain valid data. This means that the data are an accurate reflection of a student's performance of a targeted learning outcome.

There is a chance that the assessment data for students who demonstrate significant, ongoing learning challenges will be invalid simply because the student does not possess what are referred to as test-taking skills. Hence, the following discussion focuses on issues that a teacher may need to address for the purpose of ensuring that a student's misunderstanding of how to complete an assessment does not adversely impact the validity of the data obtained about the student's performance of the targeted learning outcome.

1. Whether the way that the student responds is directly and appropriately related to the behavior that is stated in the learning objective, or targeted learning outcome. When a teacher conducts a probe, they need to be certain that the behavior called for in the assessment matches the behavior that is called for in the learning objective. Furthermore, as the student

is receiving instruction, they need to be required to exhibit this type of behavior.

For instance, a learning objective that states a student will identify the correct response should result in a student being required to emit some type of recognition response during both instruction and assessment (e.g., circle the correct answer to a multiple choice question or touch the card on which a correct answer is displayed among a field of four cards). In the same way, a learning objective that says a student will name something correctly should result in a student being required to emit a generative response during both instruction and assessment (e.g., say or write the name of a picture of an article of clothing).

These instances highlight the need to address a student's vocabulary skills, particularly vocabulary that is specific to the conduct of a probe as an assessment. Chances are that one or more students in a small group who exhibit significant, persistent challenges mastering academic content will not know the meaning of some of the terms that are commonly used during assessments. This might result in them not knowing how to respond to a directive in a manner that unequivocally demonstrates to the teacher the answer that they intended to give.

2. The intentionality of a student's response. This refers to whether a student emits a response—whether correct or incorrect—that leaves no doubt in an examiner's mind that it was the one the student intended to make. If a student quickly makes one response and then just as quickly changes the response in a way that indicates the second response is the one they intended to make, the instructor may doubt the validity of the student's second response.

After touching one response card, a student repeatedly and forcefully taps a second card that is among the response choices in an attempt to indicate that this was the choice they really wanted to make.

After naming a picture incorrectly, the student immediately corrects themselves and says emphatically, "No, I meant to say that is a picture of an arm, not a leg."

3. The manner in which the assessment item is presented. There are a number of features pertaining to the way that an assessment item is presented that must be attended to for the purpose of enhancing the validity of the assessment. These include the vocabulary used, the placement of multiple response choices such that a certain placement indicates which choice is usually the correct answer (e.g., B is most often the correct answer to a multiple choice question), non-verbal or verbal indicators from the teacher (e.g., looking at the card with the correct answer), and alterations to assessment materials that indicate which answer is correct (e.g., a blemish or bent corner on a response card).

Considering the relevance of these issues to an assessment's validity, a teacher may determine that it is necessary to provide a student with explicit, systematic instruction on test-taking behaviors. These behaviors might include:

1. How to execute the exact behavior that is called for by the vocabulary in the task directive (e.g., pointing instead of touching; drawing a line from an item in the left-hand column [e.g., a term] to an item in the right-hand column [e.g., a definition]).
2. Any behavior that is appropriate to the task directive (e.g., an isolated finger point or touching an answer choice may be an appropriate behavior in response to each of these task directives: Point, Touch, Show me, Find).
3. How to engage in various response behaviors, such as making and using an isolated finger point, controlling a computer mouse, using a touch screen, and filling in the answers on a bubble sheet.
4. An appropriate wait response. This might include a sequence of behaviors, such as scanning all of the response choices once or twice and then indicating one's choice with an isolated finger point. This behavior is incompatible with the impulsiveness that is demonstrated by some students. It also allows some students to take the time they need to cognitively process both the task directive and their desired response.
5. Features of intentional behavior. Some students need to be taught how to make responses without hesitancy or quick corrections.
6. Relevant self-regulating behaviors, such as reviewing one's work to ensure that the student has answered all of the items on a probe.

A SCHOOL'S ASSESSMENT MILIEU AND ACCOMMODATIONS

Assessment Milieu

In the present era of school accountability, all students must participate in annual measures of achievement. Additionally, because most students who will receive intensive small group instruction also will be in general education classrooms, they will participate in the assessments that are administered in these locations. The various assessments that are conducted across a school comprise what can be called a school's assessment milieu. This milieu includes the following assessment activities:

1. Informal assessments that readily inform daily instruction (e.g. anecdotal data);

2. Mastery measurements that are used to assign grades (e.g., end of unit or chapter tests, mid-term and final exams, long-term projects such as a term paper);
3. High stakes tests and related assessments (e.g., subject area state tests and related exams that must be passed to earn a standard high school diploma); and
4. Assessments required for special education programming (e.g., functional behavioral assessments, eligibility determination evaluations).

As has been mentioned several times previously, one goal of this chapter is to provide an explanation of assessment as it pertains to the intensive small group instruction that some students are being provided while simultaneously explaining how this assessment fits within the larger context of all of a school's assessment activities. The main reason this relationship is highlighted here is that it naturally leads to a discussion about testing accommodations.

Because numerous students who will receive intensive small group instruction will be provided testing accommodations as part of their special education programming, teachers who present this instruction need to be knowledgeable about this topic and consider how it might apply to the assessment component of their small group instruction.

Testing Accommodations

The collection of certain assessment data will involve accommodations that are provided on behalf of certain students with disabilities. Accommodations involve a change to the conditions under which an assessment is conducted and are intended to result in a more valid indication of a student's performance than would otherwise be the case without their use.

For example, if a student's specific learning disability impairs their ability to read, the student's performance on a math test that required them to read word problems might not be a valid representation of their math skills (both math calculation and reasoning) and more a representation of their limited reading skills. Similarly, the performance of a student with a physical disability that impairs fine motor skills and ability to produce legible text on an English composition exam might not be a valid measure of their ability to actually compose an essay.

Accommodations can address the following variables: time to complete a task, the manner in which the task is presented, a student's mode of responding, and setting arrangements. The purpose for providing a testing accommodation is to ensure that a student's performance is a valid reflection of their ability to perform a targeted skill. An accommodation is not provided to give the student an advantage relative to others who are taking the same test.

Time, Input, Student Response, and Setting

As was noted previously, accommodations involve one or more of four areas: the time that a student is given to complete a task, the manner in which the task is presented to the student, the mode of responding that is required from the student, and the arrangement of the setting in which the task is to be performed. The accommodations that are provided should be predicated on a specific student's needs rather than the fact that the student has been identified as having a particular disability (e.g., providing all students with a specific learning disability an accommodation of being tested in a small group arrangement). Examples of allowable accommodations are presented in the following.

Time. Accommodations that apply to the amount of time that a student will have to complete a test include providing the student with extended time (i.e., 1.5 times as long as allowed for others), permitting the student to take the test over multiple days, and embedding breaks during the time allotted for the test.

Input. Accommodations that apply to how test items are presented include reading the directions, test items, and passages to the student.

Response. Accommodations that apply to how the student will make responses to test items include allowing the student to type responses rather than write them by hand and dictating responses to a scribe.

Setting. Accommodations that apply to the features of the location in which a student completes a test could include placement in a small group or preferential seating, such as at the front of the room and facing the instructor.

CHAPTER 6 COMPREHENSION CHECK

Now that you have finished reading the chapter, you should be able to:

Differentiate between assessment, testing, and evaluation.
Define the following types of assessment: formal, informal, criterion-referenced, and norm-referenced.
Explain what is meant by the phrase, "assessment informs instruction."
Discuss the scope of a general outcome measure and its relevance to a student who receives intensive small group instruction.

Describe the use of probes, or skill checks, with respect to the provision of intensive small group instruction.

Explain why some students may need to receive explicit instruction regarding what are referred to as "test-taking skills," and the relevant matters that may need to be addressed.

List three tangential aspects of student learning (i.e., aspects other than skill acquisition) that are important to assess with respect to the provision of small group instruction.

Explain the purpose of testing accommodations.

Provide examples from each of the following categories of testing accommodations: time, input, student response, and setting.

NOTES

1. National Center on Response-to-intervention. *RTI Implementer Series: Module 2: Progress Monitoring-Training Manual* (Washington, DC: U.S. Department of Education, Office of Special Education Programs, National Center on Response-to-intervention, 2012).

2. National Center on Intensive Intervention (NCII) at American Institutes for Research, *Data-Based Individualization: A Framework for Intensive Intervention* (ERIC Clearinghouse, 2013).

3. Mitchell L. Yell and David F. Bateman, "Endrew F. v. Douglas County School District (2017) FAPE and the US Supreme Court," *TEACHING Exceptional Children* 50, no. 1 (2017): 7–15.

Chapter Seven

Teaching Functional Content by Way of Small Group Instruction

OVERVIEW

The content that is presented in this chapter addresses two noteworthy topics with respect to small group instruction. One topic is special education. In particular, the provision of special education services is explained in terms of its relationship to small group instruction that is presented to students with disabilities and students who have not been determined to be eligible to receive special education services but have been identified as needing small group instruction. The second topic is presenting instruction that addresses what are referred to as functional skills to students with disabilities in a small group arrangement.

These are also referred to as life skills or activities of daily living, which involve tasks that enable one to meet the demands of post-secondary education, employment, and independent living, resulting in the maintenance of one's health, safety, and welfare.[1] Examples include completing personal hygiene tasks (e.g., brushing one's teeth, bathing/showering, toileting); meal preparation, including shopping for groceries; and accessing public services (e.g., riding public transportation, accessing the post office).

Key points from the chapter include the following:

1. Rather than referring to special education as a singular program into which a student with a disability is placed, it is more accurate to refer to special education as a process that results in the provision of services that are designed to enable a student to make appropriate progress in light of their particular circumstances. In most cases this progress will result in a student receiving passing marks as they advance from grade to grade.

2. Students who receive special education services are to be provided individualized instruction. This concept is not a mandate for every student with a disability to be taught in a 1:1 arrangement. Rather, it refers to matters such as the content, methodology, and delivery of instruction that are employed to address a student's unique needs.
3. The school programs for students with disabilities must address their present levels of performance regarding their academic achievement and functional performance.
4. Academic achievement refers to a student's attainment of targeted learning outcomes in traditional subject matter areas including math, English/language arts, and science, whereas functional performance refers to a student's attainment of knowledge and skills, such as being able to do a load of laundry, that enable the student to live as independently as possible in their community.
5. Small group arrangements can be used to teach students functional skills. In fact, valid reasons for using these arrangements include cost savings and the need for instructional efficiency given the limited amount of time that is available to teach these skills.
6. The basic elements of effective small group instruction that derive from those that comprise high-quality instruction in large group arrangements in general education classrooms (e.g., appropriate environmental arrangements, successful time management) also apply to the teaching of functional skills in small group arrangements.
7. Reasons why there is a relatively limited knowledge base for teaching students functional content include a history of using means testing for the purpose of permitting students with disabilities to attend a public school, the fact that most students who receive special education services experience what are considered to be mild disabilities that do not manifest as a need to receive instruction about functional content, a curriculum focus on academic content (e.g., the Common Core State Standards [CCSS]), school policies that restrict the presentation of community-based instruction, and parent involvement—assumed or otherwise—in the teaching of functional content.
8. Practical considerations that pertain to teaching students functional content include establishing a location where the instruction will be presented, unique expenses, realizing instructional efficiency by teaching a naturally occurring sequence of functional activities, and teaching students safety skills.
9. Assessment of a student's mastery of functional content can address matters including the student's ability to complete the steps that comprise a task analysis for an activity, use of a rubric to evaluate the performance

of an activity, a student's acquisition of related declarative knowledge, and measures of social validity.
10. The philosophical construct of inclusion and its implications for the use of small group instruction to teach students with disabilities functional content could serve as the basis for an entire book. Hence, only a few of the most salient issues are addressed in this chapter.

INTRODUCTION

Teaching certain students functional content must be addressed (appropriately and adequately) if the purpose of the Individuals with Disabilities Education Act (IDEA), which also has been referred to as its mission statement,[2] is to be realized. The purpose of the IDEA is to prepare students with disabilities for further education, employment, and independent living. "Further" means during their post-secondary years. Thus, addressing the need to teach certain students with disabilities functional content will mean that their teachers—along with the students' parents, school administrators, and members of their individualized education program (IEP) team—will have to account for the following issues:

1. The students who are eligible to receive special education services and need to be taught functional content. The IDEA states that each student's IEP team must document their present levels of academic achievement and functional performance.[3] Subsequently, measurable annual goals must be written for the functional content that the team determines a student needs to be taught, and appropriate services are to be provided to enable the student to achieve the goals. Among other things this means that a student's IEP team may decide that even though the student is eligible to receive special education services, they do not need to be taught functional content as part of school programming.
2. The functional content to be taught. Functional content is not operationally defined in the IDEA nor its accompanying regulations because this content covers an exceedingly wide range of knowledge and skills. Whereas academic achievement refers to a student's performance in traditional subject matter areas that have been relatively well defined, such as mathematics and science, a student's functional needs may include numerous activities (e.g., shopping for groceries, using public transportation) that are to be performed in a wide range of settings, many of which are locations beyond a school's physical campus or entities that are considered to be an extension of this campus (e.g., a school bus).

The terms "activities of daily living" and "life skills" are commonly used to refer to functional tasks. Essentially, functional content refers to all of the knowledge and skills that concern the tasks a person performs from the moment they are awake until they go back to sleep to be able to function interdependently as a member of their community.

3. The location where the functional content will be taught. Functional content can be taught in a school and in locations throughout the community. However, for a number of reasons, including budgetary constraints and local school district policies, opportunities to present instruction in community locations may be limited or non-existent. Although simulations may be contrived in a school or on school grounds (e.g., a mini store may be created to allow for the teaching of shopping skills), these arrangements increase the probability that students will not be able to generalize what they learn.

4. The time when functional content will be taught. Ideally this content will be taught at naturally occurring times and in naturally occurring places. For instance, a student will be taught how to wash their hands at the kitchen sink before they are taught how to prepare a meal. The student will then be taught how to use utensils when they consume the meal. Afterwards, they will be taught clean-up skills that are specific to fixing and consuming a meal, and they also may be taught how to update the inventory of kitchen supplies in order to prepare for constructing the next grocery shopping list.

    Given how master daily school schedules are structured and that most students will participate in other academic and non-academic instructional activities in accordance with this master schedule, teachers may be challenged to consistently teach functional content at the times when certain activities of daily living are expected to occur. Further, as was discussed previously, it may not be realistic to expect that this content will be taught consistently in the typical locations where the activities are expected to occur.

    Consistently means providing the student with the number of repetitions, through the use of systematic instruction, that they will need to be provided to master the targeted functional content. This circumstance highlights the need to consider using the instructional efficiency strategies that are available when small group instruction is presented.

5. The way that functional content will be taught. Reviews[4] have identified evidence-based practices for teaching some functional content. An example is using constant time delay as an instructional strategy to teach a student how to purchase groceries.[5] However, a comprehensive database that aligns functional content with corresponding evidence-based practices does not exist.

In fact, given the tremendous amount of functional content that could be taught, as well as the ever-changing nature of this content (e.g., the evolving ways to make a cup of coffee or prepare eggs), it is unlikely that any such database will ever exist. Rather, a reasonable approach to teaching this content would be the application of a sound, procedural framework. The use of intensive small group instruction, as it has been presented in this book, is one such framework.

TEACHING FUNCTIONAL CONTENT AS ONE PART OF SPECIAL EDUCATION

Both the rationale for teaching some students with disabilities functional content and knowing how to do so are more understandable when they are explained with respect to the construct of special education. Hence, an appropriate starting point for discussing special education is to examine what could be characterized as some of the components of the foundation of special education. In this section, three of these components are highlighted.

Special Education as Access and Opportunity

The original version of what was to become the IDEA, the Education for All Handicapped Children Act[6] (EAHCA) that was passed in 1974, was crafted to provide students with disabilities access and opportunity with respect to a public education. The EAHCA was passed at a point in time when some students with disabilities were not permitted to attend a public school. Because it was reasoned that these students—who demonstrated significant intellectual disabilities—were not capable of learning, they were not allowed to attend school. The EAHCA sought to remedy this circumstance.

Further, it was argued by proponents of the legislation that other students with specific learning disabilities were in public schools but were not being provided the services they needed to give them an opportunity to attain the learning outcomes that were associated with the general education curriculum. The EAHCA addressed this matter as well.

Special Education Is a Process

These two distinct scenarios shed light on the complex nature of the design and implementation of special education services. Contrary to popular belief, special education services are not, in every single instance, intended to be provided to erase the academic achievement differences that exist between the students who receive these services and those who do not. In other words, the sole focus of special education is not necessarily to eliminate the gaps that may exist in the attainment of targeted learning outcomes by the students who receive these services and those who do not.

Rather, instead of thinking that the provision of special education services is designed to lead a student to a pre-determined outcome, such as the awarding of a standard high school diploma, special education should be thought of as allowing for a process that includes conducting evaluations to determine which students have disabilities and are in need of special education services, identifying learning outcomes that are appropriate for these students to work to attain, and providing general and special education services in ways that are believed to be necessary to enable a student to attain the outcomes.

This process allows special education to be many things for many students. This aspect of special education is realized through the development of an IEP for each student with a disability.

1. For a student with a specific learning disability that adversely affects their attainment of basic reading skills, special education services might consist of specialized instruction that results in the student acquiring these skills and subsequently progressing through the core curriculum such that they are awarded a standard high school diploma.
2. For a student with an intellectual disability that is characterized as significant and results in noteworthy challenges mastering basic academic skills (e.g., counting to ten and writing one's name) as well as independently performing what are referred to in the IDEA as functional tasks, also known as activities of daily living (e.g., getting dressed, preparing a meal), special education services might consist of instruction intended to teach the student these types of skills but only in the context of receiving supports concurrently from an adult. This arrangement is settled upon because those who design and implement this student's school program recognize that they will need support from others throughout their entire life.
3. For students whose intellectual disability is not nearly as significant, their special education services might consist of instruction that is intended to teach them basic academic content and functional tasks that the students would ultimately perform independently. Intensive small group instruction may be provided for this purpose.

Yet the diverse nature of special education is intended to ensure that the purpose of the IDEA, which has also been referred to as its mission statement, is realized by every student with a disability. The IDEA's purpose is to prepare students with disabilities for further education, employment, and independent living during their post-secondary years.

This discussion of special education as a process that leads to the provision of needed services addresses an often-heard misstatement by school personnel who say that a student with a disability "has been placed in special education." Arguably this statement causes one to think that the term "special education" refers to a location where a wholly separate set of rules and procedures have been established for the purpose of educating the student.

This scenario is analogous to saying that someone has been put in the hospital. This statement clearly refers to a location that is separate from the mainstream of society, is governed by some unique rules, and in which specialized services are provided.

The placement, meaning location, where a student with a disability is provided educational services is a topic worthy of discussion in its own right. In fact, it is a very important topic. However, it is one of a number of important topics that, considered altogether, result in what is referred to as an appropriate education for a student with a disability.

A Deeper Understanding of Special Education and Its Relationship to Individualized Instruction

Individualized Instruction

Designing and implementing appropriate special education services is a complex endeavor for no other reason than these services must be based on the unique needs of a particular student with a disability. In the IDEA this concept is called individualized instruction, and it is important to note that this concept is separate from providing a student instruction using a 1:1 pupil teacher ratio. It is possible that the services a student needs to receive will be provided in an arrangement that involves a 1:1 pupil:teacher ratio. However, the term "individualized instruction" does not, in and of itself, mean that this will be the default instructional arrangement for every child with a disability.

Individualized instruction refers to identifying the academic and functional content a child with a disability needs to be taught, providing the services the child needs to learn this content, and monitoring the child's progress toward its attainment. Given the fact that no two students are exactly the same, no two sets of special education services will be exactly the same.

Special Education Defined

Special education is defined in the IDEA as "specially designed instruction to meet the unique needs of a child with a disability." A fundamental understanding of special education, and the outcome a student might realize if special education services are provided, can be gained by analyzing the various components of the definition.

Within the definition for special education is the phrase "specially designed instruction," which refers to three aspects of the instruction that is presented to a child with a disability: the content, methodology, or delivery of instruction. When special education services are provided, one or more of these aspects of instruction has to be addressed so that the instruction that is presented to a child with a disability is noteworthy in some way compared to the instruction that is provided to same-age peers in the general education classroom.

For instance, a sixth-grade student who is receiving special education services to address their subpar performance in reading may be taught second-grade, rather than sixth-grade, reading content because the second-grade content serves as a foundation for higher level reading skills and is at the student's instructional level. A student with an intellectual disability may need to receive instruction that enables them to learn how to toilet himself independently. Regarding the uses of methodologies that might be considered to be special education, teachers may use American Sign Language as one method for communicating with a student who is deaf or Braille with a student who is blind.

Furthermore, the definition for special education states that it is to "meet the unique needs" of a child with a disability. Principally, this refers to the fact that the services that are provided to a child must be based on an examination of the child's distinct instructional needs more so than the child's particular disability. In other words, schools cannot simply offer a generic autism program for students with this disability.

The last part of the definition for special education—"child with a disability"—refers to a student, ages three to twenty-one, inclusive, who has been found to meet the eligibility criteria for the receipt of special education services. This means that, at a minimum, special education services are to be provided beginning the day an eligible child turns three years of age through the last day they are twenty-one. Furthermore, while the phrase "child with a disability" is used throughout the IDEA, it has been established that this phrase refers to all students who have been determined to be eligible to receive special education services, which would include middle and high school students who would be referred to more commonly as young adults.

FUNCTIONAL CONTENT

As has been noted previously, a student who is eligible to receive special education services may be taught functional content. A straightforward way to identify this content is to consider the activities you perform each day from the moment your alarm goes off until you go to bed later that evening, and that enable you to maintain yourself at home and in the larger community through activities such as orientation and mobility, work, citizenship (e.g., voting, getting a car tag), and maintaining a residence (e.g., shopping for groceries, fixing a meal, housekeeping).

Various issues that are central to teaching students who need to receive intensive small group instruction to learn functional content are discussed subsequently. These issues include addressing the dimensions of high-quality instruction, developing an appropriate curriculum, existing guidance for teaching this content, practical considerations that pertain to school-based instruction, and student performance assessment.

Relationship of the Elements of High-Quality Instruction to Functional Content Instruction

The dimensions of high-quality instruction that were identified and discussed in chapter 2 are applicable to teaching students functional content using a small group arrangement. In the following, each dimension is discussed in this context.

Before reading about these dimensions in terms of teaching functional content note that, for the purpose of this discussion, the content that is presented in this section is predicated on instruction occurring in natural contexts. These contexts may be a location at school, such as the cafeteria where food preparation activities can be taught, or a location in the community, such as a grocery store.

Additionally, the content that is presented in this section is predicated on the fact that each student will not have an opportunity to independently perform each step of the activity being taught. Whereas some functional tasks can only be taught using a 1:1 arrangement (e.g., teaching a student how to independently toilet), because the focus of this book is presenting instruction using small group arrangements, this section will focus on functional tasks that could be taught using a 1:1 arrangement but are not in light of a numerous practical considerations (e.g., time and money available for instruction).

Hence, in the discussion that follows it is understood that each student in the small group will have an opportunity to independently perform some steps of a functional task but will be expected to learn how to perform others by observing a peer. For example, a group of three students could participate in a grocery shopping lesson but they would, collectively, purchase the items from one list rather than items from three separate lists. Constraints, including the time available for instruction and the money available for making purchases, are reasons for this circumstance.

Thus, during the lesson when it is time to check out, one student would unload the cart while the other two observed, another student would pay the cashier while the other two observed, and one other student would take the bagged groceries to the vehicle while the other two observed.

The following discussion is illustrative rather than exhaustive. The broad array of situations that could be addressed makes an exhaustive discussion impractical.

1. *Environmental arrangement.* Creating safe, orderly instructional environments where functional content will be taught will present more of a challenge to a teacher simply because they will present this instruction in school and non-school locations that have fixed assets that either cannot be moved or that can be moved but not in a way that permits the teacher to make changes to the environmental arrangement in the same way that they can in their classroom. Features of the environment that the teacher might like to change to increase the probability that their instruction will be effective, but that they most likely will not be able to change, include the following:
  a. The design and use of floor and wall space;
  b. The climactic conditions (e.g., the temperature);
  c. The overall aesthetic appeal; and
  d. High-traffic areas (i.e., operationally defining and locating them, and then teaching students the rules for accessing them).

  Other features of the environmental arrangement that the teacher can address, to some degree, include the following:
  a. Clear lines of sight that account for existing fixtures. Given the nature of the functional content that is being taught, a teacher may have to deal with more existing features than usual. For example, they will not be able to reposition the washer and dryer in a laundromat, the checkout line in a grocery store, or the stove in a kitchen. Yet the teacher can control how the students are positioned in the group so that they can see the instruction that is presented.
  b. Limit potential distractions. As was stated previously, to ensure that each student attends to the instruction that is being presented the teacher may have to frequently employ prompts or an attention directive. Although the teacher most likely will not be able to use interventions that involve the strategic positioning of portable floor and desktop dividers, they can position students such that they sit or stand in locations that limit as many potentially distracting stimuli as possible.

c. Though some of the instructional materials will be quite different from the papers, pencils, and books that are used in a typical classroom, they still must be nearby and ready to use.
d. Use routines that support instruction. Incorporating routines will allow for successful time management, set the stage for the teaching of appropriate social behaviors, and enable the teacher to address some of the issues identified previously. For example, when teaching students how to prepare a sandwich, the teacher could establish a routine for getting needed items from drawers, cupboards, and the refrigerator; placing the items on a counter or a kitchen island; and cleaning and returning items, as needed, to their storage locations. This routine would address the matter of having instructional materials nearby and ready for use.

2. *Successful time management.* Within the time that has been allocated for teaching functional content the teacher will want to focus on maximizing both students' engaged and academic learning time. Because the teacher often will have little to no control over the arrangement of the environment for the purpose of alleviating potential distractions, they will have to develop and rely upon other means to ensure that students are attending to instruction and maximizing their engaged time.

One strategy would be to use prompts to elicit students' attending behaviors. Another strategy would be to repeatedly present an attention directive, as necessary, throughout a lesson.

When teaching functional content, the term "academic learning time" refers to the time that a student participates in instruction that pertains to functional content that is at their instructional level. In an activity, such as learning how to wash one's hands, the student's instructional level would be the steps the student was physically capable of performing but had not learned to perform independently.

The instructional level for related content, such as counting the correct number of oranges to purchase or naming items (e.g., a banana), could be determined as a result of administrations of assessment instruments whose results are reported in terms of a student's actual academic instructional level.

One strategy a teacher could employ to maximize a student's academic learning time would be to schedule them to be the student who was attempting to perform, rather than observe, the steps of the activity that were at their instructional level. A second strategy would be to prompt the student to attend to their peers during times other students were being instructed how to perform parts of the activity that are at the target student's instructional level for the purpose of increasing the chances that they would exhibit observational learning.

Most likely a teacher will not be required to follow a pacing guide that is associated with a scope and sequence that has been designed for a global functional curriculum. This circumstance will increase the probability that a teacher will be permitted to spend as much time as is needed teaching a student functional content that is at their instructional level. In terms of students' rates of learning the teacher will have to evaluate them as best they can based on comparable experiences, such as the students' rates of learning with respect to other targeted learning outcomes.

3. *Effective instructional strategies.* Others have documented instructional strategies (e.g., constant time delay, most-to-least prompting) that have proven, through research, to be effective in teaching students with disabilities functional content.[7] These strategies can serve as the basis for teaching functional content in a small group arrangement. The resulting instruction can possibly be made more effective and efficient with the additional use of the instructional strategies that were discussed in chapter 5.

4. *Focus on curriculum content.* Strategies for getting students to focus on curriculum content were addressed previously in the discussion about maximizing students' engaged and academic learning time. A point worth emphasizing is the use of strategies that are calculated to result in each student's demonstration of observational learning. Given the complexities involved with teaching functional content and that are discussed in this chapter, it is important that teachers know about ways to teach this content effectively and efficiently in small group arrangements.

5. *Valid, reliable assessment.* As is the case when teaching academic content the teacher will use valid, reliable assessment data to inform instruction and evaluate a student's progress. Probes, also known as skill checks, that are directly related to the learning objective for the functional content that is being taught are a likely method of assessment that will be used. They are discussed in detail in chapter 6.

Probes pertaining to functional activities often consist of a checklist of the steps a student needs to perform to successfully complete the entire activity. This listing of steps is called a task analysis. A challenge will be settling upon how to conduct a probe in a timely manner on behalf of each student.

The entire probe could be conducted separately with each student. However, if there are three students in a group then three probes would need to be conducted either during one session or across multiple sessions. Another way to conduct the probe would be to evenly split the steps that comprise an activity and assess each student according to their performance of the steps they were assigned. Students could then be rotated across the sets of partitioned steps. One full probe could be completed during a session and each student's overall performance data would be attained once enough sessions were conducted to enable the student to perform all of the steps that comprise the activity.

Curriculum Limits

Others have noted that IEP teams always can identify more skills that students with disabilities need to be taught than there is time available to teach them these skills—particularly students with moderate or more significant disabilities.[8] This circumstance is relevant in three ways to the teaching of functional content in small group arrangements.

One way is that it highlights the need to settle upon the functional content that can be taught. Presently there are no CCSS with respect to functional content. However, some publications, such as the Vineland Adaptive Behavior Scales[9] and the Brigance Diagnostic Inventory of Essential Skills,[10] are examples of what could be considered the equivalent of these standards in terms of functional content.

A second way is that it requires teachers to determine what functional content must be taught in a 1:1 arrangement and what content can be taught in a small group arrangement. Some functional content, such as dressing and toileting, cannot be taught using small group arrangements. However, certain aspects of some of this content might be. This may be the case when a class goes to the restroom.

During these instances some students may need to be taught appropriate social skills, such as how to look only straight ahead when standing at a men's urinal. These skills can be taught using small group instructional strategies (e.g., a student can learn how to look straight ahead by watching a classmate perform this behavior and then receive an appropriate contingency).

The third way is that it focuses a teacher's attention on figuring out how instructional efficiency can be maximized in terms of addressing functional and academic content simultaneously. A close examination and clear understanding of instruction that addresses functional content will reveal that this instruction provides an opportunity to simultaneously address functional and academic skills. In fact, this instruction presents opportunities for students to ascertain the purpose for learning and applying academic content.

For example, when a student is taught to do a load of laundry a number of academic skills can be taught during this activity, such as identifying colors, counting objects, and labeling items and actions (i.e., teaching vocabulary). Similarly, when a student is taught how to shop for groceries, they can be taught academic skills such as labeling food items, counting the number of items to put in the shopping cart, and making change.

Individualized Education Programs and Present Levels of Academic Achievement and Functional Performance

The discussion in the previous section applies, broadly, to students with disabilities who need to be taught functional content. This section briefly discusses functional curriculum matters that are specific to an individual.

One matter that is important for you to remain mindful of is the fact that a student's particular disability does not automatically disqualify or qualify them for the receipt of instruction that addresses functional content. For instance, a student with an autism spectrum disorder who demonstrates above grade-level academic achievement may also demonstrate noteworthy deficits in the performance of certain functional tasks, such as those necessary to live independently in a college dormitory (e.g., personal hygiene, grocery shopping, meal preparation, and housekeeping skills). This student's instructional needs, and not their particular disability, would be the reason for teaching him functional content.

A second matter is allocating time during the school day to teach these skills. For some students a noteworthy challenge is constructing a schedule that allows adequate time for teaching both academic and functional content.

A third matter involves the impact of functional content instruction on a student's inter-personal relationships with peers. Issues that might need to be addressed include the negative stigma peers may ascribe to students who receive this instruction and a student not being willing to participate in this instruction because of the way their peers view the situation.

A fourth matter is how functional and academic content will be intertwined, on a case-by-case basis, during instruction. Several examples of teaching functional content while simultaneously addressing academic content were presented previously. Whereas one example involved teaching a student to make change while learning how to shop for groceries, another example would be teaching a more academically capable student how to manage a household budget using a spreadsheet in addition to how to shop for groceries.

Reasons for Limited Knowledge About How to Teach Functional Skills

Although there is a clear requirement in the IDEA to at least consider teaching certain students functional content, there exists a number of reasons why school personnel struggle to know how to teach it. For instance, years ago one reason why students who needed to be taught functional content (particularly toileting skills) were not permitted to attend school was because school personnel did not see themselves as being required to teach this content.

Rather, they saw their instructional purview as only teaching academic content. Consequently, when a student was not able to toilet independently, they were refused entry to a school and would be permitted to enroll once someone else taught them this functional skill.[11] Thus, there is a historical bias against having teachers know how to teach functional content.

Numerous reasons why teachers are challenged to know how to teach functional content are explained in the following. When one considers these reasons, it is evident that there still exists a strong bias against having teachers teach functional content and a bias in favor of having them teach academic content. This situation underscores the need to consider how to address this content through efficient, small group instruction because, in general, there does not appear to be widespread support for addressing it despite the relevant stipulations in the IDEA.

1. Mostly published curricula, such as the CCSS, focus exclusively on academic content (in fact, the CCSS do not even address school social behaviors). Furthermore, the alternate achievement standards that are targeted for students for whom these standards are appropriate—and who are the students most likely to be identified as needing to be taught functional content—are tied to the CCSS.

    Similarly, locally developed curricula may include only academic content because the stakeholders who developed the curricula believe that schools should focus almost exclusively on teaching students this content. Hence, an emphasis has been, and continues to be, placed on preparing all educators to teach students academic knowledge and skills.

2. Most students with disabilities have what are characterized as mild disabilities, resulting in their need to receive special education services that enable the students to advance from grade to grade. This, of course, means that these services will focus on academic content. Even when these students have non-academic needs (e.g., a student with autism who needs to learn school social behaviors plus functional content), there is a realization that the school calendar sets upper limits on the content that can be taught. In other words, time spent teaching non-academic content will subtract from the time that is available to teach academic content.

3. Some school's policies prohibit, or significantly limit, staff and student access to off-campus locations that could serve as venues in which students are taught functional skills. In some instances, this will prevent any

realistic opportunity for teaching a functional activity, such as using many forms of public transportation—including buses, cabs, and subways.

These policies may not necessarily be meant to restrict students' instructional opportunities. Rather, the policies account for safety concerns. Regardless the reason for them, these policies limit teachers' opportunities to develop knowledge and skills regarding how to teach functional skills.

An alternative to community-based instruction are on-campus simulations. Given the learning characteristics that are exhibited by some of these students, on-campus simulations may not result in either these students' acquisition of the functional content or their ability to generalize their learning of it.

4. Teachers, when they were students in kindergarten through twelfth grade, most likely observed their teachers present small group instruction or received this type of instruction. Hence, the teachers can use these experiences as part of the basis for how they present small group academic instruction. Conversely, there is a low probability that they had such experiences with respect to functional content.

5. Much functional content is taught by parents who willingly do so because they would rather school personnel focus on teaching the academic content that parents have not been formally trained to teach. Consequently, there are lowered expectations for schools to teach this content.

Practical Considerations

Before a teacher can begin to present instruction that pertains to teaching students functional content, they must address a number of practical considerations. Some of these are identified subsequently. Most of them will have to be addressed in concert with school administrators and students' IEP teams.

1. The location where students will be taught functional content. Within a school or somewhere on its campus, atypical locations may be where the knowledge and skills that comprise a functional curriculum are taught. Atypical means that these locations are not usually thought of as places where students are provided formal instruction—let alone intensive small group instruction.

   This means that these locations will serve as the students' classrooms during the lessons and will need to be designed in accordance with the environmental arrangement principles that apply to high-quality instruction. Examples of these locations include the cafeteria's kitchen, restrooms, and the laundry room where a school's athletic uniforms are washed.

Authentic locations off school grounds may also be places where functional content is taught (e.g., a laundromat or an apartment that is rented by the school district). While the use of these locations involves a number of special considerations that are beyond the scope of this book, it is important to note that the use of these locations may enhance a student's ability to generalize what they learn when mastering functional content.

In turn, this circumstance may promote the attainment of the IDEA's purpose, or mission statement, which is to prepare students with disabilities for further education, employment, and independent living. Oppositely, use of atypical locations within a school setting likely will necessitate that more attention be paid to the use of generalization strategies.[12]

2. Expenses that are unique to the presentation of instruction that pertains to teaching students functional content. Expenses may include the costs for transportation to and from the location where small group, functional activities instruction will be presented; materials for performing the task (e.g., laundry detergent); and fees for using equipment (e.g., coin-operated washers and dryers).
3. Increasing instructional efficiency by teaching more than one functional activity during a session. For instance, several logically related functional activities could be taught during one well-planned session: using public transportation, shopping for groceries, and then preparing a meal. Not only can this arrangement increase the efficiency of instruction, but it also can mirror post-secondary independent living.
4. If community-based instruction is employed, requisite safety skills will need to be taught. One set of these skills involves the orientation and mobility skills that are necessary for safely moving throughout a location. This includes activities such as crossing a street as well as walking through a parking lot where cars are pulling into, and backing out of, parking spaces while also driving in erratic patterns.

Another set of safety skills includes those that may be needed should a student get separated from the group and be without adult supervision. In these instances it would be important for the student to know how to identify an employee of the establishment where instruction is being presented, present personal identification information to this employee or a first responder, and reject lures from strangers.

Assessment of Student Progress Upon Being Taught Functional Content

When most people think about assessing whether a student mastered the functional content they were taught, they probably only consider whether the student has learned to independently perform a life skill, such as preparing a sandwich or making a bed. Yet, because many students who will be taught this content will exhibit relatively significant disabilities, assessment that pertains to functional content instruction should be designed to measure numerous aspects of students' progress. Each item in the following identifies one aspect of student progress that can be measured, and at least one method for measuring it.

1. *Completion of the task analysis, either independently or with prompts.* A task analysis is a listing of the steps an individual must complete in order to perform the entire functional activity.

   One way to report a student's progress in this regard would be to calculate a percentage completion score. This score could be calculated by dividing the number of steps the student completed independently by the total number of steps in the task analysis. The result would then be multiplied by one hundred to obtain the percentage completion score.

2. *Total duration for task completion.* A measure of efficiency would be whether a student could correctly complete a functional activity in less time than they did previously. A stopwatch could be used to collect duration data.

3. *Rubric for performance quality.* The completion of some functional activities can be assessed in terms of the quality of the product that is produced. In these instances, a grading rubric that lists points to be awarded based on the quality standard that was met could be used. The points could be totaled to determine an overall score, and then an overall quality standard designation that is based on this score could be assigned (e.g., the product that was produced could be regarded as being of low, medium, or high quality).

   For instance, if a student was learning how to make a peanut butter and jelly sandwich, aspects of the finished product that could be assessed include whether there appeared to be a sufficient amount of peanut butter and jelly in the sandwich, the degree to which all of the ingredients were within the confines of the perimeters of the top and bottom slices of bread, and how someone who consumed the sandwich rated its taste. A rubric that contained descriptors of the quality standards for each of these aspects could be used to determine a rating of the overall quality of the sandwich.

4. *Acquisition of declarative knowledge* (e.g., correctly identifying or else naming the utensils and ingredients used during a cooking activity). This learning outcome could be assessed during the completion of a functional activity. For example, if a student was told to get a certain utensil that was stored among a group of different utensils, the teacher could score the student's response and subsequently calculate the percentage of times during the activity that the student correctly identified a utensil.

Outside of the performance of a functional activity, this learning outcome could be measured during a probe (see chapter 6). For instance, the teacher could conduct a short, two-minute probe during which they randomly presented five utensils three times each and directed the student to "Name this item." A percentage correct score could be calculated by dividing the total number of correct responses by fifteen and then multiplying this result by one hundred.

5. *Social validity.* Social validity is a construct that deals with qualitative aspects of functional content instruction. With respect to this instruction, social validity refers to how much worth people assign to the endeavor. These people might include the teacher who presents the instruction, the students who receive it, and their parents.

Examples of two aspects of a measure of the social validity of functional content instruction would be peoples' ratings of the importance of teaching the content and their satisfaction with the outcomes of the instruction. A Likert-type scale can be used to collect social validity data.

CHAPTER 7 COMPREHENSION CHECK

Now that you have finished reading the chapter, you should be able to:

Discuss how special education refers to the provision of services to students with disabilities as opposed to placement in a generic special education program.

Describe what the term "individualized instruction" means in terms of the elements that comprise the legal definition for special education.

Define the terms "academic achievement" and "functional performance."

List two reasons for using small group arrangements to teach functional content.

List three reasons why there may be limited knowledge available to a teacher regarding how to teach functional content.

Discuss three practical considerations a teacher may have to address when they teach functional content.

List and discuss two types of assessment that can be used to measure a student's progress when a teacher presents functional content instruction.

NOTES

1. The IRIS Center, The Pre-Referral Process: Procedures for Supporting Students with Academic and Behavioral Concerns, last modified 2008, https://iris.peabody.vanderbilt.edu/module/preref/.

2. P. W. Wright and Esq Pamela Darr Wright, *Wrightslaw: Special Education Law*, second edition (Virginia: Harbor House Law Press, 2006).

3. Individuals with Disabilities Education Act of 1975, 20 U. S. C. § 1400 et seq. (1975).

4. Samuel L. Odom, Lana Collet-Klingenberg, Sally J. Rogers, and Deborah D. Hatton, "Evidence-Based Practices in Interventions for Children and Youth with Autism Spectrum Disorders," *Preventing School Failure: Alternative Education for Children and Youth* 54, no. 4 (2010): 275–82; Connie Wong, Samuel L. Odom, Kara Hume, Ann W. Cox, Angel Fettig, Suzanne Kucharczyk, and T. R. Schultz, *Evidence-Based Practices for Children, Youth, and Young Adults with Autism Spectrum Disorder* (Chapel Hill: The University of North Carolina, Frank Porter Graham Child Development Institute, Autism Evidence-Based Practice Review Group, 2014).

5. Timothy E. Morse and John W. Schuster, "Teaching Elementary Students with Moderate Intellectual Disabilities How to Shop for Groceries," *Exceptional Children* 66, no. 2 (2000): 273–88.

6. Education for All Handicapped Children Act, Pub. L No. 94-142, (1975).

7. Kathleen A. Cronin and Anthony J. Cuvo., "Teaching Mending Skills to Mentally Retarded Adolescents," *Journal of Applied Behavior* Analysis, 12, no. 3 (1979): 401–06; John W. Schuster and Ann K. Griffen, "Using Constant Time Delay to Teach Recipe Following Skills," *Education and Training in Mental Retardation* (1991): 411–19; Mark Wolery, Melinda Jones Ault, and Patricia Munson Doyle, *Teaching Students with Moderate to Severe Disabilities: Use of Response Prompting Strategies*, edited by Naomi Silverman (White Plains, NY: Longman Publishing Group, 1992).

8. Mark Wolery, Melinda Jones Ault, and Patricia Munson Doyle, *Teaching Students with Moderate to Severe Disabilities: Use of Response Prompting Strategies*, edited by Naomi Silverman (White Plains, NY: Longman Publishing Group, 1992).

9. Sara S. Sparrow, Domenic V. Cicchetti, and Celline A. Saulnier, "Vineland Adaptive Behavior Scales, (Vineland-3)," *Antonio: Psychological Corporation* (2016).

10. Albert Henry Brigance, *Brigance Inventory of Essential Skills* (North Billerica, MA: Curriculum Associates, 2019).

11. H. Rutherford Turnbull III and Ann P. Turnbull, *Free Appropriate Public Education: The Law and Children with Disabilities* (Denver, CO: Love Publishing Company, 1998).

12. Trevor F. Stokes and Donald M. Baer, "An Implicit Technology of Generalization 1," *Journal of Applied Behavior Analysis* 10, no. 2 (1977): 349–67.

Epilogue

Some students, despite consistently receiving high-quality instruction in a general education classroom, will demonstrate significant and ongoing challenges mastering targeted learning outcomes. Consequently, school staff will need to craft instructional conditions that result in the provision of effective instruction for these students. Small group arrangements allow for the possibility of creating these conditions.

However, given the nature of these students' learning challenges, it is doubtful that the use of small group arrangements, in and of themselves, will result in the presentation of effective instruction. Rather, these arrangements will provide a forum within which numerous evidence-based practices can be employed. Teachers will be challenged to determine the right mix of these practices that need to be used so that effective, intensive instruction is provided to each student in the group.

Upon finishing this book you are encouraged to consider the philosophy of teaching and learning that was put forth in chapter 1, as well as the rest of the book's content. Afterwards, develop your own philosophy and think about how it addresses the need to put every student in a situation that has been created to enable them to be successful at their job, which is to go to school and master targeted learning outcomes.

Glossary

A-B-C paradigm. A depiction of the relationship of the events that occur in an instructional exchange. In the middle of the exchange is the learner's observable behavior, which is represented by the letter B. Specifically, this is the behavior a teacher wants a student to exhibit for the purpose of demonstrating that they have mastered the targeted learning outcome. The A stands for antecedents, which are the events that precede the behavior. The C represents the consequences, which are the events that follow the behavior.

Academic content. The knowledge and skills that pertain to traditional subject matter areas (i.e., math, science, English/language arts, and social studies).

Academic learning time. The amount of time that a student participates in instruction that is at their instructional level.

Accommodation. A change of the conditions under which a student is expected to perform an academic skill, rather than an alteration of the standard that has been set for the performance of the task (which is a modification). Accommodations may include, but are not necessarily limited to, the time that a student is given to complete a task, the manner in which the task is presented to the student, the mode of responding that is required from the student, and the arrangement of the setting in which the task is to be performed. The purpose for providing an accommodation is to ensure that a student's performance is a valid reflection of their ability to perform a targeted skill. Note that accommodations can apply to instruction and assessment.

Acquisition. The phase of learning during which a student attains knowledge or learns how to perform a skill.

Active student responding. Any overt display by a student of a behavior that indicates their response to a task directive. An example is when a student shows a "thumbs up" to indicate that they believe the correct answer is true in response to a true/false question that a teacher has posed to assess students' acquisition of knowledge that pertains to the lesson's learning objective.

Allocated time. The portion of allotted time that is designated for specific instruction. During a 7.5-hour school day teachers may be required to teach language arts for ninety minutes. This length of time would be the allocated time for language arts instruction.

Allotted time. The time that is available for instruction. If a school is in session from 8 a.m. to 3:30 p.m., then the school's allotted time would be 7.5 hours.

Antecedent-based interventions. Interventions that are employed prior to a student's display of a targeted learning outcome and that are designed to increase the probability that the student will engage in the target behavior. Examples of antecedent-based interventions include the teacher's use of concise language, visual supports (e.g., picture prompt sequences and social narratives), prompting, behavioral momentum strategies, and environmental arrangements.

Assessment. The collection of information, or data.

Assessment component. The numerous ways information about the effectiveness of small group instruction is collected. A primary reason for collecting data is to inform instruction. When assessment informs instruction, it means that the assessment data are used by the teacher when they make decisions about how to present instruction differently from how they previously did with the expectation that the new way will be more effective and efficient. Assessments can inform instruction in one of two ways. One way is by providing information about students' behaviors. The other way is providing information about the teacher's behavior.

Attention directive. The behavior(s) a teacher exhibits for the purpose of communicating to students that they need to demonstrate behaviors that indicate they are attending to the teacher. An example of an attention directive would be a teacher snapping their fingers twice and then saying, "Eyes up."

Attention response. The behavior(s) a student exhibits immediately following the presentation of an attention directive by the teacher, for the purpose of demonstrating that the student is attending to the teacher. An example of an attention response is the placement of the student's hands on their lap and feet flat on the floor while looking directly at the instructor and remaining quiet.

Augmentative communication. A mode of expression that is employed to supplement or replace one's use of speech or writing.

Basic instructional strategies. The four fundamental instructional strategies, or types of planned actions, that a teacher can engage in, either singularly or in combination, when presenting instruction. The four strategies are oral, modeling, writing, and physical prompting.

Behavior. A person's observable actions, which include anything a person says or does. (See the definitions for the terms that apply to the various dimensions of behavior: frequency, duration, force, latency, locus, rate, and topography.)

Behavior management. The actions a teacher engages in to ensure that students exhibit appropriate school social behaviors. These actions are wide-ranging and include teaching students how to perform appropriate school social behaviors and putting in place environmental arrangements that set the stage for students' displays of these behaviors.

Child Find. A requirement put forth in the Individuals with Disabilities Education Act (IDEA) that public schools must seek out children with disabilities who may qualify for the receipt of special education services.

Child with a disability. As defined in the IDEA, a child with a disability is a child who meets the eligibility criteria for one or more of the categories of disability that are listed and defined in the IDEA and, because of the disability, needs to receive special education services. In other words, the manifestation of the disability adversely affects the child's educational performance. This has been referred to as the two-part eligibility standard for special education services.

Choral responding. When every student in a group responds simultaneously. This type of responding is also referred to as group, unison, and whole group responding.

Class size. Refers to the total number of students in a class. Most often this term is associated with general education classrooms in which one teacher is assigned to teach the total number of students in the class.

Consequences. The event(s) that occurs immediately after a student displays a behavior or exhibits a no response during the time they have been given to respond. These events can be referred to as consequence-based strategies because the strategy that the teacher employs is the result of a student's behavior in the A-B-C paradigm (i.e., the consequence, or the C in the A-B-C paradigm, that is used depends on the type of behavior a student exhibits).

Contingency-based strategies. The event(s) that occurs immediately after a student displays a behavior or exhibits a no response during the time they have been given to respond. These events are referred to as contingency-based because the strategy that the teacher employs is contingent upon, meaning based upon, the type of behavior a student exhibits.

Continuum of alternative placements. The various locations in which special education services can be provided to a child with a disability and which are delineated in the IDEA. These placements include, but are not limited to, general education, resource, and self-contained classrooms.

Controlled variance. The systematic change of instructional conditions, routinely, for the purpose of ensuring that a student can perform a behavior across people, settings, and conditions (i.e., the student can generalize a learned behavior).

Controlling prompt. A prompt that nearly always results in a correct student response.

Core curriculum. A listing of the knowledge and skills teachers are expected to address in the instruction that they present and that students are expected to attain. The core curriculum is to be the focus of the instruction that is presented in general education classrooms. See also General education curriculum.

Correct response. A behavior that meets the operational definition that is set forth in the targeted learning objective (e.g., the learner wrote the sum for an addition problem comprised of two single-digit addends).

Covert action. A form of active student responding that is intended to maximize a student's engaged time. A covert action is a mental activity that cannot be observed and, therefore, its performance by a student can be solicited by a teacher but not verified. Examples include having a student "use the voice in his head" for the purpose of repeating something a teacher says, such as the name of a picture of an object, or visualizing the steps the student must perform to wash their hands.

Criteria. A standard for judging a student's performance of a skill (e.g., correctly states the sum for nine of ten basic addition facts). See also criterion.

Criterion. A standard against which a student's performance is judged (e.g., correctly reading nine of ten consonant-vowel-consonant words). See also criteria.

Curriculum. A listing of the knowledge and skills teachers address in the instruction that they present and that students are expected to attain. This definition addresses the knowledge and skills teachers actually address in their instruction, which may differ from the content that comprises the core curriculum.

Curriculum-assessment alignment. A situation in which the content that is assessed is the content that comprises the curriculum a teacher taught.

Curriculum-based measurement. An assessment that involves obtaining information about a student's learning pertaining to curriculum content. The term is synonymous with curriculum-based assessment.

Data. Information. The types of data vary greatly and include everything from relatively subjective anecdotal reports to empirical, scientific measurements of more well-defined phenomena, such as red blood cell counts. Hence, data include both qualitative (i.e., descriptive) and quantitative (i.e., numerical) information.

Declarative knowledge. A discrete piece of information, such as the name for an object or stating a synonym for a word.

Delayed feedback. Feedback that is provided to the student by the teacher at a point in time removed from when the student makes a correct or incorrect response (including no response). Examples would be when a student is presented feedback after they engage in a set of trials or completes an instructional session.

Deliberate response. One in which a student behaves in a purposeful manner, demonstrating behavior called for by the teacher, without any undue hesitation, misdirection, or some other behavior (e.g., touching two response options at the same time) that disallows the teacher from confidently interpreting the student's response. A deliberate response runs counter to non-purposeful, impulsive responding.

Descriptive feedback. Teacher feedback following a student's response that characterizes the student's behavior relative to the behavior that is stated in the learning objective. An example would be the following statement to a student who incorrectly named the letter n, which is the behavior stated in the learning objective: "No, you said m but the name of this letter is n."

Diagnostic assessment. Assessment that is designed to more precisely identify the reason for a student's incorrect response. An example would be when a teacher examines a student's math worksheet and notes that the student always subtracts the smaller number from the larger number in a subtraction problem that involves a two-digit minuend and a two-digit subtrahend. The teacher would use this information to determine the student's understanding of place value and borrowing.

Differentiated instruction. Diversifying aspects of instruction, such as the content that is taught, the assignments students are to complete, and the way that students are assessed so that students' various learning needs are met.

Direct instruction lesson plan. A lesson plan format that consists of a collection of evidence-based, behavioral techniques that include stating the learning objective at the outset of the lesson, teacher modeling, and guided practice.

Discipline-specific effective teaching practices. Interventions that are specific to a subject matter area, such as math or reading, and which address either the content that is central to learning the subject (e.g., learning phonics skills during beginning reading instruction) or the instructional strategies that enable students to master this content. These interventions are supported by multiple research studies that have documented their effectiveness.

Distributed trials. Trials that are presented outside of the small group instructional session and, therefore, can be separated by a relatively lengthy period of time between the instructional session and the next time a trial is presented.

Duration. The length of time a student engages in a behavior.

Educational intervention. A change to the environment in which instruction is presented. An educational intervention is designed and implemented for the purpose of enabling a student to acquire knowledge or perform a skill that is delineated in a learning objective.

Educator. A person, such as a principal or teacher, who is involved in planning, directing, or presenting instructional services.

Effective instruction. Instruction that results in a student demonstrating mastery of the targeted learning objective.

Efficient instruction. Effective instruction that, relative to one or more other means of presenting effective instruction, requires less time, money, material resources, or effort.

Engaged time. The amount of time that a student attends to the instruction that is presented.

Evaluation. A characterization of data, or value judgment that is based upon an interpretation of the data.

Evidence-based practice. An intervention that has research which documents its effectiveness.

Evidence-based review. A protocol that is used to identify evidence-based practices. These practices are supported by research reports of their effectiveness. An evidence-based review involves identifying and evaluating the overall quality of the research.

Explicit. Clearly stated, as opposed to implied or assumed.

Explicit instruction. A type of teacher-directed instruction during which all aspects are made known to the learner. Central features of explicit instruction include the teacher selecting the learning objective and then designing a structured lesson that, as is appropriate, is comprised of direct explanation and modeling by the teacher, guided practice, independent practice, assessment, and lesson review. Each feature incorporates evidence-based strategies that enhance student learning, such as the use of clear and concise language by the teacher when they present a direct explanation and modeling, and opportunities for frequent and varied active student responding during guided practice.

Feedback. Information a teacher presents to a student. It either follows a student's response or the amount of time that has been established for making a response (i.e., no response). Types of feedback include teacher affirmation, reinforcement, and error correction.

Fluency. The rate of the performance of a behavior, expressed as amount per unit of time. Most often measures of fluency are expressed as amounts per minute (e.g., number of words typed or read per minute).

Force. The strength of a behavior (e.g., a student broke two pencils in half; the student's yelling could be heard as far as three rooms away from the classroom).

Frequency. The number of times a student engages in a behavior; a count of the occurrences of a behavior.

Functional content. Knowledge and skills that enable an individual to maintain themselves as independently as possible in an age-appropriate environment. This content is also referred to as activities of daily living and life skills.

Functional curriculum. A curriculum that is comprised of knowledge and skills that enable an individual to maintain themselves as independently as possible in an age-appropriate environment. The content that comprises this curriculum is often referred to as activities of daily living or life skills. Examples of the knowledge and skills in a functional curriculum for an adolescent or young adult include learning to read the word "Exit" and that one of its meanings is to "Go out," how to do a load of laundry, how to cook a meal, and how to mail a package. A functional curriculum is often referred to along with references to a traditional academic curriculum that is comprised of knowledge and skills from content areas that include mathematics, English, science, and history/social studies.

General education curriculum. The curriculum that has been established for students who are educated in general education classrooms to master (preschool to twelfth grade). See Core curriculum.

General feedback. Teacher feedback, such as saying "Good job" or "Nice work," that informs the student whether their response was correct or incorrect but does not make reference to the student's specific behavior.

General least restrictive environment requirement. A concept that is addressed in the IDEA and that refers to the access a child with a disability has to typical peers and the general education setting in which these peers are educated—as well as the core curriculum they are taught. Specifically, in accordance with this requirement, the general education classroom is regarded as the default placement for students with disabilities, and the core curriculum stipulates the knowledge and skills they should be taught.

General outcome measure. An assessment that serves to monitor a student's progress toward mastery of the entire curriculum that will be taught during the school year.

Generalization. Learned behaviors that are consistently performed across people, settings, and conditions.

Generative response. A response that requires the student to produce it independently. See also production and recall response.

Group response. When every student in a group responds simultaneously. This type of responding is also referred to as choral, unison, and whole group responding.

Heterogeneous group. A group in which the students are dissimilar in numerous ways that are relevant to the design and implementation of their instruction. In a heterogeneous group, students may differ with respect to their overall ability levels, the targeted learning outcomes they need to master, and their characteristics of thinking and learning.

Hidden curriculum. Refers to the knowledge and skills a student has learned inadvertently through interactions with the instructional environment. The knowledge and skills that comprise this curriculum are not operationally defined, nor are they the focus of explicit instruction.

High probability behavior. A behavior for which there is a significant chance that the student will engage in it when presented with a task directive.

High-quality instruction. Effective instruction that results from attention to multiple elements that include the appropriate design and operation of a classroom; successful time management; a focus on core curriculum content; the presentation of effective, evidence-based instructional strategies; and the use of valid and reliable assessments.

High stakes test. A test that involves the application of important consequences, such as whether a student will be awarded a standard high school diploma.

Homogeneous group. A group in which the students are similar in numerous ways that are relevant to the design and implementation of their instruction. In a homogeneous group, the ways that students may be alike include their overall ability levels, the targeted learning outcomes they need to master, and their characteristics of thinking and learning.

Immediate feedback. Feedback that is provided to the student by the teacher right after the student's response is determined to be correct, incorrect, or a no response.

Incidental learning. Refers to a student's acquisition of curriculum content that is presented during a trial but is not acted upon by either the teacher or the student.

Incorrect response. An observable behavior that does not meet the operational definition set forth in the targeted learning objective (e.g., the learner wrote an incorrect sum for an addition problem comprised of two single-digit addends).

Individual response. Refers to the times during small group instruction when only one student responds to the teacher's task directive.

Individuals with Disabilities Education Improvement Act of 2004. The federal law that directs the provision of special education services to children with disabilities in the United States. More commonly referred to as the Individuals with Disabilities Education Act or the initials IDEA.

Individualized instruction. A concept that refers to identifying the curriculum content that a student needs to be taught, providing the services the student needs to receive to learn this content, and monitoring progress toward its attainment. The term does not automatically refer to a 1:1 instructional arrangement, nor does it preclude the use of this arrangement.

Informed eclecticism. The use of a multi-component intervention that consists of multiple, evidence-based practices. The effectiveness of these practices when used together has not been established through an evidence-based review.

Instruction. The act of teaching (i.e., imparting knowledge or skills).

Instructional level. A term that refers to how a student is performing with respect to a performance standard that has been established for the student's age and corresponding grade level. For example, a student may be identified as a fourth-grade student based on age but is noted to be demonstrating a need to master curriculum content that has been established for a student who is in kindergarten, such as naming the lowercase letters of the alphabet. Consequently, this student's instructional level in English/language arts would be designated as kindergarten level.

Instructional materials. Both the tangible (e.g., counting blocks, pencil, paper) and intangible (e.g., software applications) items that are used when instruction is presented.

Instructional setting. The location where instruction is presented, as well as its configuration. Instructional settings may include global environments as well as sub-environments within the global environments. For instance, a school may be designated as the global environment and a classroom as a sub-environment within it.

Instructional strategy. The planned actions a teacher executes for the purpose of presenting instruction that is designed to enable students to demonstrate mastery of targeted learning objectives.

Integrated framework. One name for a type of multi-tier framework that consists of protocols for simultaneously and efficiently addressing students' mastery of academic content and school social behaviors.

Intensity of instruction. The concept of intensity of instruction refers to measurable dimensions/features of instruction that are correlated to relatively more individualized and prolonged student engagement during a lesson. Specifically, increases in the intensity of instruction are intended to change, in a substantive manner, how instruction is conducted with students who are not demonstrating mastery of age- or grade-level appropriate curricula such that they experience more engaged and academic learning time in a lesson that pertains to an instructional-level targeted learning objective, and this increase in engaged and academic learning time results in mastery of the learning objective. Examples of the dimensions of instruction that can be manipulated for the purpose of increasing the intensity of instruction include the use of lower pupil:teacher ratios; the allowance of more opportunities for students to engage in active student responding; the provision of more frequent and specific feedback by the teacher; the allowance for more allocated, engaged, and academic learning time; and higher rates of instructional trials per session.

Intensive instruction. Intensive instruction refers to strategically designed instruction that addresses a number of elements that allow for more individualized and prolonged student engagement. Engagement refers to a student's cognitive processing of the content that is the focus of a lesson. Intensive instruction evolves from an examination of the large group instruction that is presented in a general education classroom. This instruction is made more intense by changing certain aspects such as the size of the group, affording students more opportunities to practice performing targeted skills, and providing immediate and specific feedback to each student response.

Intervention. A change of the environment that is intended to increase a student's display of a desirable behavior or decrease a student's display of an inappropriate behavior. Examples include providing a student with feedback after every response rather than after they complete all twenty trials that are presented by the teacher and reconfiguring the assigned seating for a class so that a student who has been exhibiting a high rate of off-task behavior is seated in a spot that is not as close—as was the case previously—to a potentially distracting stimuli.

Intrinsic reinforcement. A type of reinforcement in which the successful performance of an activity functions as a reinforcer for the student who values the fact that they were able to perform it (e.g., writing the answer to a basic addition fact on a worksheet is a reinforcer for a student who responded correctly to the written task directive, "Write the answer to each problem below.")

Knowledge. Information.

Language. A rule-governed system from which rules for communication are derived.

Large group instruction. A group whose composition consists of a pupil:teacher ratio of 9:1 or higher. In most instances large group instruction refers to general education classes in which twenty to more than thirty students receive instruction from one teacher (i.e., a pupil:teacher ratio of 20–30+:1). Also referred to as a large group arrangement.

Latency. The amount of time that elapses between the presentation of a task directive, from a teacher to a student, and the moment the student begins to perform the task.

Learning. A relatively permanent change in behavior that is the result of experience.

Learning how to learn. The concept that a student becomes more efficient at learning by developing an understanding of how instruction is routinely presented. An example would be a student knowing that when new content is being presented the teacher will first model how to demonstrate acquisition of the content and then will support the student with prompts until the student demonstrates criterion-level performance.

Learning objective. A statement that describes the content from the curriculum that the student will learn, the observable and measurable behavior the student will engage in to demonstrate that they have learned the content, the conditions under which the student will perform the behavior, and the criteria for mastery.

Level of learning. To the extent that a curriculum is vertically or horizontally sequenced, the level of learning refers to an arrangement where the learning of certain skills is to precede the learning of others. In terms of grade levels, at the end of the school year when a fourth-grade student shows, on an assessment, that they have mastered only first-grade math skills, the student would be said to be performing at a lower level than a classmate who has demonstrated mastery of the fourth-grade math skills. In terms of prerequisite skills, a student who has not mastered repeated addition would be said to be performing at a lower level than a student who has mastered basic multiplication facts.

Locus. The location on a student's body where they exhibit a behavior (e.g., a student slaps the top of his right thigh with an open right hand).

Low probability behavior. A behavior for which there is a small chance that a student will engage in it at a given point in time, such as when a teacher presents a task directive.

Maintenance. The performance of a skill, over time, in accordance with the criteria that were set for mastery of the skill during the acquisition phase of learning.

Massed trials. Refers to how trials are presented during an instructional session. Massed trial presentation occurs when one trial is presented immediately after another. Once the teacher presents the student feedback the teacher initiates the next trial with the same student. The teacher continues in this manner until they have presented the number of trials intended for the student to perform under these conditions.

Master/mastery. Performing a behavior that is defined in a learning objective such that the established criterion for correct responding is met (e.g., reading ten high frequency words within thirty seconds across three consecutive assessment sessions).

Micro-analysis of teaching. The process of conducting an in-depth analysis of each variable that could, conceivably, be related to a student's mastery of a learning objective.

Mode of responding. The behavior(s) a student exhibits when they emit a response. Examples include the use of speech, written responses, pointing, properly using a computer's interface (e.g., clicking on an icon on a screen), and the successful performance of motor skills, such as those involved with independently toileting oneself.

Modification. With respect to a child with a disability, a modification refers to a learning objective that is markedly different with respect to the age- and grade-appropriate curriculum standards that have been established for the student.

Multi-tier system of support (MTSS). Some form of a multi-tier intervention framework that is employed by a school for the purpose of accounting for every student's instructional needs and educational progress.

No response. The absence of any behavior that met the operational definition for a correct or incorrect response. For example, if a student was presented with a worksheet on which was written three addition problems, each of which consisted of two single-digit addends, and was given the task directive, "Write the sums for each problem," a no response would be recorded for any problem to which the student did not write either a correct or incorrect response.

Observational learning. A student's acquisition of a targeted learning outcome for a peer as a result of the student attending to the peer receiving instruction that concerns the targeted outcome. Specifically, the student who demonstrates observational learning does so as a result of the teacher systematically directing the student to discern how they are presenting instruction, particularly prompts and feedback for correct as opposed to incorrect responses.

Operational definition. An explicit definition of the behavior a student exhibits such that two or more independent observers are able to agree upon its display by the student. The behavior must be defined in observable and measurable terms.

Overt behavior. A person's observable actions; anything a person says or does.

Pace of instruction. The rate at which instruction is presented. For instance, pace could refer to the number of targeted learning outcomes that were addressed during a unit of time.

Prereferral-to-placement process. The protocol schools follow to identify children with disabilities. It is one part of the IDEA's mandatory effort, called Child Find, to locate every child who needs to receive special education services. In many instances in schools, a pre-referral–to–placement process consists of multiple elements that include identifying children who are demonstrating low academic achievement and then providing remedial instruction to ameliorate the student's low performance. Other elements of the process include administering assessments and evaluating the data obtained, and performing administrative tasks (e.g., writing reports).

Priming. Some type of preview of upcoming instruction.

Probe. A short assessment (i.e., takes one to three minutes to complete) that consists of items that directly and extensively measures a student's performance on a targeted learning objective. The resulting data are intended to be used to readily inform instruction. See also skill check.

Procedural knowledge. A way of thinking about curriculum content that a student is to master that involves the completion of several or more interconnected steps, such as performing the algorithm to divide a four-digit number by a two-digit number. See skill.

Production response. A response that requires the student to exhibit it independently. See also generative and recall response.

Progress monitoring. A type of assessment that produces data regarding students' levels and rates of progress.

Prompt. Additional information that is provided by the teacher to the student after the task directive is presented. The primary purpose of the prompt is to increase the probability that a student will emit a correct response. For instance, after a teacher shows the student an index card on which is written the word "Cat" and presents the task directive, "Read this word," the teacher would provide a prompt by saying the first two sounds that comprise the spoken form of the word.

Prompt fading. A systematic process of eliminating the additional information a teacher presents, after delivering the task directive, to increase the probability that a student will provide a correct response. Prompt fading is, to some degree, synonymous with release of responsibility and transfer of responsibility. These latter two terms refer to a teacher no longer providing guided practice and having students engage in independent practice.

Proximity prompt. A prompt whose meaning depends on its position in space. For instance, if a student is provided two possible answer choices that are presented on index cards, and the card with the correct answer is positioned closer to the student than the card with the incorrect answer, the positioning of the first card is a proximity prompt.

Pupil:teacher ratio. The number of students per teacher, or instructor, in an instructional setting For example, 2:1 refers to two students with one teacher, whereas 8:1 refers to eight students with one teacher. In a self-contained classroom in which nine students receive instruction from a teacher and two instructional assistants, the pupil:teacher ratio would be 9:3, which is the same as 3:1.

Qualitative changes. Changes that pertain to descriptions about the characteristics of small group instruction more so than counts or measures of the characteristics. Examples include changing the composition of the group so that it is more homogeneous and having a teacher with more specialized training in the subject matter lead the group.

Quantitative changes. Changes that involve a readily identifiable numerical aspect of an intervention. Examples include increasing either the number of days per week or time per day that an intervention is provided to a student, or the number of trials the student completes during a session.

Random trial presentation. When trials are presented in an order that is based upon the teacher's discretion, meaning the trials are not presented in accordance with clearly preset criteria.

Rate. A ratio of the frequency of a student's behavior per unit of time. Usually reported as a ratio of the frequency of a behavior per one minute (e.g., answering six basic additions fact correctly in one minute).

Rate of learning. Refers to the ratio of the amount of new content learned per unit of time. For example, if twelve new math skills were learned in six weeks then the rate of learning would be two new math skills per week (twelve skills:six weeks = two skills:one week).

Recall response. A response that requires the student to produce it independently. See also generative and production response.

Recognition response. A response to a task directive that requires a student to select the correct response from two or more response choices that are provided.

Reinforcer. An event that follows a student's behavior and increases the probability that the student will perform the same behavior in the future under similar circumstances. Regarding the use of tangible reinforcers, such as edibles, it is important to note that these types of reinforcers serve as a bridge to less tangible, more infrequent, intangible reinforcement, such as teacher praise. See intrinsic reinforcement.

Reliability. Consistency across time. For example, with respect to testing, reliability refers to whether a student will attain the same score, or nearly the same score, on multiple administrations of the test across time. If so, the test is said to be reliable.

Remediate. The correction of a deficiency. With respect to learning, remediation involves teaching a student content from the student's curriculum that they should have learned at a specified performance level (i.e., criterion) at a previous point in time with respect to the scope and sequence of the curriculum.

Resource room. A classroom within a school in which children with disabilities receive instruction from 20 to 59 percent of the school day, inclusive.

Response latency. The amount of time between the presentation of the task directive and when the student makes a response.

Response-to-intervention framework (RtI framework). A multi-tiered, data-based protocol that focuses on effectively teaching the core curriculum in a general education classroom, as well as under different conditions to students who have demonstrated a noteworthy lack of progress in mastering that curriculum while being in the general education classroom.

Routines. Repeated sets of actions.

School social behavior. For the purposes of this book, social behaviors are defined as those that allow someone to share space appropriately with others. School social behaviors are those that are appropriate in a school context (i.e., while on a school's premises or an extension of these premises, such as a school bus). Each school defines appropriate social behavior for its context.

Scientifically based instruction. Refers to the use of research to validate effective interventions.

Scope and sequence. The total number of skills delineated in a curriculum (i.e., the scope) and the suggested order in which they are to be taught (i.e., the sequence).

Screen. To identify the smaller number of students, from among a relatively larger group, who need to be examined in more detail for some previously identified purpose, such as making better progress in the general education curriculum or the possibility of manifesting a disability that will result in the provision of special education services.

Screener. An assessment that is conducted to predict which students will not achieve expected learning outcomes if they continue in their current general education program, such as mastering end-of-the-year benchmarks in reading and math.

Self-contained classroom. A classroom within a school in which children with disabilities receive instruction for more than 60 percent of the school day.

Self-regulation. Various strategies that students can use to manage their behavior. These strategies include self-instruction, self-assessment, and self-reinforcement.

Semi-choral response. When a subset of two or more students in a small group arrangement respond in unison while the other students in the group do not.

Sequential trial presentation. The presentation of trials in an arranged manner that is based upon pre-set criteria.

Session. The time during which small group instruction is presented.

Skill. A way of thinking about curriculum content that a student is to master that involves the completion of several or more interconnected steps. See procedural knowledge.

Skill check. An assessment that measure a student's performance on targeted learning objectives. Typically this measure addresses very few learning objectives rather than those that comprise an entire curriculum. The resulting data are intended to be used to readily inform instruction. Also see probe.

Small group instruction. An instructional arrangement that consists of two to eight students and one or more instructors such that the pupil:teacher ratio is not less than 2:1. Also referred to as a small group arrangement.

Small group instructional arrangement. The location, as well as its set up, in which instruction is provided to a group of two to eight students and whose pupil:teacher ratio is at least 2:1 (as opposed to 1:1).

Social behavior. A behavior that involves an association with at least one other human being.

Spaced trials. Trials that are separated in time during the small group instructional session. Usually this means that, after presenting a trial to a student, the teacher presents one or more trials to one or more other students in the group before presenting another trial to the first student.

Specially designed instruction. A term that is defined in the IDEA and refers to the special education services that are to be designed and provided to a child with a disability. Specifically, the term refers to the content, methodology, or delivery of instruction.

Special education. Per the IDEA, special education is defined as specially designed instruction to meet the unique needs of a child with a disability.

Specific feedback. Feedback that identifies the behavior a student exhibited that resulted in either a correct or incorrect response.

Standardized assessment. An assessment that is conducted in a prescribed manner each time it is administered.

Systematic. Clearly defined teaching procedures that can be readily replicated by others.

Targeted. That which is focused upon.

Targeted learning outcomes. Curriculum content that is identified in a learning objective and is the focus of the instruction that is presented to students.

Task analysis. An identification and listing of the steps that comprise a skill. An example would be a list of the steps a student must complete to find the answer to a subtraction problem that involves regrouping when a single-digit subtrahend is subtracted from a double-digit minuend.

Task directive. The directions a student is to follow for the purpose of emitting what is deemed to be a contextually correct response and, therefore, a demonstration that the student has mastered a learning objective (e.g., pointing to the letter "a" when it is presented on an index card along with four other lowercase letters of the alphabet; completing a load of laundry after reading the words, "Do Laundry," that are written on an individual's list of chores).

Teacher. An individual who, after completing an approved preparation program, has been awarded a license from a designated state agency that permits the person to be employed as a teacher in a state-approved educational agency, such as a public school.

Teacher-directed instruction. An instructional protocol in which the teacher decides what will be taught, how it will be taught, how the student is to perform an activity, and when the student has mastered it.

Teaching. Imparting knowledge or skills.

Teaching assistant. A person who is not a licensed teacher but does perform various tasks that assist in the provision of educational services to students. Synonymous titles include instructional assistant, teacher's aide, and paraprofessional.

Test, testing. A means by which the presence of something is determined. In schools, tests determine the presence of things such as a student's academic knowledge and skills, or the student's ability to perform either a school social behavior or functional task. Mostly a test consists of the presentation of a stimulus, or some type of directive, to which a student must independently provide a response.

Think aloud. An instructional strategy that involves the person who is completing a task (e.g., a teacher or student) to say, out loud, what they are thinking as they do so.

Tier 1. In a multi-tier system of support framework, Tier 1 refers to high-quality, evidence-based instruction that is presented in a general education classroom. Altogether this instruction is projected to be effective with 75 to 80 percent of the students.

Tier 2. In a response-to-intervention framework Tier 2 refers to services that are provided to the 20 to 25 percent of students who did not master targeted learning outcomes after receiving Tier 1 instruction. Tier 2 services also might be presented to students whose performance on a screener indicates that they most likely will need to receive instruction that supplements the instruction that is provided in Tier 1. Tier 2 services are characterized by the use of small group arrangements and the provision of more intense intervention than was provided in Tier 1.

Tier 3. In some multi-tier system of support frameworks, Tier 3 services consist of special education services.

Topography. The location where a student engages in a behavior (e.g., in the cafeteria at school).

Trial. Refers to an instructional sequence that consists of the presentation of a task directive by the teacher, followed by an allowance for a student response (to include a no response option), the provision of feedback from the teacher, and an inter-trial interval.

Unison response. When every student in a group responds simultaneously. This type of responding is also referred to as choral, group, and whole group responding.

Universal effective teaching practices. Universal effective teaching practices mostly refer to behaviors a teacher exhibits during a lesson and are appropriate for use irrespective of the academic subject matter or school social behaviors that are the focus of instruction. Examples of these practices include clearly stating the learning objective, presenting material in appropriate chunks, frequently soliciting active student responding, and conducting a review at the end of a lesson. Universal effective teaching practices are evidence-based practices.

Validity. Refers to whether a test measures the skill (or some other construct) that it purports to measure. For instance, a test that has been constructed to measures a student's math calculation and reasoning skills via the presentation of numerous word problems that a student needs to read independently may end up being more of a measure a student's reading ability than math ability.

Visual support. Anything that a student can see and which is intended to enhance their understanding of what a teacher says (whether through speech or sign language).

Whole group responding. When every student in the group responds simultaneously. This type of responding is also referred to as choral, group, and unison responding.

Bibliography

Abbott, Mary, Cheryl Walton, and Charles R. Greenwood. "Phonemic Awareness in Kindergarten and First Grade." *Teaching Exceptional Children* 34, no. 4 (2001): 20–26.

Abbott, Mary, Cheryl Walton, Yolanda Tapia, and Charles R. Greenwood. "Research to Practice: A 'Blueprint' for Closing the Gap in Local Schools." *Exceptional Children* 83 (1999): 339–62.

Adams, Marilyn J. *Beginning to Read: Learning and Thinking About Print*. Cambridge, MA: MIT Press, 1990.

Alberto, Paul, and Anne C. Troutman. *Applied Behavior Analysis for Teachers*, ninth edition. New York: Pearson, 2007.

Algozzine, Bob, R. Putnam, and R. H. Horner. "Support for Teaching Students with Learning Disabilities Academic Skills and Social Behaviors within a Response-to-Intervention Model: Why It Doesn't Matter What Comes First." *Insights on Learning Disabilities* 9, no. 1 (2012): 7–36.

Algozzine, Bob, Chuang Wang, Richard White, Nancy Cooke, Mary Beth Marr, Kate Algozzine, Shawnna S. Helf, and Grace Zamora Duran. "Effects of Multi-Tier Academic and Behavior Instruction on Difficult-to-Teach Students." *Exceptional Children* 79, no. 1 (2012): 45–64.

Archer, Anita L., and Charles A. Hughes. *Explicit Instruction: Effective and Efficient Teaching*. New York: Guilford Press, 2010.

Baer, Donald M., Montrose M. Wolf, and Todd R. Risley. "Some Still-Current Dimensions of Applied Behavior Analysis." *Journal of Applied Behavior Analysis* 20, no. 4 (1987): 313–27.

Barnes, Aaron C., and Jason E. Harlacher. "Clearing the Confusion: Response-to-Intervention as a Set of Principles." *Education and Treatment of Children* 31, no. 3 (2008): 417–31.

Berrong, Amy Ketterer, John W. Schuster, Timothy E. Morse, and Belva C. Collins. "The Effects of Response Cards on Active Participation and Social Behavior of

Students with Moderate and Severe Disabilities." *Journal of Developmental and Physical Disabilities* 19, no. 3 (2007): 187–99.

Brigance, Albert Henry. *Brigance Inventory of Essential Skills*. North Billerica, MA: Curriculum Associates., 2019.

Brigham, Frederick J., Thomas E. Scruggs, and Margo A. Mastropieri. "Teacher Enthusiasm in Learning Disabilities Classrooms: Effects on Learning and Behavior." *Learning Disabilities Research & Practice* (1992).

Brophy, Jere E. *Teaching*. International Academy of Education and the International Bureau of Education, 1999. www.cklavya.org/edu-practices_01_eng.pdf.

Brophy, Jere, and Good. "Teacher Influences on Student Achievement." *American Psychologist* 41, no. 10 (1986): 1069–77.

Cappadocia, M. Catherine, and Jonathan A. Weiss. "Review of Social Skills Training Groups for Youth with Asperger Syndrome and High Functioning Autism." *Research in Autism Spectrum Disorders* 5, no. 1 (2011): 70–78.

Chard, David J., and Edward J. Kameenui. "Struggling First-Grade Readers: The Frequency and Progress of Their Reading." *The Journal of Special Education* 34, no. 1 (2000): 28–38.

Collins, Belva C., David L. Gast, Melinda J. Ault, and Mark Wolery. "Small Group Instruction: Guidelines for Teachers of Students with Moderate to Severe Handicaps." *Education & Training in Mental Retardation* 26, no. 1 (1991): 1–18.

Cook, Bryan G., Melody Tankersley, and Sanna Harjusola-Webb. "Evidence-Based Special Education and Professional Wisdom: Putting It All Together." *Intervention in School and Clinic* 44, no. 2 (2008): 105–11.

Cooper, John O., Timothy E. Heron, and William L. Heward. *Applied Behavior Analysis*. New York: Pearson, 2007.

Cronin, Kathleen A., and Anthony J. Cuvo. "Teaching Mending Skills to Mentally Retarded Adolescents." *Journal of Applied Behavior Analysis* 12, no. 3 (1979): 401–06.

Edmonds, Rebecca Zumeta, Sarah Powell, and Devin Kerans. "To be Clear: What Every Educator Needs to Know About Explicit Instruction Webinar." National Center on Intensive Intervention. American Institutes for Research and Division for Research. *Council for Exceptional Children*. Washington, DC. (2019).

Education for All Handicapped Children Act, Pub. L No. 94–142. (1975).

Ehri, Linnea C. "Development of the Ability to Read Words." *Handbook of Reading Research* 2 (1991): 383–417.

Ehri, Linnea C., and Alison G. Soffer. "Graphophonemic Awareness: Development in Elementary Students." *Scientific Studies of Reading* 3, no. 1 (1999): 1–30.

Epstein, Michael, Marc Atkins, Douglas Cullinan, Krista Kutash, and K. Weaver. "Reducing Behavior Problems in the Elementary School Classroom." *IES Practice Guide* 20, no. 8 (2008): 12–22.

Felton, Rebecca H., and Pamela P. Pepper. "Early Identification and Intervention of Phonological Deficits in Kindergarten and Early Elementary Children at Risk for Reading Disability." *School Psychology Review* (1995).

Fiscus, Renee Schmitz, John W. Schuster, Timothy E. Morse, and Belva C. Collins. "Teaching Elementary Students with Cognitive Disabilities Food Preparation

Skills While Embedding Instructive Feedback in the Prompt and Consequent Event." *Education and Training in Mental Retardation and Developmental Disabilities* (2002): 55–69.

Foorman, B. R., D. J. Francis, and J. M. Fletcher. *Growth of Phonological Processing Skill in Beginning Reading: The Lag versus Deficit Model Revisited.* Indianapolis, IN: Society for Research on Child Development, 1995.

Foorman, Barbara R., David J. Francis, Jack M. Fletcher, Christopher Schatschneider, and Paras Mehta. "The Role of Instruction in Learning to Read: Preventing Reading Failure in At-Risk Children." *Journal of Educational Psychology* 90, no. 1 (1998): 37.

Fuchs, Douglas, and Lynn S. Fuchs. "Critique of the National Evaluation of Response to Intervention: A Case for Simpler Frameworks." *Exceptional Children* 83, no. 3 (2017): 255–68.

Fuchs, Douglas, and Lynn S. Fuchs. "Introduction to Response-to-intervention: What, Why, and How Valid is It?" *Reading Research Quarterly* 41, no. 1 (2006): 93–99.

Fuchs, Lynn S., Douglas Fuchs, and Amelia S. Malone. "The Taxonomy of Intervention Intensity." *TEACHING Exceptional Children* 50, no. 1 (2017): 35–43.

Fuchs, Douglas, Lynn S. Fuchs, and Sharon Vaughn. "What is Intensive Instruction and Why is it Important?" *Teaching Exceptional Children* 46, no. 4 (2014): 13–18.

Fuchs, Lynn S., Douglas Fuchs, and Donald L. Compton. "Rethinking Response-to-intervention at Middle and High School." *School Psychology Review* 39, no. 1 (2010): 22.

Fuchs, Lynn S., Douglas Fuchs, Allison Gandhi, and Rebecca Zumeta Edmonds. "RTI Hits Adolescence—Will It Make It to Adulthood? A Case for Cautious Optimism." Center on Response-to-intervention. American Institutes for Research. 2016. https://rti4success.org/sites/default/files/RTIAdolescence.pdf.

Gersten, Russell, David J. Chard, Madhavi Jayanthi, Scott K. Baker, Paul Morphy, and Jonathan Flojo. "Mathematics Instruction for Students with Learning Disabilities: A Meta-Analysis of Instructional Components." *Review of Educational Research* 79, no. 3 (2009): 1202–42.

Hattie, John, and Helen Timperley. "The Power of Feedback." *Review of Educational Research* 77, no. 1 (2007): 81–112.

Horner, R. H., G. Sugai, A. W. Todd, T. Lewis-Palmer, L. Bambara, and L. Kern. "Individualized Supports for Students with Problem Behaviors: Designing Positive Behavior Plans." (2005).

Hughes, Charles A., Jared R. Morris, William J. Therrien, and Sarah K. Benson. "Explicit Instruction: Historical and Contemporary Contexts." *Learning Disabilities Research & Practice* 32, no. 3 (2017): 140–48.

Individuals with Disabilities Education Act of 1975, 20 U. S. C. § 1400 et seq. (1975).

Individuals with Disabilities Education Improvement Act of 2004, 20 U. S. C. § 1400 et seq. (2004).

Johnson, Beverley F., and Anthony J. Cuvo. "Teaching Mentally Retarded Adults to Cook." *Behavior Modification* 5, no. 2 (1981): 187–202.

Johnson, Janis L., Kelly Flanagan, Mary E. Burge, Sharon Kauffman-Debriere, and Charles R. Spellman. "Interactive Individualized Instruction with Small Groups of Severely Handicapped Students." *Education and Training of the Mentally Retarded* (1980): 230–37.

Juel, Connie. "Learning to Read and Write: A Longitudinal Study of 54 Children from First Through Fourth Grades." *Journal of Educational Psychology* 80, no. 4 (1988): 437.

Kamps, Debra M., and Charles R. Greenwood. "Formulating Secondary-Level Reading Interventions." *Journal of Learning Disabilities* 38, no. 6 (November/December 2005): 500–09.

Kamps, Debra M., Dale Walker, Erin P. Dugan, Betsy R. Leonard, Susan F. Thibadeau, Kathleen Marshall, Laurie Grossnickle, and Brenda Boland. "Small Group Instruction for School-Aged Students with Autism and Developmental Disabilities." *Focus on Autistic Behavior* 6, no. 4 (1991): 1–18.

Kanner, Leo. "Autistic Disturbances of Affective Contact." *Nervous Child* 2, no. 3 (1943): 217–50.

Kearns, Devin. "Explicit Instruction: Modeling and Practicing to Help Students Reach Academic Goals." National Center on Intensive Intervention, Module 5. 2018.

Kern, Lee, and Nathan H. Clemens. "Antecedent Strategies to Promote Appropriate Classroom Behavior." *Psychology in the Schools* 44, no. 1 (2007): 65–75.

Laugeson, Elizabeth A., and Mi N. Park. "Using a CBT Approach to Teach Social Skills to Adolescents with Autism Spectrum Disorder and Other Social Challenges: The PEERS® Method." *Journal of Rational-Emotive & Cognitive-Behavior Therapy* 32, no. 1 (2014): 84–97.

Ledford, Jennifer R., David L. Gast, Deanna Luscre, and Kevin M. Ayres. "Observational and Incidental Learning by Children with Autism During Small Group Instruction." *Journal of Autism and Developmental Disorders* 38, no. 1 (2008): 86.

Ledford, Jennifer R., and Mark Wolery. "Observational Learning of Academic and Social Behaviors During Small-Group Direct Instruction." *Exceptional Children* 81, no. 3 (2015): 272–91.

Maag, John W. *Behavior Management: From Theoretical Implications to Practical Applications*, second edition. Belmont, CA: Edith Beard Brady, 2004.

McLeskey, James, Council for Exceptional Children, and Collaboration for Effective Educator Development, Accountability and Reform. *High-Leverage Practices in Special Education*. Arlington, VA: Council for Exceptional Children, 2017.

Mellard, Daryl F., and Evelyn S. Johnson, editors. *RTI: A Practitioner's Guide to Implementing Response to Intervention*. Los Angeles: Corwin Press, 2007.

Mercer, Cecil D., and Ann R. Mercer. *Students with Learning Disabilities*, third edition. Princeton, NC: Merrill, 1997.

Mesibov, Gary B., Victoria Shea, and Eric Schopler. *The TEACCH Approach to Autism Spectrum Disorders*. New York: Springer Science & Business Media, 2005.

Moats, Louisa Cook. *Speech to Print: Language Essentials for Teachers*, second edition. Baltimore, MD: Paul H. Brooks Publishing Company, 2010.

Moats, Louisa Cook. "Teaching Reading Is Rocket Science: What Expert Teachers of Reading Should Know and Be Able To Do." Washington, DC: American Federation of Teachers. (Item no. 39-0372). (1999).

Morris, Robin D., Karla K. Stuebing, Jack M. Fletcher, Sally E. Shaywitz, G. Reid Lyon, Donald P. Shankweiler, Leonard Katz, David J. Francis, and Bennett A. Shaywitz. "Subtypes of Reading Disability: Variability Around a Phonological Core." *Journal of Educational Psychology* 90, no. 3 (1998): 347.

Morse, T. E. "Response to Intervention and the Cost of Student Achievement." *School Business Affairs* 82, no. 8 (2016): 18–20.

Morse, Timothy E., and John W. Schuster. "Simultaneous Prompting: A Review of the Literature." *Education and Training in Developmental Disabilities* (2004): 153–68.

Morse, Timothy E., and John W. Schuster. "Teaching Elementary Students with Moderate Intellectual Disabilities How to Shop for Groceries." *Exceptional Children* 66, no. 2 (2000): 273–88.

Morse, Timothy E., John W. Schuster, and Patricia A. Sandknop. "Grocery Shopping Skills for Persons with Moderate to Profound Intellectual Disabilities: A Review of the Literature." *Education & Treatment of Children* 19, no. 4 (1996): 487.

National Autism Center. "Evidence-Based Practice and Autism in the Schools: A Guide to Providing Appropriate Interventions to Students with Autism Spectrum Disorders." (2009).

National Center on Intensive Intervention (NCII) at American Institutes for Research. "To Be Clear: What Every Educator Needs to Know About Explicit Instruction." Updated February 19, 2019. https://intensiveintervention.org/resource/What-Every-Educator-Needs-to-Know-About-Explicit-Instruction.

National Center on Intensive Intervention (NCII) at American Institutes for Research. *Data-Based Individualization: A Framework for Intensive Intervention*. ERIC Clearinghouse, 2013.

National Center on Response-to-intervention. RTI Implementer Series: Module 2: Progress Monitoring-Training Manual. Washington, DC: U.S. Department of Education, Office of Special Education Programs, National Center on Response-to-intervention. 2012.

National High School Center. *Tiered Interventions in High Schools: Using Preliminary "Lessons Learned" to Guide Ongoing Discussion*. ERIC Clearinghouse, 2010.

National Reading Panel (US), National Institute of Child Health, and Human Development (US). *Teaching Children to Read: An Evidence-Based Assessment of the Scientific Research Literature on Reading and Its Implications for Reading Instruction*. National Institute of Child Health and Human Development, National Institutes of Health, 2000. http://www.nationalreadingpanel.org/Publications/summary.htm.

National Research Council. *Preventing Reading Difficulties in Young Children*. National Academies Press, 1998. https://doi.org/10.17226/6023.

O'Shaughnessy, Tam E., Kathleen L. Lane, Frank M. Gresham, and Margaret E. Beebe-Frankenberger. "Children Placed at Risk for Learning and Behavioral Difficulties: Implementing a School-Wide System of Early Identification and Intervention." *Remedial and Special Education* 24, no. 1 (2003): 27–35.

Odom, Samuel L., Lana Collet-Klingenberg, Sally J. Rogers, and Deborah D. Hatton. "Evidence-Based Practices in Interventions for Children and Youth with Autism

Spectrum Disorders." *Preventing School Failure: Alternative Education for Children and Youth* 54, no. 4 (2010): 275–82.

Plavnick, Joshua B., and Kara A. Hume. "Observational Learning by Individuals with Autism: A Review of Teaching Strategies." *Autism* 18, no. 4 (2014): 458–66.

Polloway, Edward A., Mary E. Cronin, and James R. Patton. "The Efficacy of Group Versus One-to-One Instruction: A Review." *Remedial and Special Education* 7, no. 1 (1986): 22–30.

Prince, Angela M. T., Mitchell L. Yell, and Antonis Katsiyannis. "Endrew F. v. Douglas County School District (2017): The US Supreme Court and Special Education." *Intervention in School and Clinic* 53, no. 5 (2018): 321–24.

Reid, Dennis H., and Judith E. Favell. "Group Instruction with Persons Who Have Severe Disabilities: A Critical Review." *Journal of the Association for Persons with Severe Handicaps* 9, no. 3 (1984): 167–77.

Riccomini, Paul J., Stephanie Morano, and Charles A. Hughes. "Big Ideas in Special Education: Specially Designed Instruction, High-Leverage Practices, Explicit Instruction, and Intensive Instruction." *TEACHING Exceptional Children* 50, no. 1 (2017): 20–27.

Risley, Ritamarie, and Anthony J. Cuvo. "Training Mentally Retarded Adults to Make Emergency Telephone Calls." *Behavior Modification* 4, no. 4 (1980): 513–25.

Rosenberg, Michael S., Lawrence J. O'Shea, and Dorothy J. O'Shea. *Student Teacher to Master Teacher: A Practical Guide for Educating Students with Special Needs.* New York: Prentice Hall, 2001.

Rotholz, David A. "Current Considerations on the Use of One-to-One Instruction with Autistic Students: Review and Recommendations." *Education and Treatment of Children* (1987): 271–78.

Schuster, John W., and Ann K. Griffen. "Using Constant Time Delay to Teach Recipe Following Skills." *Education and Training in Mental Retardation* (1991): 411–19.

Schuster, John W., and Ann K. Griffen. "Using Time Delay with Task Analyses." *Teaching Exceptional Children* 22, no. 4 (1990): 49–53.

Schuster, John W., Timothy E. Morse, Melinda Jones Ault, and Patricia Munson Doyle. "Constant Time Delay with Chained Tasks: A Review of the Literature." *Education & Treatment of Children* 21, no. 1 (1998): 74.

Schuster, John W., Timothy E. Morse, Ann K. Griffen, and Tim Wolery. "Teaching Peer Reinforcement and Grocery Words: An Investigation of Observational Learning and Instructive Feedback." *Journal of Behavioral Education* 6, no. 4 (1996): 511–33.

Shane, Howard C., Emily Laubscher, Ralf W. Schlosser, Holly L. Fadie, J. F. Source, Jennifer S. Abramson, Suzanne Flynn, and Kara Corley. *Enhancing Communication for Individuals with Autism: A Guide to the Visual Immersion System.* Baltimore, MD: Paul H. Brookes Publishing Co, 2015.

Simonsen, Brandi, Sarah Fairbanks, Amy Briesch, Diane Myers, and George Sugai. "Evidence-Based Practices in Classroom Management: Considerations for Research to Practice." *Education and Treatment of Children* (2008): 351–80.

Simonsen, Brandi, J. Freeman, S. Goodman, B. Mitchell, J. Swain-Bradway, B. Flannery, and B. Putman. "Supporting and Responding to Behavior: Evidence-

Based Classroom Strategies for Teachers." *USA: US Office of Special Education Programs.* (2015).

Simonsen, Brandi, George Sugai, and Madeline Negron. "Schoolwide Positive Behavior Supports: Primary Systems and Practices." *Teaching Exceptional Children* 40, no. 6 (2008): 32–40.

Sparrow, Sara S., Domenic V. Cicchetti, and Celline A. Saulnier. *Vineland Adaptive Behavior Scales, (Vineland-3).* Antonio: Psychological Corporation, 2016).

Stewart, Rachel M., Gregory J. Benner, Ronald C. Martella, and Nancy E. Marchand-Martella. "Three-Tier Models of Reading and Behavior: A Research Review." *Journal of Positive Behavior Interventions* 9, no. 4 (2007): 239–53.

Stewart, Rachel M., Ronald C. Martella, Nancy E. Marchand-Martella, and Gregory J. Benner. "Three-Tier Models of Reading and Behavior." *Journal of Early and Intensive Behavior Intervention* 2, no. 3 (2005): 115–24.

Stokes, Trevor F., and Donald M. Baer. "An Implicit Technology of Generalization 1." *Journal of Applied Behavior Analysis* 10, no. 2 (1977): 349–67.

Strain, P. S., and G. Dunlap. "Recommended Practices: Being an Evidence-Based Practitioner." (2006): 2006. http://challengingbehavior.fmhi.usf.edu/handouts/Practitioner.pdf.

Sugai, George, and Robert R. Horner. "A Promising Approach for Expanding and Sustaining School-Wide Positive Behavior Support." *School Psychology Review* 35, no. 2 (2006): 245.

Sugai, George, Robert R. Horner, and F. M. Gresham. *Interventions for Academic and Behavior Problems II: Preventative and Remedial Approaches.* Bethesda, MD: National Association of School Psychologists, 2002.

Tankersley, Melody, Sanna Harjusola-Webb, and Timothy J. Landrum. "Using Single-Subject Research to Establish the Evidence Base of Special Education." *Intervention in School and Clinic* 44, no. 2 (2008): 83–90.

The IRIS Center. Evidence-Based Practices (Part 2): Implementing a Practice or Program with Fidelity. https://iris.peabody.vanderbilt.edu/module/ebp_02. (2014).

The IRIS Center. Intensive Intervention (Part 1): Using Data-Based Individualization to Intensify Instruction. https://iris.peabody.vanderbilt.edu/module/dbi1/. (2015).

The IRIS Center. The Pre-Referral Process: Procedures for Supporting Students with Academic and Behavioral Concerns. https://iris.peabody.vanderbilt.edu/module/preref/. (2008).

The IRIS Center. "Providing Instructional Supports: Facilitating Mastery of New Skills." https://iris.peabody.vanderbilt.edu/module/sca/#content. (2005).

Torres, Caroline, Cynthia A. Farley, and Bryan G. Cook. "A Special Educator's Guide to Successfully Implementing Evidence-Based Practices." *Teaching Exceptional Children* 47, no. 2 (2014): 85–93.

Turnbull III, H. Rutherford, and Ann P. Turnbull. *Free Appropriate Public Education: The Law and Children with Disabilities.* Denver, CO: Love Publishing Company, 1998.

Vellutino, Frank R., Donna M. Scanlon, Edward R. Sipay, Sheila G. Small, Alice Pratt, RuSan Chen, and Martha B. Denckla. "Cognitive Profiles of Difficult-to-Remediate and Readily Remediated Poor Readers: Early Intervention as a Vehicle for

Distinguishing Between Cognitive and Experiential Deficits as Basic Causes of Specific Reading Disability." *Journal of Educational Psychology* 88, no. 4 (1996): 601.

Walker, H. M., E. Ramsey, and F. M. Gresham. *Antisocial Behavior in School: Evidence-Based Practices*. Belmont, CA: Wadswoth/Thomson Learning. (2004).

Whorton, Debra M., Joseph Delquadri, R. Vance Hall. "Classroom Instructional Programs with Autistic Children: Group Structures and Tutoring Models. Final Report." Federal Grant #G008300068. University of Kansas, Bureau of Child Research. ERIC Document ED 295 401, EC 202 840. (1986).

Wolery, Mark, Melinda Jones Ault, and Patricia Munson Doyle. *Teaching Students with Moderate to Severe Disabilities: Use of Response Prompting Strategies*, edited by Naomi Silverman. White Plains, NY: Longman Publishing Group, 1992.

Wolery, Mark, Donald B. Bailey, and George M. Sugai. *Effective Teaching: Principles and Procedures of Applied Behavior Analysis with Exceptional Students*. Boston, MA: Allyn and Bacon, Inc., 1988.

Wong, Connie, Samuel L. Odom, Kara Hume, Ann W. Cox, Angel Fettig, Suzanne Kucharczyk, and T. R. Schultz. *Evidence-Based Practices for Children, Youth, and Young Adults with Autism Spectrum Disorder*. Chapel Hill: The University of North Carolina, Frank Porter Graham Child Development Institute, Autism Evidence-Based Practice Review Group, 2014.

Wright, P. W., and Esq Pamela Darr Wright. *Wrightslaw: Special Education Law*, second edition. Virginia: Harbor House Law Press, 2006.

Yell, Mitchell L. *The Law and Special Education*, fourth edition, edited by Jeffery Johnston. New York: Pearson, 2016.

Yell, Mitchell L., and David F. Bateman. "Endrew F. v. Douglas County School District (2017) FAPE and the US Supreme Court." *TEACHING Exceptional Children* 50, no. 1 (2017): 7–15.

About the Author

Dr. Timothy E. Morse has worked in the field of education for nearly forty years, during which time he founded and directed a school for students with autism and held positions as a university professor, public school special education administrator, and special education teacher. He has authored nearly seventy articles in peer and non-peer reviewed journals and made numerous presentations at international/national/state/local conferences. Presently he works as a behavior support specialist and instructional coach in a public school system in Louisiana. He continues to learn about the lifelong journey of individuals with disabilities from his interactions with several family members who received special education services while in school.

www.ingramcontent.com/pod-product-compliance
Lightning Source LLC
Chambersburg PA
CBHW022012300426
44117CB00005B/144